The Cuban Democratic Experience

The Cuban Democratic Experience
The Auténtico Years, 1944–1952

Charles D. Ameringer

University Press of Florida
Gainesville · Tallahassee · Tampa · Boca Raton
Pensacola · Orlando · Miami · Jacksonville

Copyright 2000 by the Board of Regents of the State of Florida
Printed in the United States of America on acid-free paper
All rights reserved

05 04 03 02 01 00   6 5 4 3 2 1

Library of Congress Cataloging-in-Publication Data
Ameringer, Charles D., 1926–
The Cuban democratic experience: the auténtico years, 1944–1952 / Charles D. Ameringer.
p. cm.
Includes bibliographical references (p.-) and index.
ISBN 0-8130-1755-6 (alk. paper)
1. Cuba—History—1933–1959. 2. Democracy—Cuba—History. I. Title.
F1787.5 .A6975 2000
972.9016'3—dc21   99-087367

The University Press of Florida is the scholarly publishing agency for the State University System of Florida, comprising Florida A&M University, Florida Atlantic University, Florida International University, Florida State University, University of Central Florida, University of Florida, University of North Florida, University of South Florida, and University of West Florida.

University Press of Florida
15 Northwest 15th Street
Gainesville, FL 32611-2079
http://www.upf.com

To Jean

CONTENTS

Acknowledgments ix

Introduction: The Authentic Revolution 1
1. "La Jornada Gloriosa": The Glorious Journey 16
2. The Ministry of Scandal 32
3. The Torrid Season 42
4. Passing the Torch 60
5. The Cordial President 74
6. The Democratic Bulwark 90
7. New Directions 106
8. Sugar and Vinegar 121
9. "Crazy Eddy" 144
10. Conclusion: 1952 167

Notes 191

Bibliography 213

Index 219

ACKNOWLEDGMENTS

Numerous persons and entities have assisted me over the years I spent in the preparation of this book. I am grateful in particular to the History Department and Research Office of the College of the Liberal Arts of Penn State University for funding and leave for research and travel. I am strongly indebted to Jack Harrison, Jaime Suchlicki, and Ione Wright of the University of Miami, Coral Gables, for their assistance and collegiality. I thank my wife, Jean, for her skillful editing of the manuscript and for her encouragement.

Introduction

The Authentic Revolution

Specialists in the history of Cuba from its birth as a nation generally divide it into three periods: the Plattist Republic, 1902–33; the era of Fulgencio Batista, 1934–58; and the rule of Fidel Castro, 1959 to the present. This division overlooks a distinct period of Cuban national history, the time from 1944 to 1952, when Cuba experienced four democratic elections, civilian government, and freedom of expression, marked by the rule of the Cuban Revolutionary Party-Auténtico, PRC-A. One reason for this oversight may be that Batista's political career and the emergence of the Auténtico Party originated in the same set of circumstances, the overthrow of the dictator Gerardo Machado and the Revolution of 1933.

When elements of the Cuban army removed Machado in August 1933, they were unwittingly engaged in the more difficult task of containing a movement that regarded Machado as the latest, if worst, representative of a failed system in place since 1902. This system was characterized by subservience to the United States under the Platt Amendment, which gave the United States the unilateral right of intervention in Cuban affairs. The quip of the American humorist Mr. Dooley (Finley Peter Dunne) that under the Platt Amendment "Cuba was free, but not free to make mistakes," was not funny in Cuba. For three decades a "Plattist mentality" governed Cuban affairs, beginning with a military that was shaped by American instructors after the Liberation Army was disbanded and sent home.[1] This relationship with the United States continued under a string of Cuban presidents who competed for a place in history with a series of American overseers—Leonard Wood, William Howard Taft, Charles Magoon, and Enoch Crowder—and encompassed U.S. economic domination of the sugar industry and commerce and of the railroads, public utilities, and banks.

Gerardo Machado aggravated this unhappy situation by adding tyranny to the mix. Assuming the presidency in 1925, he advocated reforms designed to liberate the economy from foreign domination and remove Cuba from under the American thumb. Three years later, emboldened by the popularity that his avowed stance appeared to give him and by an improved economy and achievements in public works, Machado schemed to continue his term in office by installing a new Constitution that provided for his reelection and extended the presidential term to six years. Machado intended to govern for a total of ten years, until 1935. "Not one minute more, nor one minute less," he pledged.[2]

This act outraged even the obsequious caudillos and politicians who had been playing by the rules of the Plattist republic. Their dissent, bolstered by opposition from among Havana University student groups and the National Labor Confederation (CNOC), evoked a harsh response from Machado that worsened as the economic collapse of 1929 exacerbated the political crisis. Machado sponsored the formation of the Patriotic League, or Porra (bludgeon), a paramilitary group that assaulted and murdered those protesting against the regime.[3]

Amid the deepening crisis, a small group of students at Havana University, never more than thirty-six in number, formed the 1930 University Student Directorate (DEU) in September of that year. They sought to revive the student anti-Machado movement, leaderless since the earlier crushing of the 1927 DEU. Initially, the 1930 DEU planned street demonstrations to demand "the termination of the present regime and the immediate resignation of the President of the Republic."[4] In November, its message expanded to nothing less than "a total and definitive change of regime," following the martyrdom of the student Rafael Trejo.[5]

The 1930 DEU quickly became one of the principal elements in the evolving revolutionary spirit, expressing goals beyond the removal of the tyrant, calling now for a total break with the past, meaning the abrogation of the Platt Amendment, and amounting to a "new declaration of independence."[6] The young people of the 1930 DEU, especially the emerging leaders Carlos Prío Socarrás, Rubén de León García, and Manuel Antonio ("Tony") Varona Loredo, were the vanguard of a new generation—the Generation of '30—that had grown up under the miasma of the Platt

Amendment and had lost respect for its kowtowing elders. They were born between 1898 and 1912 and, although they represented all six provinces, the predominant element came from the Vedado section of Havana. At that time Vedado was a white, middle-class suburb located west of the old port city, bounded by the principal government buildings and abutting commercial district, the Malecón seawall, Havana University, and the Colón Cemetery. The 1930 DEU represented a socioeconomic element distinct from the residents of Old Havana and the newer suburbs of Miramar and Marianao. Its influence grew as that of the old-style caudillos and politicians diminished.

From the beginning, certain "traditional" politicians had challenged Machado's illegal rule, but their purpose was to restore the old order, not to destroy it. The most prominent among this group were Colonel Carlos Mendieta, the leader of the Nationalist Union Association (AUN), dissidents from Machado's own Liberal Party; former president general Mario G. Menocal, the head of the Conservative Party; and former mayor of Havana Dr. Miguel Mariano Gómez, the son of former president general José Miguel Gómez. Believing that they could rally elements in the armed forces, the caudillos attempted to organize a military insurrection in August 1931, the so-called Río Verde affair, but they misjudged their support and the operation collapsed almost immediately. Their failure ended their influence "in the revolutionary process." According to Justo Carrillo of the 1930 DEU, "With the mystical power of the caudillos broken, the doors of history opened to the younger generations."[7]

A group of young professionals passed through those doors more swiftly than the 1930 DEU. Joaquín Martínez Sáenz, a thirty-year-old Havana lawyer, organized the ABC Revolutionary Society in October 1931, with the aid of Carlos Saladrigas, Jorge Mañach, and Francisco Ichaso. Confronted with Machado's intensified oppression in retaliation for Río Verde, the ABC adopted an underground strategy, organizing secret cells among various elements of the population and engaging in clandestine propaganda and acts of terrorism. The ABC mounted a campaign that resembled "a state of civil war in the country."[8] Luis Aguilar insists that the accounts of ABC-*porrista* violence in 1932 were overdone and "melodramatic,"[9] but there is no denying that the ABC's derring-do captured the popular imagination and undermined Machado's ability to govern. The 1947 movie *We Were Strangers,* starring John Garfield and Jennifer Jones, depicting an ABC plot to assassinate Machado, demonstrated how far its fame had spread.

At the invitation of the ABC, the 1930 DEU appointed two representatives to the society's Directing Cell, which brought the principal student movement under the ABC's umbrella. The ABC also prepared a revolutionary manifesto, giving structure to the vague pronouncements and menu of demands that the 1930 DEU had been circulating up till then. Both the 1930 DEU and the ABC were significantly influenced by the program of the American Popular Revolutionary Alliance (APRA), the organization founded by the Peruvian exile Víctor Raúl Haya de la Torre in Mexico in 1924.[10] The Aprista doctrine, fully committed to democracy, condemned imperialism, both Yankee and Russian, and took a multiclass approach to the resolution of economic and social problems. Ironically, in the brutal struggle of 1932, more 1930 DEU students were thrown in prison, because of their visibility, than ABC terrorists, who operated clandestinely.[11]

The Modelo Prison on the Isle of Pines served as a revolutionary school for seventeen members of the 1930 Directorio. There, these students interacted with other sectors involved in the struggle, including certain middle-aged professionals and teachers and a group of noncommissioned officers caught up in the rebellion. The "camaraderie" they developed with their fellow prisoners had a profound effect on ensuing events.[12] They incorporated into their ranks Eduardo ("Eddy") Chibás, a leader of the 1927 DEU, and were mesmerized by Dr. Ramón Grau San Martín, the medical school dean, who embodied the nationalistic spirit. Their fraternization with the soldiers influenced their actions the following year in support of the "Sergeants Revolt."[13] At the same time, they were fervently anticommunist, regarding the Student Left Wing, the communist student organization, as a rival, not an ally, despite Machado's efforts to redden them all. Machado's failure to end the crisis, other than filling the jails, led the United States finally to enter the fray.

The new American president, Franklin D. Roosevelt, dispatched Assistant Secretary of State Sumner Welles to Cuba in April 1933 in an effort to restore peace on the island. Despite the Plattist implications of the move, most oppositionist elements welcomed the action on the grounds that the previous administration of Herbert Hoover had supported Machado and that Roosevelt was a liberal-minded politician and had announced a Latin American policy of the "Good Neighbor," implying a noninterventionist stance. At first, the 1930 DEU went along with the ABC and the "traditional" politicians, acceding to the "popular clamor" for unity to topple the dictator, but in June it withdrew. It realized that it was improper to sit at the table with representatives of Machado's illegal government and that Welles's mediation perpetuated the notion that Cubans were incapable of settling their own affairs.[14] The 1930 DEU split with the ABC and issued a statement that denounced "any kind of American intervention in Cuban affairs" and demanded "the future annulment of the Platt Amendment."[15] It now stood outside the mediation along with the Cuban Communist Party (PCC), which had not been invited to participate in the first place.

Nonetheless, Welles pushed on in his resolve to remove Machado, as necessary for ending the violence, and to arrange a succession that would avoid social revolution. Machado became defiant when he realized Welles's purpose, declaring that he was not going to be "thrown into the street" and challenging the American president to come and get him.[16] Seeming to invite armed intervention with such bravado, Machado lost what remaining support he had. The army deposed him on August 12, 1933, when he appeared unable to settle a general strike. It acted to protect its interests in any post-Machado government and to avoid U.S. armed intervention.[17] Welles immediately engineered the choice of Carlos Manuel de Céspedes, a "safe" elder statesman and son of the "Father of the Country," as provisional president.

The Céspedes government fell far short of the 1930 DEU's demand for "a total and definitive change of regime." Too much blood had been shed, too many passions engendered, and too many ideas floated for it to survive. The status quo parties—Liberal, Conservative, and Popular—remained intact, and most "elected" officials, bureaucrats, and military rank and file, except those who had rebelled earlier against Machado, retained their posts. Machado and a few notorious *porristas* fled, but Céspedes showed no disposition to bring to justice *machadista* collaborators who stayed behind. "What should have been a revolutionary government turned out to be . . . `a Machadato without Machado.'"[18]

It should have been obvious that the Céspedes government was doomed. The country was disrupted by strikes, land seizures, mob action against suspected *machadistas,* and parades and demonstrations. After ten days of this agitation, the 1930 DEU knew that the revolutionary momentum had not abated. It issued a manifesto reiterating that the overthrow of the despotic government was not enough and charging that the provisional government had been "manufactured in the diplomatic recesses of the American embassy." It warned that it would not be deprived of "its right to accomplish an *authentically revolutionary program.*"[19] Céspedes appeared to yield to the students' message.

Within forty-eight hours, he issued a decree restoring the Constitution of 1901, in effect annulling all acts of the Machado government and terminating the mandate of every elected official, and setting elections for a new government for February 24, 1934. The 1930 DEU, however, denounced the decree as a trap designed to perpetuate the colonialist regime, particularly the notion of elections in 180 days, with the status quo parties intact and having every advantage. It would not be satisfied by anything less than the "Authentic Revolution." Sergio Carbó, the editor and publisher of *La Semana*, returning from a two-year exile, smelled blood. He renewed the publication of his newsmagazine on August 26, exhorting students, workers, and soldiers to unite and demanding, "What are you waiting for to start the revolution?"[20] He did not have to wait long.

Events moved rapidly in early September, and chance played a large role. On September 1, a hurricane struck Cuba, and Céspedes undertook a tour of Santa Clara and Matanzas, the provinces that were hardest hit, taking with him the acting army chief of staff General Armando Montes. The recent appointment of Montes had not been well received by an army already unnerved by uncertainty; Montes had served in the Alfredo Zayas administration (1921–25) and had a reputation for downsizing and pay cutting. It was not a good time for him to be absent.

On September 3, the noncommissioned officers (NCOs) at Camp Columbia, the principal army base in Havana, requested permission to hold a meeting the next day to talk about salaries and promotions in the midst of distressing rumors. The meeting was intended to be a gripe session, dealing with pay and working conditions and small matters such as substituting leather for canvas puttees, but it inexplicably assumed the character of a mutiny. When the NCOs had drawn up their grievances, under the leadership of a new actor on the scene, stenographer Sergeant Fulgencio Batista, they could find no one in authority to receive them because the officers had abandoned the post and reassembled in the Hotel Nacional, where Welles was residing. Batista, although terrified by the prospect of being ruled insubordinate, urged his fellow NCOs "to hold the post" until the high command agreed to hear their demands.[21] At this point, certain members of the 1930 DEU arrived at Camp Columbia.

Carrillo, Rafael García Bárcena, and Juan Antonio Rubio Padilla had heard via the grapevine and the radio that "something strange" was occurring at army headquarters, and they decided to see for themselves. There had been no prior understanding between the sergeants and the students, but Carrillo and his companions were more than just curious: "We had gained a great deal of confidence; we were on the point of overthrowing Céspedes; and this movement at Camp Columbia might be the vehicle for that overthrow."²² When they arrived they encountered other members of the Directorio already intent on transforming the sergeants' unionist action into a political coup d'etat. The students and sergeants united to form the Cuban Revolutionary Association (ARC), and the NCOs endorsed the 1930 DEU's August 22 manifesto as a plan for proceeding with the revolution. The 1930 DEU came to regret its collaboration with the unknown Batista, but Carrillo explained that subconsciously a bond existed between the students and the enlisted ranks going back to their time together in the Modelo Prison.²³ The Revolution of 1933 was an untidy affair, without a heroic leader astride the barricades.

That was the way the 1930 DEU wanted it. The Directorio did not have a president, only a secretary, and its August 22 manifesto proclaimed that its members would not occupy any position in the new government. In Carrillo's opinion, the DEU committed the "tremendous error of aspiring to power so that, upon assuming it, [the DEU] could promptly delegate it."²⁴ Idealism prevailed, and in the early hours of September 5, the now functioning ARC determined who would govern. The August manifesto provided for the creation of a five-person Executive Commission inspired by the Uruguayan concept of a plural executive designed to discourage *caudillismo*. Two of the persons selected, Grau San Martín and José Miguel Irisarri, were totally unaware of what was happening and had to be aroused to receive the news. The only member whom the sergeants insisted on appointing was Carbó.²⁵ But the "Pentarchy" idea did not work. It was a "bad time," Carrillo said with regret, "to introduce to Cuba the Executive Commission as a system of government."²⁶ In five days it had to be scrapped, and the DEU, revoking its vote of confidence in the commission, designated medical doctor and professor of physiology Grau San Martín as provisional president.

The military institution was not functioning during this time either. The sergeants were in nominal control of Camp Columbia, but they were used to taking orders not giving them, and the barracks were a disgrace. The officer corps was ensconced in the Hotel Nacional, literally "under the protection of the Stars and Stripes."²⁷ The DEU needed to create an armed force loyal to the revolution and proposed to do so by reinstating Colonel Julio Aguado and four young lieutenants who had been court-martialed in October 1931 for conspiring against Machado. They would next rebuild the officer corps by promoting a group of academy officers, with whom the students had been exchanging views discreetly for the last several months. Since no officer was available to recall the colonel and lieutenants, Carbó suggested promoting Sergeant Batista to colonel and appointing him chief of staff for the *sole* purpose of signing the order, after which he would resign. The first step was accomplished on September 8, but Batista refused to take the next, remaining in command and promoting his NCO supporters to the commissioned ranks to create an army beholden to him. The revolution had produced two principal leaders, Grau and Batista, but each had distinct interests and ambition.

The Grau government exercised power for 127 days (though it was commonly referred to as "the Government of 100 Days"). It was troubled from the beginning to the end. Its most formidable foe was the American envoy Welles, who resented the overthrow of his handiwork and "consistently painted a black—and, at times, red—picture of what was happening in Cuba."[28] Initially, he urged his government to intervene militarily. He advised Secretary of State Cordell Hull on the telephone on September 5 that "it was important that a battle cruiser be sent to Havana at once" and that "it would be wise to land a certain number of troops from the American ship."[29] President Roosevelt and Secretary Hull declined, aware of the growing sentiment in Latin America against any form of intervention and anxious to achieve improved relations for the purpose of expanding trade. Thwarted, Welles pursued a policy of nonrecognition, which weakened the Grau government considerably and encouraged its enemies to conspire.

The ABC, now completely estranged from the DEU, proclaimed its opposition to the revolutionary government because of "its origins in the sergeants' barracks." The Communist Party (PCC) denounced the Grau government as a "bourgeois-landlord government . . . placed in the presidential chair by the petit bourgeoisie and by the army."[30] Though the PCC opposed the revolution, its efforts to establish *soviets* in sugar mills and the armed forces created an illusion that served Welles's red-baiting and strengthened his hand in Washington. At the same time, the former army high command and officers assembled in the Hotel Nacional constituted a "counterrevolutionary center" that threatened the stability of the Grau government.[31] Batista knew that the deposed officers were as much a danger to him as to Grau, so he willingly obeyed orders to storm the hotel on October 2. Again, Batista did things his way, reportedly lining up at least seventy officers and shooting them after they had surrendered. The Grau government had traded a pimple for a boil.

Now that Batista was thoroughly in military control, Welles believed that he might be the man to restore conditions to the way they had been. Ignoring Batista's behavior at the Hotel Nacional—in fact, holding the Grau government responsible for the atrocity—Welles met with Batista on October 5 and told him that he was "the only individual in Cuba today who represented authority."³² He assured Batista that "the leaders of the important political factions," namely, Mañach of ABC and Mendieta of the Nationalist Union, "were in accord that his control of the Army as Chief of Staff should be continued." He stated flatly that the Grau government did not meet any of the conditions necessary for recognition by the United States.³³ Welles had planted the seed of sedition that he continued to nurture throughout October, meeting with Batista on numerous occasions and getting him to agree by October 29 that "a change in government [was] imperative."³⁴ But the 1930 DEU got wind of the conspiracy.

On November 3, Carlos Prío informed the Directorio that a coup d'etat directed by Welles and Batista was imminent. The students convened the ARC and, with Grau's approval, set in motion a plan to arrest and execute Batista. They set a trap for him that evening in Carbó's residence in Vedado, but Grau, after confronting Batista and excoriating him, inexplicably permitted him to depart with no apparent change in his status. Grau advised the students, who were dumbfounded and aghast, not to worry, Batista would no longer be a threat; he had been "scared to death."³⁵ The students "rebuked" Grau, who reminded them, "I give the orders here and Batista will continue as Chief of the Army."³⁶ The 1930 DEU immediately went into an all-night session and decided by a simple majority to disband. Rubio Padilla considered this action of the DEU "its most grave error,"³⁷ abandoning the revolution and facilitating the design of Batista and Welles to overthrow Grau. But before that happened, the Grau government placed a mark on the conscience of Cuba that could not be erased.

Despite the unstable political conditions of the 127 days, Grau issued an avalanche of decrees intended to fulfill the promise of the revolution. In this respect, the students had not erred in selecting Grau as president, even though some had not fully anticipated the outcome. Felipe Pazos wrote to Carrillo that the DEU had little reason to expect Grau, "a doctor of the aristocracy [and] a near millionaire," to carry out the social reform he did.³⁸ In contrast, Eduardo Suárez Rivas argued that Grau was "the interpreter, the maximum leader, of the generation of '30," maintaining that a generation was "not a matter of biology" but a "philosophical concept" that included persons of all ages.³⁹ In achieving this reform, Grau was guided by three cabinet ministers in particular: Angel Alberto Giraudy (labor), Antonio Guiteras (interior), and Carlos Hevia (agriculture).

Working feverishly, these three prepared an abundance of decrees for Grau to issue on his own authority. Certain acts were key to the "Authentic Revolution," such as the "nationalization of labor," the so-called 50 percent law that required all enterprises to maintain a labor force of at least 50 percent native Cubans. The "nationalization of labor unions" gave legal status to workers' organizations, requiring that all union officers be Cuban citizens (aimed against the Communists) and be qualified to work in the trade they represented. And a series of decrees provided for the progressive nationalization of industry and lands by reducing the number of foreign holdings and limiting the size of sugar lands. Collectively, these decrees established a system of production quotas, fixed prices, wage formulas, profit sharing, and wages in cash, under the authority of the newly created Colonos (sugar farmers) Association to balance the existing Hacendados (mill owners) Association. Other decrees with long-range effects included autonomy for Havana University, increased teachers' salaries, the creation of a national paper currency, the fixing of ten centavos as the maximum rate for a kilowatt of electricity nationwide—amounting to a 45 percent reduction in the costs of electricity and gas in the city of Havana (a blow to the American-owned Cuban Electric Company, which was also obliged to install lines throughout the republic at its own cost)—the right of women to vote, be elected, and hold diplomatic positions, the eight-hour workday, and workers' compensation.[40] Hundreds of decrees were issued, including ones providing for the functioning of the provisional government and for the election of a constituent assembly to chart the future government of Cuba.

Although Grau did not issue a decree specifically abrogating the Platt Amendment, his intention was clear. At his inauguration on September 10, he refused to swear to the Constitution of 1901, which contained the offensive provision, thereby giving notice that Cuba was "free, independent, and sovereign."[41] To make this firm, the Grau government took advantage of the Seventh International Conference of American States, which met in Montevideo in December 1933. Its delegation included Giraudy, the labor minister; Herminio Portell Vilá, a Havana University history professor and specialist in U.S.-Cuban relations; and Carlos Prío and Rubio Padilla, two members of the erstwhile 1930 DEU, who, though feeling betrayed by Grau, went in the hope of salvaging the primary goal of the revolution. Montevideo was the site of the climactic showdown between the United States and Latin America over the issue of intervention. It was there that Latin America achieved U.S. acceptance of the principle that "no state has the right to intervene in the internal or external affairs of another," which removed the juridical underpinning of the Platt Amendment. Although the Montevideo conference was a triumph for Cuba, it also created a circumstance that worked to the disadvantage of the Grau government.

Secretary Cordell Hull led the American delegation at Montevideo, and in his absence from Washington, Welles personally pressured President Roosevelt to endorse his nonrecognition policy. Hull had resisted a public statement in support of nonrecognition as not in the spirit of the Good Neighbor. While Hull was en route to Montevideo in mid-November, Welles hastened to Warm Springs, Georgia, where the president was resting. He persuaded Roosevelt to issue the "Warm Springs Declaration" on November 23. It stated, "We have not believed that it would be a policy of friendship and of justice to the Cuban people as a whole to accord recognition to any provisional government in Cuba unless such government clearly possessed the support and the approval of the people of the Republic."[42] The declaration implied that Welles was correct to withhold recognition of the Grau government as not having the confidence of the Cuban people. It gave Welles the green light to continue his efforts to replace the Grau government.

Welles and his successor Jefferson Caffery moved in for the kill. They urged Batista "to bring down Grau."[43] Although Batista had been damaged by the confrontation in Carbó's home on November 3, he regained control of the army just five days later as the result of a bungled coup attempt by the ABC and the Nationalist Union. The 1930 DEU's defection, Batista's suppression of the November 8 insurrection, and the Warm Springs Declaration made the former sergeant "master of Cuba."[44] During December Batista organized his forces and lined up support, and on January 18, 1934, with the connivance of Caffery, he overthrew the revolutionary government, installing Mendieta in the presidency, the first of three puppet presidents. The revolution was halted, but its essence persisted, signifying "a break with the past"[45] and affecting subsequent events on two tracks.

Batista moved on one track, aided from the beginning by the abrogation of the Platt Amendment. Although Batista's rule during the 1930s was repressive, it was qualified by his origins as a peasant from Banés and his service in the enlisted ranks. Batista promoted a vigorous anti-illiteracy campaign, albeit under the auspices of the army, using soldiers as instructors and military posts for schoolrooms. He sponsored the Sugar Coordination Law of 1937, which, in the spirit of the authentic revolution, governed the nature of the sugar industry for the next two decades, giving Cuba greater control over production and protecting the interests of small growers and wage earners. And he facilitated the development of organized labor into one of the strongest groups on the island. To accomplish this, he allied with the Communist Party, which, following the Popular Front strategy of the late 1930s, cooperated and established the Cuban Workers Confederation (CTC) in 1939. Under the leadership of Lázaro Peña as secretary general, the CTC and its affiliates made significant gains in membership and benefits. But although the Communist Party provided leadership for the trade unions, it failed to create Communist trade unions.[46] Batista saw to that; he imposed a speed limit on his "populist" track.

Running on the other (faster) track was the Cuban Revolutionary Party-Auténtico (PRC-A), founded on February 8, 1934. The party was founded by the deposed leaders of the revolution ("blessed be the defeated"),[47] particularly members of the Generation of '30, although only Carlos Prío, Tony Varona, and Rubén de León from the 1930 DEU participated. The Auténtico Party took its inspiration from APRA, adopting the democratic, multiclass, reformist model, but was also rooted in the Cuban experience in its determination to stem the expansion of latifundium (corporately owned agroindustrial combine). This meant eliminating the twin evils of "foreign capital and imported cheap labor."[48] Grau was in exile in Mexico when the party was created, but he returned to Cuba in May and agreed to serve as its president. He affirmed that the party's doctrine was essentially "nationalist, socialist, and anti-imperialist."[49]

The party's beginnings were difficult. Batista's police hounded its organizers, forcing the party to go underground and driving Grau and members of the Organizing Committee into exile, this time in Miami. The militants who remained in Cuba formed the Auténtica Organization (OA) as an action arm in the spirit of the anti-Machado struggle. At the same time, Guiteras, the most charismatic of the Generation of '30, formed Young Cuba (Joven Cuba), another armed group in the fight against Batista. These elements gave a rough edge to *autenticismo* that became a liability in time, but Grau nonetheless was deeply grateful for their sacrifice.[50] Guiteras himself was killed in 1935, attempting to flee the island following a failed general strike in March. In 1937 his followers, among them Orlando León Lemus and Rogelio Hernández Vega, formed the Guiteras Revolutionary Action (ARG), a clandestine revolutionary organization that focused on the trade unions, doing battle with Batista's police and the Communists.[51] In the meantime, the Auténtico Party continued to perfect its message in the hope of winning the allegiance of the Cuban people.

The "Political Doctrine" of the Auténtico Party, as drafted by Enrique

C. Henríquez, was enunciated by Grau in a series of three speeches during a Pan-American conference in Panama in August 1935. The central theme was anti-imperialist. Guiteras had proclaimed that "a movement that was not anti-imperialist in Cuba, was no revolution."[52] And Grau, revealing the scars of recent experience, declared, "Today, with greater insistence than ever, we demand an end to the bloody, onerous, underhanded intervention that, without any visible responsibility, is deeply responsible for all the ills occurring in Cuba today."[53] Grau sounded the battle cry, "Cuba for the Cubans," charging that Cubans had been dispossessed of their lands and jobs by foreigners. This displacement was the result, he affirmed, of "financial imperialism," with the collaboration of the "old" politicians and the "mercenary" army. The solution rested with the "economic liberation" of Cuba and the restoration of its "lost economy" by means of a simultaneous struggle against the "three fundamental causes of Cuba's indisposition"[54] (foreign capital, Plattist politicians, and the army). In outlining a program that called for "the intervention and control of the national economy by the State" and for "the direct intervention by the wealth-producing classes in the direction of the State," Grau disavowed any connection between *autenticismo* and communism, fascism, or nazism.[55] He concluded by exhorting the Cuban people to join the ranks of the PRC-A, to take part in the "march against reaction." Grau's message began to take effect toward the end of the decade, as the two tracks carrying Batista and the Auténtico party converged.

By 1939, political attitudes and tensions were easing as a result of changes in Cuba and worldwide. The Great Depression was abating, improving the economic outlook. Organized labor was domesticated, "appeased" by Batista's paternalism in cooperation with the Communist Party.[56] Franklin Roosevelt, the New Deal, and the Good Neighbor softened the image of *Tío* Sam, taking the bite out of the anti-imperialist argument. The rise of Hitler and Mussolini tended to unify the political left in condemnation of fascism. Many Cubans volunteered to go to Spain to fight against Franco in the civil war. The lack of success of the action elements of the Auténtico Party and allied groups, particularly the crushing defeat in the 1935 general strike, strengthened the hand of moderates in the party (and attracted new members) favoring a political solution. Given the improved *ambiente,* Batista believed he could risk playing the democratic statesman and restore legitimate government. He convoked elections in November 1939 for a constituent assembly to draft a new constitution, and the Auténticos abandoned their previous abstentionist tactics and agreed to take part. In fact, they won a plurality of seats, allying next with other oppositionist elements to control the assembly and elect Grau initially as presiding officer.

The Cuban Constitution of 1940 has been described as "one of the most liberal and progressive ever written in the American hemisphere."[57] It was a remarkable document, putting on paper the essence of the ten-year crisis that Cuba had just passed through. The social democratic philosophy of the Auténticos dominated the charter, but it also bore the influence of the six Communist delegates in the convention and the populist program of Batista. While guaranteeing the broadest exercise of individual freedom and rights, the charter gave the national government the power of the collective will to intervene in the economy and manage fiscal and monetary policy and made it responsible for providing social security and economic well-being.[58] Sixty-eight of its 286 articles dealt with economic and social issues, including family and culture, labor and property, and education. It strengthened representative democracy by extending the suffrage to all citizens and restricting the power of the presidency (as a safeguard against *caudillismo*) by installing a "semiparliamentary system," with a prime minister and cabinet ministers subject to congressional review.[59] The promise of the Constitution of 1940 was postponed, however, by the election of Batista as president in 1940, even though he won fairly over Grau.

As hard as he tried, Batista could not shed his strongman image, nor did he display serious commitment to the Constitution by urging the passage of complementary laws to make it effective. Admittedly, he maintained his alliance with the Communist Party, supporting its leadership of organized labor and appointing Juan Marinello and Carlos Rafael Rodríguez, party stalwarts, to positions in his cabinet. But the arrangement on both sides was opportunistic, not ideological. What made the interlude between the passing of the old and the beginning of the new at least tolerable was the extraordinary period of World War II.

The struggle against the Axis powers promoted national unity and caused the economy to boom. Cuba could not produce enough sugar to satisfy the war effort. Scarcity economics was put on hold, and the United States suspended the sugar quota in 1942 for the duration of the war. Batista enjoyed certain popularity as the beneficiary of U.S. propaganda designed to strengthen hemispheric solidarity. But good times also gave political insiders more to steal, and the Batista government was notoriously corrupt. U.S. ambassador Spruille Braden deplored the lack of "honest and competent" government in wartime Cuba.[60] Ernest Hemingway's protagonist Thomas Hudson in *Islands in the Stream* complained about food shortages and the added suffering of the poor, while government officials enriched themselves dealing in the black market.[61] Batista lined his pockets for four years and did little to improve the lot of ordinary Cubans and advance the cause of social justice.

With his fortune made, and caught up in the rising tide of democracy in the closing years of World War II, Batista was disposed to abide by the no-reelection provision of the Constitution. Handpicking Carlos Saladrigas, his prime minister and a founder of the ABC, as the government's candidate for president in 1944, Batista felt confident that he could win even in a free election. But he miscalculated. Given the opportunity to choose, the Cuban people flocked to Ramón Grau San Martín and the Auténticos as more firmly identified with the ideals of the Revolution of 1933 and the Constitution of 1940.

The election of 1944 was a referendum on the "Authentic Revolution." It represented the culmination of the ten-year struggle for political democracy and economic and social justice. Nostalgia was Grau's most powerful weapon. His platform was a recitation of "the laws of the 100 days." As Eddy Chibás, Grau's principal spokesman, stated, the Auténtico program was not written on "fancy paper" but was inscribed "on the cheapest pulp in the world." It was printed in the *Gaceta Oficial de la República*, containing the "Auténtico Laws," and was "stamped on the soul of the people."[62] To foresee what Grau and the Auténticos were going to do in four years of normal government, Chibás affirmed, one had only to observe "what we were capable of achieving in four months of revolutionary government."[63] On this promise, Grau won the election handily.

Scholars have treated the years 1934 to 1958 as a seamless era dominated by Batista. They overlook the fact that he was in eclipse for eight of those years, beginning in 1944. During that time Cuba experienced democratic rule under two Auténtico presidents, constituting a separate and distinct period of Cuban history. The Auténticos have been the object of so much criticism that one feels defensive in writing anything positive about them. But this book is not an effort to rehabilitate the Auténticos. The intention is to examine the eight-year period of Auténtico government in its entirety to achieve a sense of the only time in their history when Cubans had the opportunity to be free. What they made of that opportunity is complex and contradictory.

1

"La Jornada Gloriosa"

The Glorious Journey

Eddy Chibás called it "la jornada gloriosa," a ten-year march of restoration. On June 1, 1944, Ramón Grau San Martín of the Auténtico Party won the Cuban presidential election with 1,041,822 votes to 839,220 for Carlos Saladrigas, representing the Batista-sponsored Democratic Socialist Coalition. It was truly a glorious day for Grau, more a personal victory for him than for the Auténticos, who had formed an alliance with the Republican Party and had ceded the vice presidential slot to Raúl de Cárdenas. Furthermore, the Auténticos did not achieve a majority in either house of the Congress. Grau would put in place the "Authentic Revolution" and end the corruption of the Batista administration. The expectations for him were exceedingly high. There was "an explosion of popular jubilation never seen before in Cuba."[1] He was the "apostle of rising expectations."[2] An American journalist on the scene commented that "the masses have a blind faith that Dr. Grau can cure all their ills. They idolize him with a frantic frenzy that must be seen to be believed."[3] Grau's campaign had been based on "Cubanidad" ("an essential Cuban way of being") and his record in the "100 days," but he appealed to more immediate concerns as well. Cuban women, whose vote was "decisive" in Grau's victory, proclaimed that "now, there will be an end to standing in line [for food and scarce goods] and [an end to] the black market."[4]

Although Grau's magnetism and promise to fulfill the 1933 Revolution made him the popular choice, he won the election for other reasons as well. First, Fulgencio Batista kept his word and did not interfere in the election.[5] He did not use the army "to secure a corrupt election."[6] His disappointed supporters charged that he "sacrificed" Saladrigas so he would "look good" for history.[7] Second, the attitude of U.S. ambassador Spruille Braden was critical. He deplored what he described as the corruption and inefficiency of the Batista government (in which nothing ever got done),[8] which alienated the business community because it was concerned about the deterioration of public services.[9] Braden displayed no animosity toward Grau, however, meaning that he found Grau at least acceptable and appeared neutral toward the election, even admonishing the members of the American Chamber of Commerce of Cuba "not to contribute even a five-cent piece to a Cuban candidate."[10] Batista regarded Braden's neutrality as hostility and vainly sought his recall at the end of 1943, whereas Chibás praised his "genuine democratic attitude" and "strict observance of the principle of non-intervention."[11] Despite Braden's insistence that the United States not interfere in the election, Guillermo Belt (who served Grau as ambassador in Washington) asserted that Grau could not have become president "without the de facto approval of the United States."[12]

Finally, Grau was helped greatly by the alliance of the Auténticos with the Republican Party. Gustavo Cuervo Rubio, Batista's vice president, bolted the Democratic Party (which was part of the government coalition) and formed the Republican Party when Batista chose Saladrigas over him.[13] "Ostensibly," Cuervo Rubio and his fellow Democrat Guillermo Alonso Pujol, outspoken anticommunists, broke with Batista over his collaboration with the Communists.[14] Thus the Popular Socialist (Communist) Party's backing of Saladrigas may have contributed to his defeat; indeed, it influenced Braden's position toward the election.[15] In any event, the "new" conservative Republican Party (not to be confused with a former Republican Party active in the 1930s) may have provided Grau with his "margin of victory."[16] Of Grau's votes, 771,599 were recorded in the Auténtico column, while 270,223 came from the Republican line. Though the Auténticos insisted repeatedly that they had not modified their program—that they remained committed to "nationalism, anti-imperialism, and socialism"—the alliance with the Republicans gave them a conservative cover that they had not had in 1940, when Grau received only 42 percent of the vote. Grau won by promising "candy for everyone"[17] over the "dry" and "boring" Saladrigas,[18] but circumstances also worked in his favor.

Conditions remained stable between Grau's election (June 1) and his inauguration (October 10, the "Grito de Yara," Independence Day). The outgoing president, Batista, remained on good behavior. On June 9, he removed General Manuel Benítez Valdés, the National Police chief, because of a rumor that he was planning a coup to prevent Grau from becoming president. Apparently, Ambassador Braden made it clear that the United States would not tolerate any antidemocratic act at that moment: World War II was entering a critical stage; the Allies landed in Normandy on June 6.[19] Grau, however, refused to recommend any Auténtico to participate in Batista's lame duck cabinet, either to ease the transition or as a symbol of wartime unity, and he was reluctant to relax his opposition to Communist leadership of the Cuban Workers Confederation (CTC), giving in only at Braden's urging. Though Grau was not disposed to forgive Batista, he appeared to soften his attitude toward the United States. Grau, who had said, "I fell because Washington willed it,"[20] was suggesting by August 1944 that the U.S. air bases built in Cuba as a wartime measure might remain indefinitely as part of the hemispheric defense system.[21] At the end of the same month, he made an obligatory visit to Washington, where he met President Franklin Roosevelt, who quipped, "And to think that I did not recognize you eleven years ago." Roosevelt accepted Braden's assurances that Grau "was not the same man."[22] There was irony in that evaluation inasmuch as Cuba was counting on Grau to renew the revolution.

In his inaugural address and in his first message to Congress, Grau gave no indication that he had changed. Speaking at noon from the balcony of the Presidential Palace, he told the assembled throng in the Plaza del Pueblo below, "This Government, amigos, is the will of the people. No, it is more, it is the Cuban people themselves who are going to rule their destiny."[23] And that evening, in the Capitolio (the Capitol building), Grau reaffirmed before the full Congress his commitment to "the economic and social imperatives of contemporary democracy." These imperatives were state intervention in the economy, the codification of social laws, and the efficient and honest administration of the Ministries of Treasury, Education, and Health. He urged the immediate passage of the complementary laws of the Constitution, principally the creation of the Tribunal of Accounts (General Comptroller), the Civil Service, and the National Bank.[24] Grau had set for himself and the Congress a strong challenge, but before he could determine a course of action, even if he were serious, he had to consider the larger picture and adjust to or eliminate certain elements therein.

In the first place, Cuba was locked in a straitjacket economy dictated by sugar. Though overproduction was not a concern of the moment, with Cuba enjoying "free *zafras*" (unrestricted harvests) since 1942, the structure of the sugar industry was a legacy of the 1920s and 1930s. During the first two decades of the twentieth century, technology (increased grinding capability) and demand (World War I) spurred the extraordinary growth of the sugar latifundium (the corporately owned, agroindustrial complex). There was concern that the Cuban farmer and rancher were being displaced and that the Cuban rural way of life was fast disappearing. The huge mills and ever-expanding cane lands of the latifundium, nurtured by foreign capital and serviced by imported cheap labor from Haiti and Jamaica, threatened to transform Cuba into a vast plantation, duplicating the sugar and slave Caribbean colonies of England, France, and Holland in the seventeenth and eighteenth centuries. Ramiro Guerra y Sánchez described what he believed was happening to Cuba in 1927:

> For four centuries [Cubans] had been settling the country little by little, clearing it and making it a healthy place to live in. They imported its principal commercial crops; they adapted cattle and domestic livestock to its climate; they found suitable locations for towns and cities on its coasts and in its interior; they courageously defended the island against invasion; they allotted and divided its land among farmers; they laid out and built its modern railways as well as its old but useful country roads; they fought for liberty and independence in the hope of establishing a vigorous republic that would be shared by and would serve all; and, thanks to the genius of a Cuban—Finlay—not only Cuba but the whole world was freed of one of its worst plagues [yellow fever].
>
> When all this toil of centuries seemed to be almost completed and the fruits could at last be enjoyed by the children, the sugar latifundium, which had ruined the West Indies with its two formidable instruments, foreign capital and imported cheap labor, invaded the island. Its appearance marked the beginning of the wholesale destruction of our small and medium-sized properties and the reduction of our rural landowners and independent farmers, backbone of our nation, to the lowly condition of a proletariat being stifled by that economic asphyxiation which afflicts the country today from one end to the other.[25]

At about the same time that Guerra expressed his alarm, the problem almost took care of itself with the collapse of sugar prices. Overproduction and the worldwide economic depression caused sugar prices to fall from 3.37 cents a pound in 1927 to 0.57 cents a pound in June 1933.[26] Sugar had sold for 22.5 cents a pound in May 1920, its best price during the so-called dance of the millions. As early as 1926, Gerardo Machado had attempted to restrict sugar production voluntarily and in 1931 created the Cuban Sugar Stabilization Institute to impose controls on Cuban sugar exports in an effort to defend the international price of sugar. Inspired by Guerra's thinking, Grau, during his first government in 1933, issued the "nationalization of labor" decree, aimed at stemming the immigration of field hands. Likewise, Carlos Hevia wrote a series of decrees against latifundium by setting production quotas, limiting the size of landholdings, and creating the Colonos (sugar farmers) Association to counterbalance the Hacendados (mill owners) Association.

The United States also had concerns during the period about the price of its agricultural commodities, including sugar. Up until 1934, it had employed tariff policy to protect domestic producers, but in 1934, when that proved inadequate, it introduced production and import quotas as a solution—the Agricultural Adjustment Act (AAA) domestically and the Jones-Costigan Act to cover imported sugar. In the same year, the U.S. Reciprocal Trade Agreements Act authorized a preferential tariff for Cuban sugar in exchange for tariff reductions for four hundred American products in the Cuban market. In effect, Cuba abandoned its nonsugar economic sector just when it needed to stimulate it (diversify) to reduce its reliance on the sugar industry.[27]

In 1937, Cuba determined to codify the various measures it had been taking to regulate production and stem the growth of latifundium by passing the Sugar Coordination Act. The measure mandated a fully regulated sugar industry, with fixed zones for the *centrales* (sugar mills), production quotas for the *hacendados,* and guaranteed access to grinding at a fixed price and on a permanent basis for the *colonos.* In addition, the act contained reforms designed to "redistribute" earnings by reducing "the share of total income going to foreigners" and shifting income "from upper-class Cubans to workers and small farmers."[28] Critics called the system "irrational" and warned that it threatened the "stagnation" of the sugar industry.[29] Conceding that the regulation of the sugar industry "went completely contrary to the `natural' process of survival of the fittest," Ramiro Guerra's son José Antonio wrote in 1942 that it represented "the triumph of national interest over the private interests of large corporations."[30] Indeed, in time, the Sugar Coordination Act had the effect of increasing Cuban ownership of sugar lands and mills and of breaking up large holdings.³¹ "Administration cane" (cane produced on mill-owned lands and worked by hired labor) virtually disappeared.³² Grau was not disposed to interfere with such developments, which coincided with his own wishes, despite dire warnings that the absence of competition and market forces promoted inefficiency and obsolescence. For the time being, the ongoing Second World War created conditions that mitigated the system's flaws.

The second element of the larger picture that Grau needed to consider was his lack of a parliamentary majority. The Batista-Saladrigas Democratic Socialist Coalition (which was neither democratic nor socialist) controlled both houses, potentially strengthened by the Communists, who held a few seats in the Chamber and a seat in the Senate (Juan Marinello), and by other opposition parties, such as the Liberals, led by Eduardo Suárez Rivas. The Liberal Party was the only "traditional" party to survive the Revolution of 1933. Moreover, Grau did not have firm control over his own party's representatives and those of his allies in the Republican Party. The alliance between the Auténticos and the Republicans in the presidential election campaign was viewed as an old-fashioned political deal not in the spirit of a revolutionary party. Rubén de León, a founder of the PRC-A and one of the few 1930 DEU members still active in the party, complained about this development. He asserted that the Auténticos had changed, being influenced by the "new Auténticos," those who joined the party beginning with its reduced militancy after 1938, and who "introduced" professional politics into the party.³³ Grau failed to achieve a working relationship with Congress during his presidency. Once, in frustration, he declared that "the legislative bodies are in the street," with the people.³⁴

Allied to Grau's problems with the Congress was the Communist leadership of the Cuban Workers Confederation (CTC). Grau was not comfortable with the Communists in control of labor and earlier, in 1943, had sought to replace Lázaro Peña as secretary general of the CTC with his own candidate, Eusebio Mujal. After he won the presidency, however, the U.S. Embassy persuaded him to let Peña stay on, in the spirit of "wartime unity."³⁵ In 1942, the Communists had committed the CTC to a no-strike pledge for the duration of the war and the next year changed their name to the Popular Socialist Party (PSP). Grau could not be too aggressive toward the Communists in the struggle for trade union supremacy if he had any hope of wooing their votes in the Congress. On the occasion of his inauguration, the PSP offered Grau "collaboration in any initiative favorable to the country, unconditionally."³⁶ This pledge was probably as sincere as that of the armed forces, extended during their "luncheon of confraternity" with the president-elect on August 25.

The army, as a remnant of the Batista years, was the most serious institutional challenge that Grau faced. At Camp Columbia, La Cabaña, and other military posts in and around Havana treachery lurked. The "Sergeants Revolt" of September 4, 1933, "did not replace the traditional army with another of a revolutionary character," that is, one "forged in the revolutionary struggle."[37] Instead, Batista had purged the old officer corps and promoted his comrades from the enlisted ranks, transforming the army into a "mercenary organization,"[38] loyal solely to the man who "raised the soldiers' pay and built the modern brick barracks."[39] He politicized the army in a way totally alien to the Cuban experience, creating a situation that Grau could not permit to persist if he expected to govern Cuba and fulfill his promises to the Cuban people. During Grau's first six months in power, there were repeated rumors of a military coup, causing Ambassador Braden to warn Washington in January 1945 that it could happen.[40]

Although the revolution had not produced an army, it had generated action groups that engaged in acts of violence against the Machado dictatorship and later against Batista. These groups had participated in the struggle that ended in victory for the Auténticos, and Grau felt indebted to them. They were Grau's "boys,"[41] but old habits were hard to break and a culture of violence and spirit of revenge had crept into Cuban politics. Grau should have disarmed the "trigger-happy boys," but instead he appointed them to positions in the bureaucracy and police, believing they would be a "counterweight" to the perceived threat of Batista's army[42] and that they could be "rehabilitated" by being given responsibility.[43] He erred; *pistolerismo* (political violence) deteriorated into *bonchismo* (gang violence on the University of Havana campus) and gangsterism (organized criminal activity). During Grau's presidency, three principal action groups competed for influence and spoils, while claiming to be revolutionary, "fighting for social justice and freedom."[44] These groups, the Guiteras Revolutionary Action (ARG), led by Eufemio Fernández Ortega; the Revolutionary Socialist Movement (MSR), headed by Rolando Masferrer; and the Revolutionary Insurrectional Union (UIR), under Emilio Tró, served Grau badly, "transforming liberty into license."[45] But he refused to crack down on them, believing "that freedom is strengthened with more freedom."[46] Using toughs for political purposes was a blot on Grau's otherwise positive record of maintaining "a climate of civil liberties."[47]

Finally, though not part of the larger picture but a factor that affected his performance as president nonetheless, Grau carried baggage of a personal nature. Grau was stubborn and vain, quick to take offense and hold a grudge, but susceptible to flattery and given to playing favorites. In 1940, U.S. ambassador George Messersmith had doubts about Grau's ability to judge character, asserting that he was more likely to follow "the worst influences around him" than to be influenced by "the decent men" of his party.[48] Grau was a bachelor, but nepotism still ran rampant in his administration; his cousins, nieces, nephews, and in-laws were scattered throughout the government. Paulina Alsina *viuda de* Grau, the widow of Grau's brother, served as "First Lady." Paulina de Grau had tremendous influence over the president and presided over a "palace clique" that influenced cabinet appointments and dispensed favors and *botellas* (sinecures).[49] Because Grau was "*el Maestro*" and "*el Viejo*" and so much was expected of him, few anticipated the corruption that emanated in time from the "third floor" (the presidential offices area) of the Presidential Palace. But Grau also had good men and women in the Auténtico Party, and he did listen to them.

Grau's term could be called the "Vedado years," in reference to the section of Havana where so many of the Generation of '30 grew up, as well as home to many of the figures of the Revolution of 1933 and the "100 days." The "reformist" bourgeoisie (who grew up despising the Platt Amendment) lived there, as distinct from the "colonial" bourgeoisie (who perceived their well-being to be dependent on the Yankee dollar) residing in the newer suburbs of Jaimaintas, Miramar, and Marianao.[50] Moreover, Vedado of the 1940s was distinct from the tourist center (of the big hotels and night spots) that it became in the 1950s, as described by Guillermo Cabrera Infante in *Tres tristes tigres*. In the 1940s, the family home of Eddy Chibás at 17th and H, just a couple of blocks from Grau's at 17th and J, was frequently the site of political conclaves.

At the end of December, after two months in office, the Auténtico senators met there with Grau. The senators were concerned that the president was ignoring Congress. Carlos Prío did the talking, expressing dismay that the executive branch had not come to Congress to present its program. He criticized Prime Minister Félix Lancís, remarking that he had appeared before Congress only twice: once, to take the oath of office; and a second time, to request funds to clean up after a hurricane at the end of October. "That is not semi-parliamentarianism," he complained.[51] In truth, parliamentary government, semi or otherwise, did not work well in Cuba. Although Grau was no caudillo, presidential authority was not diminished in practice by the ministerial form of government mandated by the Constitution of 1940. Grau got around his lack of a majority in Congress by ruling by decree. He had done it in 1933, and he was doing it again in 1945. In fact, when Grau completed his term in October 1948, Carlos Lechuga, writing in the weekly magazine *Bohemia,* noted that "in four years, Congress [had] not worked more than a total of three months."[52] This situation was not entirely Grau's fault; the Senate rarely had a quorum, though Senator Eddy Chibás showed up almost every day for work.[53]

Chibás was Grau's most faithful and articulate spokesman at the beginning of his presidency. If Grau's relations with Congress were poor, Chibás kept the Cuban people fully informed of the president's actions and latest decrees. In 1945, Chibás's Sunday evening news and commentary program on radio CMQ was the most popular broadcast on the island. In 1946, he also took over the Auténtico Party's fifteen-minute spot on radio COCO. Only a month after Grau had been in office, Senator Suárez Rivas joked that Cuba had three premiers (PMs): Chibás, the "presidential" premier; Lancís, the "constitutional" premier; and Prío, the *"casi"* (almost) premier.[54] What he meant was that Eddy Chibás was the presidential spokesman, and Carlos Prío was the rising star of the Generation of '30. Thus it is possible that the meeting of the Auténtico senators with Grau at Chibás's house in late December was not limited to the issue of Grau's relations with Congress.

In the early hours of the New Year 1945, Chibás announced that Grau was moving against Batista's army. He reported the "retirement" of Brigadier General Francisco Tabernilla y Dolz, the commander of La Cabaña fortress, though leaving little question that the root cause was "insubordination."[55] Tabernilla was one of Batista's closest confidants. Batista wrote to "Pancho" not to take it personally, noting that it was the start of "vengeance and reprisals."[56] He may have been right. Toward the end of February, Grau acted again, "retiring" General Manuel López Migoya, the chief of staff, and replacing him with Major General Genovevo Pérez Dámera. Pérez Dámera was clearly Grau's creation. In less than six months, beginning in October 1944, Pérez Dámera experienced five promotions, going from major to major general and chief of staff. The columnist Ramón Vasconcelos, writing in *Prensa Libre,* asked, "What Caesar, what Napoleon, what Washington, what Bolívar, what Maceo, Foch, MacArthur, or Montgomery" had a more "meteoric rise"?[57] If there was any question about democracy in Cuba under Grau, or at least freedom of expression, one had only to observe how the media treated the new army chief of staff.

Pérez Dámera was the perfect foil for *Bohemia*'s caricaturist, "Davíd" (Juan Davíd). *Bohemia* delighted in poking fun at Pérez, who was short of stature and overweight. On its humor page, "Picadillo a la criolla" ("Cuban Hash"), the satirist "Vergara" published "Genovevo's diary," with the general entering in it, among other things, "Wednesday—I spent the day rearranging and polishing my medals."[58] Humor was not *Bohemia*'s only genre, nor was the office of the once-feared army chief of staff its only target. One of Latin America's leading magazines, its "en Cuba" pages edited by Enrique de la Osa were freewheeling, usually scathing, commentary on contemporary politics. And it regularly published opinion pieces and essays by a variety of political writers, namely, Juan Bosch, Rafael Estenger, René Fiallo, Francisco Ichaso, Jorge Mañach, Carlos Márquez Sterling, José Pardo Llada, and Herminio Portell Vilá. *Bohemia* was one of the "five aces of Cuban democracy" that included *El Mundo*, radio station CMQ, *Diario de la Marina,* and *Alerta*,[59] amid a full deck of newspapers, magazines, journals, and radio stations (and in 1950, TV) of every political tendency. And cultural life also seemed to come alive in Grau's restoration.

In 1944, José Lezama Lima, in collaboration with José Rodríguez Feo, began publication of *Orígenes*, a literary magazine. At the time, there were no book publishing houses in Cuba, but Lezama Lima assembled a stable of writers and poets that constituted "a cultural galaxy," including Virgilio Piñera, Gastón Baquero, Fina García Marruz, Eliseo Diego, and Cintio Vitier. They formed a close-knit intellectual community, a kind of Bohemian colony, that flourished during the period of the Auténtico governments.[60] Some of the artists were homosexual, but they suffered no official harassment or persecution as, for example, Piñera did under Fidel Castro almost two decades later.[61] The *Orígenes* group looked for a particular means—poetry—to express "Cubanidad." Nearby, in Vedado, the Lyceum Lawn Tennis Club, an association of women activists, headed by Gloria Jaime de Domingo, Conchita Garzón, and Angélica Planas, maintained "a performance *salle* (for lectures, plays, and chamber music), an exhibition hall, and the first circulating library in Cuba."[62] All its activities were open to the public and enjoyed complete freedom under the Auténticos; the Lyceum chose the lecture topics and the causes to support, such as the Dominican exile movement against the dictator Rafael Trujillo.

The exile community was another element that flourished under the Auténticos. Grau and most of the Auténtico leaders had experienced exile in places like Mexico and Miami, so they had firsthand knowledge of exile politics and intrigue. Refugees from tyranny in Spain, the Dominican Republic, and Nicaragua, to name a few of the nationalities involved, added to the political and intellectual life of Cuba in the mid-1940s. The Dominicans Juan Bosch and Juan Isidro Jiménez Grullón and, later, the Venezuelans Rómulo Betancourt and Rómulo Gallegos plotted in Cuba against dictatorships in their homelands and, as writers, frequently contributed to *Bohemia*. The sympathy of the Auténticos toward these exiles, especially toward leaders of Aprista-style parties akin to the PRC-A, strongly influenced Cuban foreign relations (particularly in the area of covert action). Chibás's residence was headquarters for a congressional group opposed to the Trujillo regime in the Dominican Republic, and Senator Agustín Cruz was the leader of the Congressional Committee Pro the Spanish Republic.[63] These two leaders were outspoken in their opposition to dictatorial governments, arguing that Cuba should have nothing to do with them, even if it affected hemispheric solidarity.

As World War II was winding down, the American nations met in Mexico City in February and March 1945 to determine the future of the inter-American system. The Inter-American Conference on Problems of War and Peace (the Chapultepec Conference) was the prelude to the San Francisco Conference scheduled to meet at the end of April to draft the United Nations Charter. The American nations were prepared to join the world organization en bloc but wished to preserve the integrity of the regional system by creating an organization of American states that provided for economic cooperation and hemispheric defense. The sticking point was whether to permit Argentina to participate in the San Francisco Conference. The Auténticos had little inclination to forgive Argentina for remaining neutral during the war, indeed, for being pro-Nazi. Despite Argentina's eleventh-hour declaration of war on the Axis powers (March 27), Portell Vilá, for example, argued that the Edelmiro Farrell–Juan Perón regime in Argentina was "frankly totalitarian" and its participation in the postwar conferences would be a betrayal of "democratic principles."[64] In this context, the inclusion of Eddy Chibás in the Cuban delegation at the Chapultepec Conference created a sensation. Batista's foreign minister, Jorge Mañach, the ABC leader, opposed the appointment, saying that Chibás's "disrespect" toward certain Latin American governments was well-known and that, above all, the Latin American governments ought to unite, "creating a bloc of governments in defense of their interests."[65] Though Chibás failed to prevent Argentina's charter membership in the United Nations, Cuba's position at Chapultepec signaled its postwar activist role in the struggle for democracy, particularly in the Caribbean. As will be seen, it was a policy that conflicted with that of the United States, suggesting that the Auténticos were no pushovers for the Yankees. While postwar political concerns were large in the international community, Cuba, for its part, was focused on its economic future.

The Auténtico programs were dependent on national control over the sugar industry as the financial underpinning of economic planning and social reform. Following the practice of the war years, the entire 1945 sugar harvest was sold to the United States at a fixed price of 3.10 cents per pound. There had been wrangling over the price and quotas for raw and refined sugar and certain sugar derivatives, but sugar was still a rationed commodity and Cuba enjoyed a certain advantage, at least through 1945.[66] Prominent Cuban businessmen and economists interviewed by *Bohemia* in September 1945 generally agreed that Cuba would have another "two or three" good *zafras* (sugar harvests).[67] They were not too far off; Cuban sugar sales and prosperity stayed high for the remainder of Grau's term.

José López Fernández, the president of the American Continental Bank, argued that Cuba needed to diversify production, ending its dependence on sugar exports. During the war, Cuba had accumulated a substantial reserve, but López noted that there was also pent-up demand for automobiles, appliances, radios, and other consumer goods. He feared that instead of investing in new industries and products and purchasing only immediate necessities, Cubans would go on a spending spree, fueling inflation, and exhaust the wartime savings earned at great sacrifice.[68] He opposed the Auténticos' mixed-economy approach but vigorously urged the creation of the Central Bank in compliance with the Constitution of 1940. The Central Bank, he believed, was necessary for resolving postwar economic problems and would enable Cuba to fulfill the international monetary commitments it had made under the Bretton Woods agreements.[69]

Frank Fernández, the vice president of General Electric in Cuba, echoed López's sentiments that Cuba ought to act now in good times to reduce its dependence on sugar, but he feared it would not happen because Cubans trusted too much in luck. "We shouldn't forget," he said, "that they call Cuba `*La Isla de Corcho*' [the Island of Cork]. Whenever Cuba is in poor economic shape because it can't export its principal products, something unexpected turns up . . . and it floats again."[70] But just in case, he agreed strongly with Juan Ulloa, the manager of a Havana automobile dealership, that Cuba ought to take advantage of the projected three years' lead time and revitalize its tourism industry.

Tourism, a major source of income in the 1920s and 1930s, disappeared from Cuba during the war. The principal casinos (Sans-soucí, Montmarte, and Gran Casino Nacional) were padlocked, and the facilities for tourism—the docks and the airport—were run-down and in need of refurbishing.[71] Ernest Hemingway, who spent portions of World War II in Cuba hunting submarines, described the inner harbor of Havana as badly polluted by oil seepage from tankers and vessels moored along the old docks.[72] He described Havana as poverty-stricken and dirty and was moved by the many homeless persons living in the streets. They were still there in 1945, a problem that *Bohemia* urged the government to resolve, "for humanity's sake more than any other," before bringing in tourists.[73]

The Grau government tended to be improvident. Grau, and the Auténticos for that matter, were mesmerized by the idea that economic liberation and salvation depended on the control of the principal product, sugar. They did not trust the free market economy, believing that history showed they could not compete with the vast resources of foreign capitalists. Despite the disadvantages of monoculture and the cartelization of the industry, as long as the good times lasted, Grau lacked any sense of urgency. He tended to follow the advice of politicians, namely, Inocente Alberto Alvarez, rather than that of economists, such as Justo Carrillo and Felipe Pazos. Alvarez, the minister of commerce, attempted to solve the shortage of goods (the queues had not been eliminated) and simultaneously expand the market for sugar through a program of *trueques* (barter deals). In principle, there was general agreement with the policy of barter as a means of acquiring much-needed commodities and of expanding into the Latin American market. Chibás believed the policy would bring Cuba "economic independence."[74]

Under the terms of the 1945 sugar sale to the United States, Cuba was permitted to retain a portion of the crop for domestic consumption and 150,000 short tons for free export. Beginning in February, Alvarez fashioned a series of deals, bartering sugar with Ecuador for rice, with Mexico for black beans, and with Argentina for tallow. While the *trueques* alleviated the shortages of these commodities, they also produced the first major scandal of the Grau administration. Alvarez, in collaboration with private sugar producers and brokers (among them, José Manuel Casanova, the head of the Cuban Sugar Stabilization Institute and president of the Hacendado Association), took advantage of the spread between the price of crude sugar and that of refined to realize a handsome profit in the barter.[75] Using evidence gathered from wiretaps, Major Mario Salabarría of the National Police broke the case in October, delivering a fifty-page brief before the Chamber of Representatives, which quickly (on October 8) voted "no confidence" against the accused minister. There were immediate calls for Alvarez's resignation, but Grau dug in his heels, proclaiming, "First I go before Inocente!"[76] The *trueques* scandal did indeed force the favorite's resignation, but he was not jobless for long, being compensated with the post of foreign minister. Among those calling for Alvarez to step down were the students of Havana University. Manolo Castro, the president of the University Students Federation (FEU), speaking for the student body, and Rafael García Bárcena, representing the faculty, condemned Alvarez. They declared that he had "done more harm to the Government of the Revolution" than all the attacks of the opposition, all the congressional inquiries, and all the military conspiracies combined.[77]

Amid the *trueques* scandal, the University of Havana began its new school year. Nineteen-year-old Fidel Castro entered the university that year. In 1945, the university was a dangerous place. Looking back, Castro said it was "more dangerous" than the Sierra Maestra, where he waged guerrilla warfare twelve years later.[78] From a personal standpoint, he was probably right. The graceful entrance of the university belied the violent goings-on within. Proceeding up the hill on San Lázaro Street through Vedado, one approached the magnificent 163-step *Escalinata* (stairway), dominated by the statue of the seated Alma Mater and a gateway of Doric columns, without a hint of the rough-and-tumble atmosphere within. The university, enjoying autonomy, was off limits to the police, meaning that the academic community shared its sanctuary with action groups running rackets (contraband, black market, drugs, protection, and the like) and hiding out.[79] The campus was a battleground among rival gangs (*bonches*) that dictated university affairs, from determining the FEU presidency to "passing examinations at pistol point."[80] Allegedly faculty members were deeply involved as well. According to Suárez Rivas, certain professors "sponsored" *bonchismo* as a means of "obtaining appointments or political prominence."[81] The *bonches* were affiliated in one way or another with either of the two major *pistolero* groups, MSR or UIR.

In fact, while many MSRistas and UIRistas traced their origins to the anti-Machado struggle and Joven Cuba and ARG, the groups themselves sprang from campus politics in the early 1940s. At that time, a group of faculty and students, among them Ramiro Valdés Daussá, Mario Salabarría, and Eufemio Fernández Ortega, formed the Committee for University Supervision (CSU) in an effort to bring the *bonches* under control.⁸² Rather than achieving its purpose, the gang warfare intensified, resulting in the murder of Valdés and causing the CSU to split into two rival factions.⁸³ One, the UIR faction led by Emilio Tró, favored the *bonches* as an element in the revolutionary struggle; the other, made up of left-wing and Communist elements, opposed the gangs and the use of the campus as a staging area for action against the government. In 1945, when Rolando Masferrer broke with the Communist Party, he organized the latter group as the MSR and quickly made it the dominant force on the university campus.

The difference between the MSR and UIR was more personal than ideological. Both groups were linked to Grau and the Auténticos, and the leaders of each held positions in the government, particularly in the police forces, which gave them an excuse to carry arms and shoot people. Major Emilio Tró of the UIR was the director of the National Police Academy. He had fought in the Spanish Civil War and during World War II served in the U.S. Army in combat at Guadalcanal. His bitter enemy from their student days was Major Mario Salabarría of the MSR, the chief of the Enemy Activities Investigating Bureau of the National Police. Masferrer, the leader of MSR, had also fought in Spain against Franco. Before he split with the Communists, he wrote for the party newspaper, *Hoy*. Cabrera Infante described him as "one of the best journalists that Cuba has ever produced, writing a dynamic and audacious prose that he borrowed from the Spanish anarchists, as did Hemingway."⁸⁴ At the time, Masferrer was editor and publisher of *Tiempo en Cuba*.

When young Castro arrived on campus, he joined UIR, challenging MSR's "hegemony."⁸⁵ Manolo Castro (no relation) tried to get him to join MSR, but Castro, influenced by charges of corruption in the Grau government, declined. Salabarría, unwilling to take no for an answer, told Castro "either to tone down his opposition politics or get off campus for good."⁸⁶ Castro remained on campus, but he "packed a pistol" from that point on, becoming a *bonchista* and taking part in the mayhem that was "the leitmotiv of behavior of the times."⁸⁷ Actually, there is a debate as to whether Castro was a card-carrying member of UIR. Jesús Diéguez, a top UIR leader, said he never identified "publicly" with UIR,⁸⁸ and Lionel Martin, a biographer, insisted that Castro "used" the UIR in his political activities on campus, but followed an "independent line."⁸⁹ Based on their research, Nelson Valdés and Rolando Bonachea are convinced that Castro "enrolled in the UIR."⁹⁰ In any case, whenever young Castro's name appeared in the newspapers, it was usually in connection with a UIR event or affair. Moreover, in whatever capacity, there is sufficient evidence that

Castro took part in the very same antisocial behavior for which he subsequently condemned the Auténticos. He and his fellow *bonchistas* did little to enhance Cuban democracy.

Eddy Chibás used his weekly radio broadcast to criticize the thuggery on the University of Havana campus, angry in particular over the FEU's attacks on Grau in the Alvarez affair. When he was at the university, he observed, the leaders represented the students, not their own personal interests.[91] Stung by his criticism, FEU snapped back that Eddy was not a graduate of the university. The feisty Chibás answered that he never said he was. "I am a graduate of the University of the jail," he said, explaining that Machado closed the university when he was a student and that after Machado's fall he remained in the trenches against Batista. Chibás stood by Grau. Speaking at Antonio Guiteras's grave at the end of the year, Chibás deplored the actions of some in the police, the army, and the cabinet, but affirmed, that "in general terms, the work of the government is honest and constructive."[92] The events of the coming year caused him to change his mind.

Grau's first year in office was disappointing. *Pistolero* violence, the *trueques* scandal, and the lack of a working relationship between the president and Congress took the shine off the "glorious journey." Cubans enjoyed unprecedented freedom of expression, the war was over, and economic prospects seemed good (for a few years at least), but Grau's toughest task was living up to expectations, and there he had fallen short. "Perhaps [we] expected too much too soon," noted Jaime Suchlicki.[93]

2

The Ministry of Scandal

One of the principal objectives of the Revolution of 1933 was to provide for the education of Cuba's youth. Consequently, the Constitution of 1940 mandated free and compulsory primary education and established that the budget of the Ministry of Education should be most favored, that is, no less than the ordinary budget of any other ministry.[1] Furthermore, in accordance with *Inciso* K (Paragraph K) of Law Number 7, April 5, 1943, and its amendment by Decree Number 3603, December 13, 1943, a nine-centavo tax was assessed on each sack of sugar produced and assigned to the Ministry of Education. When Ramón Grau San Martín took office on October 10, 1944, education had the potential for being the most effective element of government, or the most corrupt.

The first year was quite successful. Luis Pérez Espinós served as minister during that time. In addition to being an Auténtico militant, having taken part in the clandestine struggle against Machado and in Joven Cuba, he had earned a doctorate in pedagogy. He was an idiosyncratic figure, traveling the length and breadth of the island, visiting the most remote areas, bringing "shoes and caramels to his children," along with a good measure of "tears and kisses."[2] He coined the slogan, "Everything for the children," and he honored it, overseeing the construction of more than two thousand classrooms and expanding the school lunch and health programs and building dining halls and dispensaries. His philanthropic approach to education, "transforming the Ministry into a branch of the

Three Kings,"[3] made him too popular for his own good. Grau and all those with presidential ambitions viewed Pérez Espinós as a threat and conspired to force his resignation after one year in office.

While Pérez's quick rise to national prominence had been a factor in his removal, the large amount of money at his disposal also caused the vultures to circle. His successor, Diego ("Dieguito") Vicente Tejera, a senator from Matanzas, was more political in his orientation and used the funds of *Inciso* K to make more appointments than any other minister of government, distributing *botellas* (sinecures) to "friends and enemies" alike.[4] Because Tejera had close ties to certain action groups, these elements became a significant part of the education bureaucracy, and Tejera also diverted funds away from educational purposes to finance campaign activities in the upcoming midterm elections in June 1946. But Tejera lacked the vision to be a grand thief. In fact, he stayed away from the ministry as much as possible, traveling about Havana and Pinar del Río provinces in a caravan of automobiles, not for the purpose of visiting schools but to avoid the nuisance of job-seekers, and earning the title of "phantom minister."[5] In his absence, José Manuel Alemán, the chief of budgets and accounts, ran the ministry and schemed to replace his boss.

In 1946, Alemán had been in the Ministry of Education for almost twenty years. His father, General José Braulio Alemán, one of the founders of the republic, had been secretary of public instruction and fine arts under Machado, dying in office in 1930. The younger Alemán, a graduate in accounting from West Chester Normal School near Philadelphia, initially served in the ministry under his father in various capacities, rising to chief of personnel and property in the early 1930s and to chief of budgets and accounts later in the decade. Although Alemán worked clandestinely in the ABC against Machado, he had no role in the revolutionary government and after its overthrow returned to the ministry to serve under Batista.[6]

When Grau was elected president, Alemán expected to lose his job. He was not an Auténtico, being in fact a registered Democrat and having supported actively Carlos Saladrigas. But he survived. With Pérez Espinós out visiting schools and Tejera busily running away from his duties, someone had to administer daily affairs, and each minister came to rely on the experienced bureaucrat Alemán. In time, the palace clique on the "third floor" discovered that they could get results with a simple phone call to the "active functionary."[7] He was the golden accountant who knew where the money was and how to tap into it. His influence grew to the extent that at the end of 1945 Grau appointed him director general of technical instruction against the wishes of Tejera, who had earmarked the position for his brother.

Alemán used this position to flatter Grau and win his favor. Aware that Grau despised Batista, he removed references to Batista's civic-military programs in education, changing the name of his own directorate from technical instruction to polytechnic instruction and the name of the Civic-Military Institute to the Superior Polytechnic School, all "inspired" of course by the president. He tore down the Congrejeras military barracks to build an elementary polytechnic school named in honor of the "First Lady," Paulina Alsina *viuda de* Grau.[8] Such blatant sycophancy completely charmed Grau. "Alemán succeeded in convincing the professor-physiologist [Grau] that only he was capable of directing the department where he had served for more than twenty years."[9] Tejera had served barely six months when Grau forced him to resign on May 5, 1946, holding him responsible for attacks by the opposition that the ministry had been transformed into a "means for distributing jobs and favors."[10] Grau immediately appointed Alemán to succeed him.

The transition did not go smoothly. The action groups, concerned that they might be dropped from the payroll, occupied the ministry building and barred the entrance to the new minister. They objected that Alemán was not an Auténtico, that he had not made the sacrifices of the decade-long struggle, and that the position ought to go to one of the "old guard."[11] They did not have to worry; Alemán did not invent thievery in the Ministry of Education, but he would raise it to unprecedented levels. He had already enlisted as allies two powerful Auténticos, the senator from Las Villas and presidential aspirant Miguel ("Miguelito") Suárez Fernández, and the future vice president of the republic, Guillermo Alonso Pujol. Pointing out his revolutionary credentials through militancy in the ABC, they arranged a meeting in the Presidential Palace between Alemán and a commission of *pistoleros* wherein the minister pledged "to respect their interests."[12] Realizing that he had had a close call, Alemán determined that in the future the guns would be on his side.

Although Alemán had met with Orlando León Lemus of Guiteras Revolutionary Action and Emilio Tró and Jesús Diéguez of the Revolutionary Insurrectional Union he decided that his best bet lay with the Revolutionary Socialist Movement. He became the power behind MSR chieftain Rolando Masferrer, and he appointed Manolo Castro, the MSR leader on the University of Havana campus and FEU president, to be director general of physical education and sports. In time, he commanded a private army of hired guns that threatened his critics and even discharged bullets into the senate chamber on one occasion.[13]

Alemán's use of strong-arm tactics in directing his ministry and his diversion of public monies for personal and political gain were scandalous. His avarice undid the very system for which he was responsible. He did terrible harm particularly to rural education, which could afford it least, taking over and destroying the José Martí Rural Normal School, closing the peasant children's homes, and ending the educational missions that visited remote areas to provide student and social assistance.[14] These missions had included a teacher-trainer, a dentist, a veterinarian, an agricultural extension agent, a radio technician, a nurse, and a home economics teacher.

Alemán's betrayal of rural education may be observed in the numbers. Despite an outlay of $58.38 million for education in 1947 (over one-quarter of the national budget), six years later the illiteracy rate of the population over ten years of age was still 23.6 percent. Specifically, the illiteracy rate in 1953 was 11.6 percent in urban areas in contrast with 41.7 percent in the countryside. The figure for the rural population of Oriente province was even higher, reaching 49.7 percent, demonstrating that those educational resources not diverted to other purposes continued to be concentrated in the western provinces, particularly Havana.[15] In education, as in other programs, the Auténticos failed to alter the unequal pattern of development that produced "an island with two histories," that is, "Cuba A" (Havana and the western provinces), flourishing and prospering, and "Cuba B" (the eastern part of the island, particularly Oriente province), exploited and impoverished.[16]

Alemán used the "savings" from collapsing relevant programs to bloat the payroll with patronage jobs and *botellas* and to become the major source of political campaign funds. He institutionalized this graft by forming the BAGA (Bloque Alemán–Grau Alsina), joining with Francisco Grau Alsina, Grau's favorite nephew and "third floor" gatekeeper. At the same time, he amassed a personal fortune, acquiring among other properties the *finca* America, formerly owned by President General José Miguel Gómez. The power of the purse enabled Alemán to become the eminence grise of the Grau government, extending his influence to other ministries and exercising "almost omnipotent authority."[17]

The general deterioration of educational services and school buildings caused a public outcry, but apparently Grau was deaf to it, believing that "the best minister, the hardest worker, the most selfless was the señor of inciso K."[18] Alemán's money pot only partially explained his Svengali-like hold over Grau. *Inciso* K had facilitated the Auténticos' victory in the midterm elections (June 1, 1946), enabling the party to gain control of the Congress and win the important mayoralty of Havana. But Alemán cajoled Grau, telling him that it was his victory, a referendum on his presidency, and he promoted the idea of possible reelection, even though the Constitution forbade it.

The reelection issue was divisive, and Alemán knew it. He enjoyed seeing his rivals squirm, especially the presidential hopefuls among the Auténticos, who had to oppose the idea of amending the Constitution to permit Grau's reelection without offending Grau. The presidential bug had not yet bit Alemán, but he was in effect leading a counterrevolution, returning Cuba to the former ways of corruption and *continuismo*. At the end of the year, Foreign Minister Inocente Alvarez held a meeting in his home with party leaders including Miguel Suárez Fernández, Lincoln Rodón, Segundo Curtí, and Carlos Prío to protest Alemán's baneful influence. They told Grau that "it was either them or Alemán."[19] Grau sided with Alemán, and Alvarez resigned his position, causing a mild cabinet crisis, but none of them left the party. Some other Auténtico leaders were less willing to go along.

As Alemán's power in the Grau administration grew, that of Eddy Chibás declined. Chibás had long been Grau's loyal spokesman, but he was also a mixture of principle and presidential ambition. When *Bohemia* asked prominent Cubans in its June 23 and 30, 1946, issues whether the Constitution should be amended to permit the president's reelection, Chibás stated his opposition unequivocally, affirming that it would be a "betrayal" of the revolution.[20] By year's end his relations with Grau were nearing a breaking point, and Alemán's intrigues and corruption were the essential causes. During his December 12 broadcast, he called Alemán "a crook," charging him with misappropriation of public monies. He demanded to know, "What have you done, bandido, with the funds allocated to pay for the paper, pencils, and other supplies for the public schools? . . . You are, Alemán , the most thieving Minister of Education that the Republic has ever had. You are speculating with even the students' lunch."[21] Alemán was a stain on Grau's presidency, but he could get away with only so much in a political climate that was striving to be democratic and there were no restraints on the freedom of commentators and politicians such as Chibás to speak out.

Actually, Chibás and Grau had begun the year in close collaboration. Even though "I am going to tell Chibás" had become the refrain of real or imagined victims of injustice, Chibás devoted his considerable energy in support of any Grau initiative in behalf of the revolution. In February 1946, Grau issued Decree 308 establishing the sugar differential by which the government appropriated the difference in the price acquired by the sale of "free export" sugar and that fixed in the sale of sugar to the United States. The plantation owners and sugar farmers objected to this levy, but Grau determined that the differential represented an excess profit that ought to be distributed among the sugar workers "as their share in the earnings of the industry."[22] He further justified his action by the so-called escalator clause of the 1946 sugar agreement with the United States that tied the wages of sugar workers to the cost of imported foodstuffs, "guaranteeing to the worker a salary increase always in proportion to the cost of living." Senator Suárez Rivas declared that the sugar differential was Grau's "most important revolutionary act."[23] Chibás defended it just as vigorously, broadcasting that Auténtico socialism "does not seek to lower the standard of living of the rich, but to raise that of the poor."[24]

Frequently, when controversy arose, Chibás used his Sunday evening broadcast, to which most radios in Cuba were tuned, to support Grau. Even in cases of *pistolero* violence for which police officials appeared responsible, Chibás denounced the "trigger-happy caballeros" but did his best to keep Grau out of it. One such event involved the murder of the student Hugo Dupotey Nico in the cabaret Bar Criollo on March 11, 1946. It was one of sixty-four *pistolero*-related murders that occurred during Grau's term. Initial reports named Major Pablo Suárez Aróstegui, the husband of Grau's niece "Tata" Grau Alsina, as the killer, but Chibás said the major was innocent and that he personally would find the assassin.

As suspense built, he announced on April 1 that next Sunday he would reveal the killer of Hugo Dupotey. When the radio hour came, all ears glued to the set, he failed to come up with the name, revealing only that present in the cabaret at the time of the shooting were several persons, including Eufemio Fernández Ortega (ARG) and Manolo Castro (MSR). Manolo "knows the guilty party," Eddy maintained, "and it is not Pablo Suárez." He suggested that it could be Mario Salabarría, the MSR chieftain, or "at least" his driver, Alfredo Aguerreberre, who "has disappeared."[25] In not carrying through, Chibás revealed a characteristic that proved his undoing in the end. He was a tireless crusader for honesty in government, but he was also overzealous, prone to exaggerate and to make claims that he could not support.

Chibás's relationship with Grau remained strong through the midterm elections of June 1946. He even hailed the appointment of José Alemán as minister of education.[26] He also supported enthusiastically the Auténtico candidate for mayor of Havana, Manuel Fernández Supervielle, who had a reputation for honesty as minister of the treasury and was campaigning on a pledge to build an aqueduct for Havana. Water was a chronic problem in Havana, and in past elections candidates routinely promised an aqueduct but never made good. In 1944, while drinking a daiquiri in his favorite haunt, La Floridita, a Cuban politician told Thomas Hudson (Hemingway), one can always get money for an aqueduct, so promise it, but don't build it. "Would you kill the goose that lays the golden aqueduct?"[27] Supervielle was different. He intended to build it.

Chibás campaigned hard for Supervielle, defeating the candidacy of Carlos Miguel Céspedes, whom Eddy denounced as a *machadista*. But Supervielle's victory was bittersweet for Chibás because it encouraged the movement for Grau's reelection. Among Grau's supporters, Chibás was the most outspoken of any in opposition to a constitutional reform permitting presidential reelection or extension of power. He opposed it in 1927, he reminded everyone, and still opposed it. It was "a question of principle," he stated in a broadcast on July 23. But Eddy's opposition to Grau's reelection was clouded by his own presidential ambition. Just a week earlier, in speaking against extending the Auténtico-Republican pact, Chibás argued that the PRC-A could win in 1948 on its own with the right candidate, adding, "And I'm it."[28]

Chibás's open criticism of *pistolerismo* and corruption in government and his opposition to the reelection movement and the alliance with the Republicans were affecting Auténtico unity. Those positions brought him into conflict with Tony Varona, Rubén de León, and Carlos Prío, his "old companions from student battles,"[29] each a founder of the PRC-A and an original member of the 1930 DEU. Varona deplored his attacks on the Auténtico-Republican alliance as "divisive," and De León said he was "pugnacious," comparing him to the popular Cuban boxer Kid Chocolate (Eligio Sardiñas).[30] Always a powerful orator, Chibás described the division as one between "sound revolutionary radicalism" and "rank traditionalist reactionaryism."[31]

The split became nearly irreparable during the mayor's race in Camagüey in September, when Chibás attacked the Auténtico candidate, Aguilar Recio, as a "dastardly *machadista*" and threw his support to the opposition candidate, Ramón Pereda Pulgares. "All the Al Capones of Cuban politics are with the candidate Aguilar Recio," Chibás intoned. "All the best leaders of the PRC, the Revolution, and Camagüey are with Pereda."[32] Following the election, which Aguilar Recio won by a scant three thousand votes, Chibás and Varona got into a raucous exchange on the floor of the senate, which nearly came to blows, Chibás charging that the Camagüey election had been "bought" and Varona shouting, "That is false and despicable!" After order was restored, the two men agreed to a duel on October 26. It was the fifth in a total of ten duels that Eddy fought between 1945 and 1950 with such rivals as Varona, Inocente Alvarez, Francisco "Paco" Prío, Carlos Prío, and the sugar baron José Manuel Casanova. Chibás and Varona fought with sabers, Eddy receiving a slight wound on the forearm, after which, with honor restored, the two men had lunch together in the restaurant Kasalta.[33] But the political wounds were not as easily healed. By the time that Chibás called Alemán a crook in December, a so-called Ortodoxo group in the PRC-A was considering the creation of a new party. Although Chibás resisted the formation of a new party, insisting that he preferred to remain within the party in order to save it, a further crisis arose over a different gang of crooks.

The notorious Mafia chieftain Lucky Luciano arrived in Havana in October 1946. He had been serving a long prison term in the United States but was released suddenly and deported to Italy the previous February, apparently because of his assistance to U.S. intelligence during the war in counterespionage activities on the New York docks and in collecting information and making contacts that facilitated the invasion of Sicily. He was not content to remain in Italy, so his partner-in-crime Meyer Lansky arranged his move to Cuba. Lansky had been the Mafia's man in Cuba during the Prohibition era, overseeing rum-running operations. After repeal, he stayed behind and shifted his activities to gambling, taking charge of the Gran Casino Nacional in 1937 and paying Batista "millions of dollars a year."[34] Lansky urged Luciano to come to Cuba. "You could operate from the island the way you did in the old days," he told him.[35] Although Lansky served as Batista's "banker," transferring his share of gambling receipts to an account in Switzerland, his influence also extended into the Grau government. He enlisted the support of Minister of the Interior Alfredo Pequeño and Chief of Secret Police Benito Herrera in bringing Luciano to Cuba.[36]

Cuba was only the first step in Luciano's plan to return to the United States, but to reassert his authority, he decided to hold an "underworld convention" in Havana in December 1946. It was the first general meeting of the council of the Unione Siciliano in more than a decade. Luciano took over the top four floors of the Hotel Nacional to host a gallery of notorious crime figures that included Joe Adonis, Albert Anastasia, Joe "Bananas" Bonanno, Frank Costello, Carlo Gambino, Vito Genovese, Tommy Lucchese, and Santo Trafficante.[37] For entertainment, Frank Sinatra came to give a Christmas concert, providing a legitimate image for the "meet." Luciano told the delegates that he was "making his way back to America" and that "arrangements" had been "fixed up" with the government for him to stay in Cuba "for as long as necessary."[38] He subsequently confessed that he had another reason for "pickin'" Havana as his halfway home: "The war bein' over, people was beginnin' to flock there, what with the place bein' wide open, the gamblin' good and the broads beautiful. With a combination like that, Lansky and his friend Batista was rakin' the dough in and I had no intention of bein' left out of that. Batista wasn't president no more, but he had his own guy in there, a doctor named Ramón Grau San Martín; Lansky and Batista had him strictly in their pockets."[39] Luciano's assertion that Grau was in the "pocket" of his archenemy Batista was an exaggeration, but the mobster's presence in Cuba caused a scandal nonetheless. His flamboyant lifestyle, plus rumors that he intended to take over the Isle of Pines and convert it into a Caribbean Monte Carlo,[40] attracted attention and led to demands that he be expelled.

Among those calling for his expulsion, Henry Anslinger, chief of the U.S. Bureau of Narcotics, charged that drug trafficking had increased since Luciano's arrival in Cuba. He urged President Harry Truman to put pressure on the Cuban government to send Luciano back to Italy.[41] Pressure from Washington only stiffened the resolve of the Grau government in its usual stubborn and independent attitude toward the north, but Eddy Chibás saw a darker side. He led the fight in Cuba to get rid of Luciano. He accused the Mafia chieftain of "dealing in drugs, gambling, and prostitution" and claimed that the Grau government was reluctant to deport him out of fear that he would reveal the names of his "Cuban associates," who, Chibás alleged, included Francisco "Paco" Prío Socarrás, the brother of the prime minister. This charge led to a fistfight on the floor of the senate, "Paco" punching Eddy and shouting, "Lucky Luciano sends this to you," followed by the inevitable duel on the field of honor.[42] The Grau government finally did detain Luciano and return him to Italy, but by the time that "Paco" Prío and Chibás had their altercation in March 1947, Chibás was almost completely estranged from Grau and the Auténticos.

Earlier, in January, Chibás had written a letter to Grau in which he sharply criticized "his work of government." He revisited the issue of the *trueques*, affirming that Alvarez had deceived him. "Inocente was not innocent," he wrote. And he accused the present minister of commerce, César Casas, of dealing on the black market. He claimed that Grau's closest advisers were reaping huge fortunes on the black market and in illicit sugar sales, "while the children in the public schools go without their `School Lunch.'" You are, he told Grau, in the midst of such a stench that your nose has been desensitized and you cannot smell it. Furthermore, he demanded that Grau disavow the reelection campaign, which he charged was being carried on by certain ministers using misdirected public funds. In the past, he warned Grau, such campaigns had led to civil war. He reminded the president that he had been his "most devoted" partisan for twenty years but that now he wanted an explanation for why he had "abandoned" the goals of the PRC-A and "turned his back" on its "principles."[43] After he had addressed the proud Grau in this manner, it was evident that Chibás's days in the Auténtico Party were numbered, even though he resisted calls to abandon the "sinking ship" for several months.

Chibás's friends, having formed the *grupo ortodoxo* (Ortodoxo group), urged him to consider forming a new party, but he held out, insisting that he had faith in the "great moral resources of *autenticismo*." He invited all Auténticos to join him in rescuing the party from "enemy hands."[44] His followers, including Mario Castillo, José Pardo Llada, Evelio Alvarez del Real, and Emilio Ochoa, disagreed, saying that they had no future in the party. Grau would never forgive them for crushing his "reelection dreams" and would bring down the full weight of his anger against them "budgetary and bureaucratically." At the same time, they realized that they could not proceed without Chibás. Starting a new party without him, Alvarez del Real declared, would be like making *"arroz con pollo sin pollo"* (like making chicken with rice without the chicken).[45]

Nonetheless, as the old year ended and the new began, it was evident that the "Authentic Revolution" was about to divide. The Grau government had triumphed in the midterm elections in June, but its standing had declined by December with the rise of the corrupt minister of education José Alemán. Though Grau maintained his mystique as *el Maestro* and *el Viejo,* the constitutional order prevailed, resisting his ambition for reelection. Critics like Eddy Chibás had their say, and political affairs were freewheeling. R. Henry Norweb, the U.S. ambassador, reported to Washington, "The Grau administration has not covered itself with glory, but on the other hand it is undoubtedly the most democratic regime in Cuban history."[46] Having a different view, Inocente Alvarez, of all people, after resigning as foreign minister in December, confided to Chibás, "The present government is the most corrupt in the history of the republic."[47] The year ahead promised to be very stormy.

3

The Torrid Season

The third year of Grau's presidency was the most tempestuous yet. The year began with Eddy Chibás's letter accusing Grau of abandoning the PRC-A program and surrounding himself with corrupt ministers and advisers. And events piled on from there. While dissident Auténticos had already formed the Ortodoxo group and wanted Chibás to lead them out of the party, party stalwarts, such as Segundo Curti, tried to persuade him not to break ranks. Curti insisted that the talk of Grau's ambition for reelection was exaggerated, and he teased Chibás for his reputation as "el loco" ("the crazy one").[1]

Chibás was a wild character. Short of stature and wearing ultra-thick lenses to overcome his poor eyesight, he raced around Havana in a Packard convertible, ignoring traffic signs and speed limits. He was just as impetuous and erratic in his public statements, but he was scrupulously honest and ingenuous. He was "easy to ridicule," but he seemed to delight in his image as "Crazy Eddy."[2] He was a "tortured soul"; he was more Auténtico than the "thieves and fifth columnists" who had taken over the party, but he faced the dilemma of having to leave the PRC-A to save its program. Chibás told his radio audience at the end of March that he would not form a new party and that he was still determined to fight from within.[3] A week later, however, he voted with the dissident Auténticos in the Senate to approve a resolution to interpellate ministers José Manuel Alemán (education) and César Casas (commerce). They wanted to confront Alemán with allegations of embezzlement and misappropriation of funds and Casas for alleged conspiracy in the customs service to abet smuggling and the operation of the black market in goods and foodstuffs.

The semiparliamentary system established by the Constitution of 1940 enabled the Senate and the Chamber of Representatives to summon ministers of government for formal questioning. The process, intended to restrain the president, appeared to work in October 1945, when the Chamber interrogated Commerce Minister Inocente Alberto Alvarez for seven hours and voted "no confidence" in view of his "mistaken and prejudicial" conduct in the matter of the *trueques* (barter deals).[4] Admittedly, Grau had the last word, immediately appointing Alvarez minister of foreign affairs. When the Senate moved to summon Alemán and Casas, Grau was incensed and refused to present them. Casas told the president that he was "terrorized" by the thought of a public appearance; "I have stage fright," he explained.[5] Alemán took another tack, ordering his *pistoleros* to fire into the Senate chamber. Refusing to be intimidated, the Senate voted no confidence against the entire cabinet. Ever resourceful, Grau eventually frustrated the action, appointing a subcabinet made up of deputy ministers and then restoring the original cabinet after the Senate had adjourned. He further relied on a constitutional provisional that prevented a new vote of no confidence for six months to a year.[6] Nonetheless, the very occurrence of this "institutional crisis" demonstrated a new dynamic in Cuban political affairs, whereby the legislative branch contested the executive branch with some success.

In the midst of this clash, Manuel Fernández Supervielle, the mayor of Havana, committed suicide. Like Chibás, he was an honest man, came from the old Cuban bourgeoisie, and was a "political populist."[7] He had promised water to the city of Havana but failed, being "torpedoed" by the central government in his efforts to build an aqueduct. His suicide, according to Guillermo Cabrera Infante, "was an expression of personal failure."[8] His widow told Chibás that Grau was to blame. "He! Only he! He is responsible for [my husband's] death!"[9] And she asked Chibás "to open the eyes" of the Cuban people. Supervielle's suicide coupled with Grau's obstinate defense of the corrupt Alemán and Casas led Chibás finally to break with Grau and leave the Auténtico Party. One may argue that Chibás's driving ambition for the presidency tainted his break with Grau and the Auténticos, or that his program lacked "a serious analysis" of the "social roots of corruption in Cuba."[10] But one may not deny his deep revulsion for the dishonest practices emanating from the third floor of the Presidential Palace. R. Henry Norweb, the American ambassador, had a dimmer view of these shifts in political allegiance, which revealed more about the ambassador than about Cuban politics: "We now have the familiar spectacle of the same people jockeying for place and power, first in one alignment and then another. The combinations or re-combinations change, but the main participants seldom, and I am unable to recall a significant or plausible public statement of any principles involved in these shifts. To invoke principles might indeed have been too cynical."[11]

On May 11, 1947, using the microphones of CMQ, Chibás announced his intention to form a new party. He proclaimed that Grau had abandoned the ideas and program of the PRC-A—"nationalism, anti-imperialism, and socialism." He lamented that he could no longer fight "the irregularities, vices, and frauds" of Grau and his ministers from within.[12] Four days later, Chibás met with other disaffected Auténticos, among them Pelayo Cuervo Navaro, Emilio Ochoa, Manuel Bisbé, Agustín Cruz, Luis Orlando Rodríguez, Luis Conte Agüero, Charles Simeón, and Rafael García Bárcena, in the headquarters of the Auténtico Youth Section. They appointed an organizing committee and gave Grau seventy-two hours to convoke the National Assembly of the PRC-A as one last gesture toward reconciliation.

By the end of the month, when Grau had not responded, Chibás created the Cuban People's Party (PPC)—Ortodoxo. He stated that he acted for the purpose "of rescuing the program of the PRC-A and the Auténtico doctrine—economic independence, political liberty, and social justice—conducting our activities within the democratic regimen established in the Constitution."[13] Always one for symbolism, Chibás set up the Ortodoxo headquarters in the former gymnasium of Kid Chocolate, the popular Cuban featherweight boxer. Though his rivals might refer to him as "punchy," he preferred to be seen as "pugnacious," a scrappy underdog, ready to take on the *"caciques"* (bosses) and grafters. It was also an effort to attract the Afro-Cuban community, which had been ignored generally by the political parties except for the PSP (Communist Party), which had a large black membership. The new party purposely ignored the *pistoleros*, unless one counted Fidel Castro.

The student Castro was present at the May 15 meeting and became a founding member of the PPC. Strongly critical of Grau and the Auténticos and in deep trouble with Mario Salabarría and the MSR, Castro was perceived as UIR and may actually have been one of the *bonche*. He came to the meeting attracted by Chibás's effective use of radio and admiring his "fearless style of moral denunciation," but he was not attuned to his nonviolent approach to politics or to his strong anticommunist stance.[14]

As a result, he formed a splinter group within the Youth Section of the party known as the Ortodoxo Radical Action (ARO) made up largely of former UIR members and "action groups" that favored armed revolt.[15] It was uncharacteristic for Chibás to tolerate this situation; on one occasion, when Castro tried to enter Eddy's Packard, he was ordered out. In response to queries as to what had happened, Chibás shrugged: "Nothing, but I don't like people to see me with a gangster in my automobile."[16] Despite Chibás's apparent disapproval, Castro remained an Ortodoxo throughout the democratic experience, learning a great deal from Chibás and studying his propaganda techniques and use of symbols.[17]

In reference to symbols, while the Ortodoxo Party was in the process of formation, someone stole the diamond set in the floor of the Capitol rotunda. The diamond, valued at from thirty to forty thousand dollars, marked the zero point for determining distances to all parts of Cuba. In early June, it turned up on the desk of President Grau, with the implication that he was the biggest thief of them all. Chibás adopted a broom as his symbol to demonstrate his determination to "sweep away" the corruption of the Auténticos.[18] Not to be outdone, and showing that he was learning fast, Fidel Castro brought the Demajagua Bell from Manzanillo to the University of Havana campus in November 1947.

The Demajagua Bell, first used in 1868 to initiate the War of Independence, making it Cuba's "Liberty Bell," was the perfect symbol in Castro's thinking to announce "a war against government graft."[19] With the connivance of local officials, Castro and fellow students Lionel Soto and Enrique Ovares traveled to Manzanillo to bring the three-hundred-pound bell to the University of Havana on November 5, planning to hold a rally and ring-in the war against corruption the next day. The bell was "stolen" overnight, however, only to be "retrieved" several days later by Grau and returned to Manzanillo. But Castro still had his day, addressing the rally on November 6 and denouncing Grau for "betraying" the 1933 revolution.[20] While Grau was beset by diamonds, brooms, and bells, along with insurgency in Congress and division in his party, he launched an offensive to oust the Communists from leadership of the Cuban Workers Confederation (CTC).

The CTC was a holdover from the populism of the Batista dictatorship of the 1930s. It was a corporatist go-between, representing workers' interests in the Presidential Palace and handing out government concessions in the Workers Palace (constructed in 1946 with a $772,000 grant from the Grau administration). It provided the government in power with political support and industrial peace in return for mandated wage hikes, favored working conditions, and job security for organized workers. Because the CTC was essentially a political organization, it frequently promoted labor practices that deterred economic development, such as featherbedding and resistance to technological innovation. For example, throughout 1946 the Grau government was locked in a bitter battle with Seatrain Lines, Inc., a U.S. containerized cargo shipping company. The dispute revolved around the dockworkers' demands that they either be allowed to unload cargo in port for reloading unto Cuban railway cars or "to be paid as much for servicing Seatrain . . . [as for] actually unloading cargo from the holds of conventional ships."[21] This controversy persisted throughout Grau's term and that of his successor, causing turmoil on the docks and checking economic growth, though offset by the joy of hamstringing a Yankee company. Though Grau was unabashedly pro-labor, he was uneasy over Communist leadership of the CTC.

Grau's collaboration with the PSP was a marriage of convenience. On the day of his election, he declared that the CTC was "a product of the authentic revolution" and announced his intention to restore it "to its rightful owners."[22] But this was sheer bravado; his position was too precarious, especially in the early going, to risk a fight with organized labor over the question of leadership of the CTC. He adopted a pragmatic course, entering into a pact with the PSP that enabled Lázaro Peña to continue as secretary general of the CTC in return for enlarged Auténtico representation on the Executive Committee (the Communists called it a "Trojan horse"). This arrangement suited Grau's political ends, but the true-blue Auténticos—the 1930 Generation Auténticos, such as Carlos Prío and Tony Varona—opposed it and worked to undermine it from the beginning. Being social democrats, they were firmly anticommunist, believing in the Aprista approach of reform without sacrificing individual freedoms. The advent of the Cold War gave added intensity to the struggle, marked by Prío's affirmation: "We must remove their masks [the Communists'] and expose their aims of world domination."[23]

The Auténticos' labor arm, the National Workers Committee (CON), under the leadership of Eusebio Mujal, Francisco Aguirre, and Juan Arévalo, took on the job of breaking the Communists' hold over the CTC. CON proposed Aguirre for secretary general and began fieldwork among the member unions of the CTC aimed at securing a majority of delegates to the V National Congress scheduled for December 1946. To facilitate this task, José Alemán provided money, and the ARG's Eufemio Fernández provided muscle. Alemán supported the campaign with an infusion of twenty-three thousand pesos monthly, and Fernández was on hand to protect the organizers and bully the opposition. Unique among the action groups or *pistoleros*, the ARG possessed an ideology, being anarcho-syndicalist in orientation and focusing on the labor movement. Mujal's efforts were further aided by the American Federation of Labor (AFL), which was leading the Cold War campaign to organize democratic trade unions in the hemisphere to displace the Communist-sponsored Latin American Workers Confederation (CTAL), led by the Mexican labor leader Vicente Lombardo Toledano. In early 1946, Mujal, Aguirre, and Arévalo met in Miami with Serafino Romualdi, the AFL's "roving ambassador" for Latin America, and Arévalo, head of the Cuban Maritime Union and the CTC's foreign secretary, maintained contact with Matthew Woll, the AFL's vice president and head of its Free Trade Union Committee. Jay Lovestone, who had close links to U.S. intelligence agencies, was the committee's executive secretary. Receiving covert funding from U.S. clandestine services, the AFL provided monetary and technical support to CON in its organizing activities. It expected in return that the "cleansed" CTC would withdraw from Lombardo Toledano's CTAL and join the AFL-sponsored Inter-American Confederation of Labor (CIT), then in the process of formation (and later replaced by the Inter-American Regional Organization of Workers [ORIT]).[24] Despite this support and intrigue, CON failed to win a majority of delegates during 1946 and prevailed on the Grau government to force a postponement of the CTC's national congress until the following April.

During the first three months of 1947, the campaign heated up considerably. The battle shifted to the Credentials Committee, where Aguirre, representing CON, blocked the certification of PSP delegates. CON also enlisted the support of the CTC's "independent" faction, sponsoring "in secret" the formation of the Independent National Workers Committee (CONI) under the leadership of Angel Cofiño.[25] Still, Mujal and his colleagues were coming up short, leading to a great deal of frustration and the outbreak of violence. On April 5, an armed clash took place at a sugar workers local, and Félix Palú, an Auténtico sympathizer, was killed. Two days later, on the pretext of needing a cooling-off period, the Grau government suspended the convocation of the V Congress for a second time, appointing an official commission to examine the credentials of the delegates. But the CTC Executive Committee secured a restraining order, charging that the government's action violated the constitutional rights of the organization.

Following the May Day celebrations, Peña convoked the CTC congress. CON and CONI boycotted the sessions, and in their absence Peña won reelection as secretary general. The days of PSP control over the CTC were numbered, however. On April 30, Prío had become minister of labor, and he encouraged Mujal and Cofiño to call a CTC congress composed of any delegates they could round up. "Even police officers and Auténtico councilmen from diverse localities of the island were seen in the role of delegates."[26] The rump congress met on July 6, 7, and 8 in the auditorium of Radio-Cine and elected Cofiño as secretary general. Though CONI was a sham, the election of the "independent" and former Communist Cofiño provided some cover for the high-handed tactics of Grau and the "cetekarios" (CTK, so-called because of the use of *Inciso* K funds to finance the outcome).[27] Thus at the very time that Eddy Chibás was splitting the authentic revolution in two, Grau was dividing the Cuban labor movement. But in the latter case, the fight was unequal.

Although the PSP gave Cuban labor efficient leadership, it failed to instill a "class consciousness," that is, "to educate the workers in defense of their interests," maintaining loyalty instead through the delivery of benefits in partnership with the government in power.[28] The loss of official recognition reduced Peña's CTC, which had relied on government favors, to an empty shell. At the end of July, Prío "evicted" Peña and his followers from the Workers Palace. In protest, or retaliation, Peña ordered strikes and work slowdowns across the island, but such actions were counterproductive (and notably ineffective), providing Prío with the excuse for cracking down harder. He filled the jails with Communist strikers and on October 9 issued a decree recognizing the Cofiño CTC.[29] Several days later, he seized the PSP's newspaper *Hoy* and shut down its radio station, Mil Diez (1010). The Auténticos had succeeded in taking over the CTC, even if the labor movement was in certain disarray.

The Cuban scholars Oscar Zanetti and Alejandro García accuse the Auténticos of "toeing the line of the United States cold war policy" and of employing "the dirtiest gangster tactics" in ousting the Communists from the leadership of the CTC.[30] They forget that the Cold War context merely reinforced a rivalry that had its roots in the Cuban experience. While the Auténticos suffered exile and martyrdom in the 1930s, the Communist Party collaborated with the dictator Batista in creating the CTC in 1939 and in cashing in on the labor and social decrees of the "100 Days." When Grau first tried to remove Peña as head of the CTC in 1944, United States ambassador Spruille Braden asked him to refrain in deference to wartime unity. In renewing the campaign against Peña in 1946, Grau proclaimed, "The CTC cannot be in hands other than those of patriotic workers, because the CTC is the legitimate daughter of the first Auténtico administration. I never thought it would fall into the hands of those who upheld doctrines that introduced alienating customs in the country."[31] The further assertion that the Auténticos sought to "divide" labor so as to render it "obedient to the owners and the dictates of Washington"[32] denies the legitimacy of the ideological stand of the Auténticos as social democrats against communism. And it belies the pro-labor policies of the Grau administration that caused powerful resentment on the part of U.S. businesses on the island. As the party in power, the Auténticos had a responsibility to control the violence, which they failed to do, marking the most serious contradiction in the recognition of the Auténtico governments as truly democratic. The most egregious case was the murder of Jesús Menéndez, president of the National Federation of Sugar Workers (FNTA), by a military officer in January 1948, allegedly for resisting arrest. Still, Juan Manuel Márquez, a municipal councilman of Marianao, introduced a resolution calling for the removal of Pérez Dámera as army chief of staff and the arrest and punishment of army captain Joaquín Castillas, the actual shooter.[33]

The Grau government's violations of civil liberties in the CTC takeover and use of ARG "shock troops" were a throwback to the eras of Machado and Batista, except that two branches of government continued to function as guarantors of the constitutional order. Cuba's higher courts defended the rights of the PSP as a legal political party, ordering the release of imprisoned strikers and restoring PSP ownership and operation of *Hoy* and *Mil Diez*.[34] In addition to the action of Councilman Márquez, the national Senate approved resolutions that ordered the interpellation of Labor Minister Prío and condemned President Grau for "administrative immorality and violation of the Constitution."[35] In his appearance before the Senate in October, Prío stood tall, realizing that public sentiment supported his anticommunist position. He reiterated his previous statements, declaring that the Communists "are a fifth column preparing Cuba for the USSR's war on the USA, and must therefore be eliminated from Cuba."[36] His purge of the Communists from the CTC had made him a front-runner for the Auténtico presidential nomination in 1948, and he announced his resignation as labor minister to enable him to concentrate on his presidential bid. The Auténticos had achieved a clean sweep; Aguirrre succeeded Prío as labor minister, and Mujal eventually replaced Cofiño as secretary general of the CTC. Arévalo did not fare as well, being the victim of labor violence in September 1948; all sides played rough. As for Prío, he could not rest on his laurels, as his rivals for the PRC-A nomination were busy on other fronts.

Coincidentally with Prío's takeover of the CTC, José Alemán was engaged in a foreign intrigue, which, if successful, would make him a national hero. With the blessings of Grau, Alemán was in charge of a covert operation intended to overthrow the dictator Rafael Trujillo in the Dominican Republic. In 1947, the largest concentration of Dominican exiles resided in Cuba. They had fled Trujillo's tyranny and taken advantage of Cuba's freedoms to organize a political opposition and devise means to duplicate those freedoms in their homeland, by force if necessary. The Auténticos overwhelmingly sympathized with their purpose; in fact, the program of the Dominican Revolutionary Party (PRD), founded in exile in Cuba in 1939, was close enough to that of the PRC-A to be a carbon copy. Enrique Cotubanamá ("Cotú") Henríquez, a Cuban politician of Dominican heritage and Prío's brother-in-law, was the author of both programs, drawing heavily on Aprista and social democratic formulas.[37] In February 1947, the Dominican exiles in Cuba began the organization of an armed expedition to overthrow Trujillo in the Dominican Republic.

The principal leader of the expedition was Juan Rodríguez García, a Dominican millionaire cattle rancher, who had only recently fled the Dominican Republic. He provided the "spark" and money that got the movement going. The plan foresaw the preparation of a liberation force to attack the Dominican Republic by sea from Cuba and link up with an Internal Front awaiting the arrival of the invaders as the moment to rebel. Longtime Dominican exiles such as Juan Bosch and Angel Morales already had ties with Auténtico leaders and pledges of support. In addition to ideological sympathies, Grau, Prío, et al. favored a policy of overthrowing Latin America's dictators, not just Trujillo, as a threat to democracy and as a means of finishing the job of World War II. In this purpose they enjoyed the active support of presidents Rómulo Betancourt of Venezuela and Juan José Arévalo of Guatemala. With the connivance of the latter, Rodríguez purchased a thousand Mauser rifles and a million rounds of ammunition indirectly from Juan Perón of Argentina.[38] Bosch also busied himself in arms procurement, acquiring small aircraft and conspiring with Cuban customs officials to bring in "war surplus" weapons purchased in the United States.[39]

By the summer of 1947, the movement had ballooned into a grandiose plan to create a Liberation Army of America to eliminate all the dictators in the region, adding Anastasio Somoza of Nicaragua and Tiburcio Carías Andino of Honduras to the list. Though Rodríguez remained commander in chief of the Liberation Army, Grau had placed Alemán in charge of Cuba's clandestine support of the Dominicans, and the "señor of *Inciso*

K" got carried away. In addition to the invasion from Cuba by sea, he envisioned a combined operation of air raids on Ciudad Trujillo (Santo Domingo) and a land incursion from Haiti. To promote his plan, he funneled three million dollars of his ministry's funds to the movement and provided school buildings and other venues and trucks and buses.[40] Initially, the José Martí Sports Park and Havana Sports Palace were used as recruiting stations and drill grounds. To oversee the day-to-day preparations, he assigned Rolando Masferrer, the head of MSR, and Manolo Castro, the national sports director, full time. Masferrer, a former Communist and Spanish Civil War veteran, proved a tough drill instructor, and Manolo Castro traveled to the United States to procure aircraft and high explosives and to recruit fighter pilots. He succeeded in bringing back some of the legendary Flying Tigers, who established their headquarters in the Hotel Sevilla, a block from the Presidential Palace and almost as close to Sloppy Joe's and La Floridita. By mid-July, a force of twelve hundred men had been amassed, in which Cubans outnumbered Dominicans two to one. Most of the Cubans were MSR, though a few recruits belonged to other *bonches*. Fidel Castro was one, volunteering after first receiving guarantees through FEU president Enrique Ovares that his life would not be in danger.[41]

All this commotion, especially in public buildings and places, removed whatever secrecy the movement ever enjoyed. Héctor Incháustegui Cabral, the Dominican chargé in Havana, reported to Trujillo that he did not need "special sources" (spies) to learn what was happening because he heard it "on the street, in cafés, from bootblacks and taxi drivers," and read it in the newspapers "every day."[42] Even the mothers of some of the recruits published a petition calling on Grau to halt the expedition. U.S. secretary of state George C. Marshall, in the midst of preparations for a conference in Rio de Janeiro to draft an inter-American defense treaty, was alarmed over the reports and instructed Ambassador Norweb to remind Cuba of its commitment to the principle of nonintervention. He told Norweb to go directly to President Grau and insist that he investigate the reports of the plot, with the expectation that if he found it to exist, "he would crush it rapidly and effectively."[43] In follow-up meetings with Foreign Minister Rafael Pérez y González Muñoz, Norweb was certain that Cuba was stonewalling and "unwilling to cooperate with the United States on this or any other matter."[44] ("Any other matter" was a reference to Norweb's difficulties in negotiating a treaty of friendship, commerce, and navigation.) Grau was still displaying his nationalistic colors and refusing to be a toady of the Yankees, but within Cuba denial was less easy to sustain, especially as knowledge of Havana's worst-kept secret spread.

In July, the Dominican foreign minister, Arturo Despradel, lodged protests about the invasion plot in Havana, Washington, and New York (before the United Nations), to little avail. Thus, the twenty-third of the month, the Dominican army chief of staff, General Fausto E. Caamaño, sent a telegram directly to his counterpart in Cuba, General Genovevo Pérez Dámera, stating, "Although I assume you are aware of the military preparations taking place in Cuba for the purpose of invading our territory, I wish to notify you officially for the record."[45] Though it is hard to believe that Pérez Dámera was unaware of the preparations, he confronted Grau with the message, and Grau likewise expressed surprise that he had no knowledge of the conspiracy and asked Alemán "to bring the General up-to-date."[46] Pérez Dámera was loyal to Grau, he owed him everything, but he regarded Alemán as a delinquent, sponsoring political corruption and street violence, and he had to react. He insisted that the expedition "had to leave Cuba soon," or he would disband it as a "threat to the peace."[47] The protests of the United States and the Dominican Republic failed to move Grau, but Pérez Dámera's warning was more serious. Under instructions from Grau, Alemán moved the recruits first to the campus of the Polytechnic School in Holguín and then to Cayo Confites, a key off Cuba's northeast coast, near Nuevitas.

In August 1947, Cayo Confites was a barren islet that was home to an old fisherman and his family and a few goats. During World War II, the Cuban government used the key as a coast-watchers' station with a few personnel and a radio transmitter. Hemingway's protagonist in *Islands in the Stream*, Thomas Hudson, took on supplies there during his tragic pursuit of the survivors of a doomed German U-boat. In any event, it was not suitable for accommodating twelve hundred men for very long. But the expedition got stuck there for six weeks, long enough to cause its failure. The United States, which had been unable to get Grau to cooperate, contributed to this outcome by impounding the vessel *Patria*, a war surplus LCI that Rodríguez had purchased in Baltimore. Until Rodríguez could get permission for this vessel to leave the United States, his invasion plans were on hold. Masferrer kept the troops busy drilling and practicing landings, but boredom and the lack of sanitation caused morale to sink. Cotú Henríquez, for one, had to be taken to the mainland, suffering with acute gastroenteritis caused by the swarm of flies that infested the camp.[48] The delay exacerbated existing divisions; Masferrer, dubbed "the tiger" for his ferocity, did not get along with Bosch and threatened his life, and

Fidel Castro, under similar circumstances, survived by keeping out of sight. The Dominicans were motivated by patriotism but suspected that their Cuban allies had other purposes in mind. They feared that certain Cubans planned to go on a "looting spree" in Ciudad Trujillo, having heard rumors that they had maps of the city marked with the locations of banks and jewelry stores.[49] Even Grau's decision to give Alemán a sixty-day leave of absence from his ministerial duties, presumably to enable him "to devote more time to the solution of the Dominican problem," did not change matters.[50] He had lost his chance, and a seemingly unrelated episode made it a certainty.

On September 15, the most spectacular shoot-out in the history of Cuban *pistolerismo* took place in the Orfila section of the Marianao suburb of Havana. For almost three hours that afternoon, two groups of uniformed policemen representing the rival MSR and UIR gangs exchanged gunfire that killed six people and wounded eleven. The fight began when MSR gunman and chief of the Enemy Activities Investigating Bureau of the National Police Major Mario Salabarría went to the home of Major Antonio Morín Dopico, chief of police of Marianao, with an arrest warrant for UIR leader and director of the National Police Academy Major Emilio Tró, charged with the murder of Captain Raúl Avila, chief of police of the Ministry of Health, three days earlier. Tró resisted arrest, and the shooting began. While the battle raged, newsreel cameramen filmed the event, providing documentary evidence that Tró and Morín's pregnant wife were shot in cold blood after the flag of surrender had been raised.[51]

Grau showed little inclination to interfere in the struggle, but its length and intensity left him no choice. With great reluctance, he ordered the army to intervene and requested General Pérez Dámera to return from Washington, where he was on an official visit. Pérez did not get back to Havana until 3 A.M., hours after the gun battle had ended, but he went to work immediately to smash *pistolero* presence in the National Police and, coincidentally, to quash the Dominican invasion plot. He appointed a military supervisor for the National Police and, after viewing the newsreels, arrested the "assassin" Salabarría. He occupied the National Police Academy and searched the Sevilla, but the Flying Tigers had already flown, having been spirited away on a Pan Am flight to Miami by the American embassy. He even sent a search party to Hemingway's finca, Vigía, east of Havana. The author was a friend of Manolo Castro and supposedly was billeting some American pilots and hiding weapons for the expedition.[52] But Pérez's most spectacular move occurred on September 20, when he raided Alemán's finca, América, and seized thirteen truckloads of arms and military equipment. While Alemán was procuring weapons for the Cayo Confites expedition, he amassed a huge arsenal of his own on his estate outside Havana. Eddy Chibás wryly noted the minister of education's "art of magic" in converting "pencils, paper, and text books" into "machine guns, rifles, and grenades" and suggested that Alemán and Grau were using the Dominican invasion plot to conceal plans for a "golpe de estado" to remain in power.[53] Whatever the truth of this assertion, Grau and Alemán had no choice but to admit what they had been denying—that they were involved in a plot to invade the Dominican Republic—unless they wanted to be charged with treason. The deeply embarrassed Grau summoned Juan Rodríguez from Cayo Confites to inform him that he had twenty-four hours to leave Cuba.[54]

The collapse of the expedition was not a tidy affair. Masferrer, after abandoning the key, first set sail for Havana, possibly intending to reinforce Alemán and the MSR and restore Grau's authority over Pérez, but Grau radioed him to stop at Cayo Santa María and await Rodríguez there. After taking on supplies on September 25, the expedition wandered aimlessly along the Cuban coast. Masferrer seemed bent on salvaging the operation, mentioning Haiti as a possible landing site, claiming that "six tanks and forty trucks" were waiting there to cross the frontier into the Dominican Republic.[55] But the game was up, and on September 29, Cuban warships overtook the two vessels commanded by Rodríguez and Masferrer and took them into Antilla on Nipe Bay. The expeditionaries were placed in boxcars and shipped to Havana, except for Fidel Castro, who dove into Nipe Bay and swam ashore, fearful that Masferrer might take advantage of the confusion to kill him.[56]

Once the argonauts were back in Havana, their defeat was transformed into triumph. They were greeted as heroes, and Supreme Court magistrate Evelio Tabio ordered their release, ruling that they had not threatened the constitutional order and that the armed forces overreached in arresting them and seizing their property. Against the vehement protests of the Dominican government, Grau permitted Rodríguez to recover most of his weapons and depart for Guatemala, where he could plot anew. Pérez was recast from the "man of the hour" to a "Judas." There were rumors that he had gone to Washington to receive a two-million-dollar bribe from Trujillo and that his efforts to disarm the *pistoleros* were a smoke screen for his real purpose of suppressing the expedition. The American ambassador observed that at the very least the "portly" general "ran away with the ball" and embarrassed the president and "his favorite," Alemán.[57] Of those involved, only Alemán was unable to capitalize on the sympathy of the Cuban people toward the Dominican rebels. In response to a Senate vote of "no confidence" against him on October 1, he organized a "confidence rally" for himself a week later, but protesters showed up and a high school student was killed in the melee. Fidel Castro, back on campus after his adventure, led a demonstration to display the youth's body before the Presidential Palace, challenging Grau to "come out and see your handiwork."[58] The Orfila and Cayo Confites affairs were a watershed in a way in the Auténtico rule—not just the winding down of the Grau presidency but an irreconcilable breach, engendering demagoguery and gang warfare. The only constant was the heavy influence of the United States in the Cuban economy.

In the midst of the fight over the CTC and the buildup of the Cayo Confites expedition, President Harry Truman signed the Sugar Act of 1948 on August 8, 1947. This measure, replacing the Sugar Act of 1937, due to expire at the end of 1947, provided Cuba with essentially the same quota it had before. The United States had reneged on its promise to reward Cuba "for its excellent production performance during the war."[59] Even worse, Section 202e of the act authorized the U.S. secretary of agriculture "to retain or reserve any increase in the sugar quota of a foreign country that denied fair and equitable treatment to United States citizens, their commerce, navigation, and industry."[60] Guillermo Belt, the Cuban ambassador to the United States, complained that Section 202e was "a violation of the Act of Chapultepec, Pan-Americanism and the United Nations Charter."[61] Even Sumner Welles concluded that this so-called good behavior clause was "a vicious joker solely intended to coerce the Cuban government."[62] Clearly, the Grau government had been distracted, but there was a further explanation for this unfortunate turn of events.

U.S.-Cuban relations had been strained since the beginning of 1947, when the United States proposed a draft Treaty of Friendship, Commerce, and Navigation. American business executives in Cuba had been pressuring the U.S. embassy in Havana and the State Department in Washington throughout 1946 for a commercial treaty. John Duys, president of the American Chamber of Commerce of Cuba, argued that such a treaty was necessary to put an end to "the abusive treatment of American businessmen in Cuba."[63] His members complained especially about the "Nationalization of Labor" law, insisting that it denied them the opportunity to hire "indispensable American personnel."[64] One member, F. Adair Monroe, president of the Cuba Company (a corporate conglomerate controlling sugar mills, lands, and the Consolidated Railroads of Cuba), went further, demanding a treaty that would "roll back all objectionable practices resulting from aggressive nationalism."[65] These businessmen had been very helpful in the past, doing more, in fact, than Cubans themselves to obtain favorable prices and quotas for Cuban sugar. With the strong endorsement of Ambassador Norweb, the so-called Havana Boys prevailed on the State Department to draft a treaty that, they affirmed, would make the Good Neighbor Policy a two-way street.[66]

The reception given the treaty by the Grau government demonstrated that, in foreign affairs and particularly in relations with the United States, it had not abandoned the principles of the Revolution of 1933. On August 1, 1946, the State Department consulted with Ambassador Belt about Article 1 of the proposed treaty, which was concerned with abating alleged discriminatory labor practices affecting U.S. citizens. Belt promised to respond in one week but had not done so by January 27, 1947, when Ambassador Norweb presented the draft treaty to the Cuban Foreign Ministry. When Pérez y González Muñoz assumed the position of foreign minister a few days later, on February 1, Norweb shuddered, informing the State Department that Pérez "had a reputation for being secretive, indecisive and reluctant to take action."[67] Pérez was adept in the art of procrastination; in his hands, the treaty languished. He had no intention of acting on it. Finally, at the end of March, when the U.S. Congress was beginning to consider the new sugar act, Belt conferred with Grau in Havana and proposed linking the treaty negotiations with an enhanced sugar quota for Cuba. The State Department had a similar idea, but an impasse occurred because neither side would act first. "Cuba argued that the quota must precede the treaty, and the United States insisted that the treaty must precede the quota."[68] As a result, Cuba lost out both ways.

The Sugar Act of 1948 was written without any input from Cuba, and the State Department imposed Section 202e in lieu of a treaty of friendship. U.S. beet sugar interests virtually wrote the sugar bill; no spokesman for Cuba took part in the congressional hearings on the measure.[69] Top officials in the State Department—Spruille Braden and Ellis Briggs—who had argued at length that Cuba should be given a larger sugar quota in recognition of its contribution to the U.S. war effort reversed their position in frustration over failing to secure a commercial treaty. Not only did they fail to fight for an enlarged sugar quota for Cuba, but they actually proposed Section 202e—the State Department's principal contribution to the sugar bill. Briggs bluntly informed Braden that the purpose of Section 202e was "to bring Cuba to the negotiating table to sign the Treaty of Friendship, Commerce and Navigation."[70] In urging President Truman to sign the Sugar Act of 1948, Secretary of State Marshall stated that Section 202e was "indispensable" for attaining "the protection of United States sugar mills and the conclusion of a treaty to protect U.S. businesses from nationalism."[71]

Grau and his successor, Carlos Prío Socarrás, never agreed to a commercial treaty with the United States, nor did they ever modify the prolabor legislation stemming from the Revolution of 1933 and the Constitution of 1940. Grau lashed out at the "economic aggression" of the United States implicit in Section 202e, condemning it as "the unilateral use of economic pressure by one state against another."[72] Belt presented this "Grau Doctrine" before the Inter-American Conference on the Maintenance of Peace and Security in Rio de Janeiro (the Rio Conference) in September 1947. The impact of these events, especially the disappointment over the sugar quota, tended to be lessened because 1947 was a peak year for the Cuban economy, fueled by sugar sales amounting to $662.7 million, second only to those of 1920.[73] And 1948 was almost as good. In the postwar era, Cuba was supplying one-quarter of the world's sugar production.[74]

Overlooked as part of the entire dynamic was the tremendous influence of American businessmen on Cuban affairs. Though they supported the idea of dangling an increased sugar quota as a means of achieving a commercial treaty, they did not want to go too far in punishing Cuba if it failed to comply. Those in the sugar business stood to profit from enhanced sales, and those with products to sell in Cuba realized that Cubans could not be good buyers if they were not successful sellers. The American Chamber of Commerce of Cuba had argued the latter point in a letter to Braden in May 1947, stating, "Since American exports to Cuba [are] directly dependent upon Cuba's ability to market her sugar, any undue protective measures whether in the form of high tariffs or low sugar quotas [will] deprive American farmers and manufacturers of millions of dollars of export trade with Cuba."[75] Not part of any grand conspiracy, businessmen like Maurice McGovern, president of General Electric Cubana, enjoyed the preferences of U.S. reciprocal trade policies, permitting him to penetrate the Cuban internal market. Nonetheless, reciprocity had the effect of diminishing Cuba's chances of diversifying its economy and rendering it increasingly dependent on sugar export sales.[76]

Despite the booming economy, it was a time of transition and for planning ahead for less prosperous times. For the preservation of its democratic order, Cuba needed to face the problem of its sugar-based economy.

According to Cabrera Infante, 1947 was a time of transition of another sort. The "last days" of 1947 were "the end of an era and the beginning of literature."[77] Cabrera was on the staff of *Hoy*, but that year he read Lino Novás Calvo and experienced an "awakening" and *Bohemia* published his first short story. In this democratic era he noted that one could get books. "By books I mean free books, literature, those that offer you adventures in reading."[78] He lived at 408 Zulueta Street, on the line dividing Old and Central Havana, just doors from Trocadero, where José Lezama Lima maintained his writers' commune and produced *Orígenes*. Even though these places were in Havana's tenderloin district, Cuba's bohemians, literati, and gunsels seemed to leave one another alone. "Despite the gang wars," according to Cabrera's experience, "Havana had always been a peaceable city."[79] Within this awakening, Cabrera contradicted another notion, affirming, "American influence never really amounted to much in Cuban cultural life, which was oriented towards Europe, especially to France and Spain."[80] He acknowledged that American films were "truly" influential, even if "only at a popular level." U.S. movie stars Errol Flynn and Tyrone Power were highly popular at the time, but, although the Cuban film industry had difficulty competing with that of the United States or Mexico, there was no contest with regard to radio. Cuban soap operas (*novelas radiofónicas*) over CMQ and RHC, regarded by some as "trash," were actually quite creative and produced writers, actors, and technicians. As the public listened to romances and westerns, it heard Richard Strauss or Gustav Mahler as background music.[81] In the evening hours, radio brought dramatizations of works like *Rebecca*, *Doña Bárbara*, and *Sangre y Arena* (*Blood and Sand*) and, of course, commentary by Chibás and José Pardo Llada. Thus, as José Rodríguez Feo, the financial "angel" of *Orígenes*, noted, Cuban cultural life began to flourish as Grau neared the end of his term, "despite the crisis of our civic institutions, the political and administrative corruption, the public indifference to culture, and the scarce official support of the government."[82]

Grau's third year in office had been highly contentious. It was a tribute to Grau's stamina that he withstood so many crises. And it was a measure of the growing strength of Cuban democracy that it did not fold in the face of this turmoil. It was encouraging, too, that so many civilian politicians were lining up at year's end to succeed Grau as president, trusting fully in the electoral process. But the events of the year would not make the future president's path easy. The effects of the defection of Chibás, the takeover of the CTC by the Auténticos, the Orfila shoot-out, the Cayo Confites debacle, and the Sugar Act of 1948 persisted and created dangerous conditions that threatened the stability of the democratic order.

4

Passing the Torch

In Cuba 1948 was a presidential election year. Ramón Grau San Martín was ineligible for reelection under the Constitution, and it was anticipated that he would deliver the sash of office and pass the torch of the authentic revolution to his elected successor. Democracy was intact, but there was a sense that Grau had diminished the presidency and betrayed the revolution and that the torch had been reduced to a "candle."[1] Francisco Ichaso, one of the founders of the ABC, described Grau's last year in office "as one of the most corrupt periods in the history of the Republic."[2] Eddy Chibás, Grau's harshest critic, faulted Grau "more for the good that he left undone than for the evil he did."[3] He was referring to Grau's failure to enact the complementary laws to give vitality to the Constitution of 1940, such as the creation of a Central Bank and a Tribunal of Accounts. Others concentrated on the evil, naming specifically BAGA, *Inciso* K, the black market, the looting of the Lottery Fund, the bloated bureaucracy (*botellas*), and *pistolerismo*.[4] Given the debased status of the presidency, it was possible that no one would want the job, but such was not the case. There was a spirited contest for the highest office.

The competition for the PRC-A nomination was very lively. There were four principal candidates: Carlos Prío Socarrás, Miguel "Miguelito" Suárez Fernández, José "Pepe" San Martín, and José Manuel Alemán. Prío was the strongest. Justo Carrillo writes that one must distinguish among the 1930 University Student Directorate (DEU), the 1930 Generation, and the Auténtico Party; they were not synonymous. But Prío embodied all three. He was part of the student Generation of `30, he had been a member of the 1930 DEU, and he was a founding member of the PRC-Auténtico. Prío distinguished himself in the struggle against Machado and was imprisoned numerous times. He served in Grau's 1933 government and again in 1944–48. In Grau's cabinet, he held the offices of prime minister and minister of labor, in the latter capacity winning control of the CTC for the Auténticos against the Communists. Prío was the first of the Generation of `30 to reach the threshold of power.

Miguelito Suárez lacked the revolutionary credentials of Prío but had the advantage of fewer ties to Grau. As president of the Senate and head of the Provincial Assembly of Las Villas, Suárez was based in the legislative branch, and he showed great skill in assembling parliamentary majorities. He was one of the politicians whom U.S. ambassador Norweb faulted for "jockeying for place and power," with no strong party loyalty, but Suárez displayed independence, and many in the PRC-A admired him for his actions in the Senate, in which he frequently criticized the Grau administration. In April 1947, for example, he resigned as Senate president in protest over Grau's refusal to present Alemán and César Casas for interpellation.

José "Pepe" San Martín was the cousin of Grau San Martín and served in the cabinet as minister of public works. In assessing Grau's term, *Bohemia,* one of the president's severest critics, concluded that "Pepe" San Martín was the only bright spot in the Grau government.[5] San Martín administered the ministry honestly and fairly, free of *botellas* and peculation, and undertook works projects in all provinces, without favoritism. Given the reputation of the Grau government for corruption, San Martín's honesty won him a place in the national political scene. In fact, his rise to national prominence aroused the envy of the ubiquitous José Manuel Alemán, who conspired against him in the Presidential Palace. He managed to reduce the appropriations for public works, which led to the abandonment of certain projects and consequently to protest demonstrations in the affected communities, tarnishing San Martín's public image.

It was a tribute to the adage "hope springs eternal" that Alemán dared to think of himself as a presidential candidate. He was the most notorious of the corrupt officials of the Grau government, but as he confided to Guillermo Alonso Pujol, the head of the Republican Party, "Grau vetoes Miguel, `Miguelito' vetoes Carlos Prío, and the third floor vetoes `Pepe' San Martín. The only one who does not have problems is *yo* [I]."[6] He was fooling himself. Alemán was not popular, being known as the man who stole the children's "school lunch." He had control of a huge political fund (BAGA), but in an electoral situation he could only be a president-maker, not president. He had a personal army—MSR—but a coup was unthinkable because the number one military man, General Genovevo Pérez Dámera, detested him. In the aftermath of the Cayo Confites affair, Ambassador Norweb wondered how much longer Grau could keep apart "such strange cats" as Alemán and Pérez.[7]

After trying every conceivable combination to make a deal with Suárez Fernández, Alemán accepted defeat and, following Grau's wishes, threw his support to Prío. Grau later affirmed that he "made" Prío president of the republic.[8] He had said he would "pass the torch [only] to a legitimate Auténtico."[9] But he made Prío kowtow first. He made the "caramel" bitter, even though he had no intention of endorsing Suárez Fernández, whom he did not consider a "legitimate" Auténtico and whom he resented for being among the first to oppose the idea of his reelection.[10] In April, Prío won the Auténtico nomination, but Grau kept him jumping through hoops to the very end.

At the beginning of the year several of the opposition parties considered uniting behind a single candidate as a means of defeating the incumbent Auténticos. The Liberal, Democratic, and Republican Parties negotiated the "Pact of Florida" and hoped to unite behind the candidacy of Liberal Party leader Ricardo Núñez Portuondo for president and the Republican Alonso Pujol for vice president. Eddy Chibás "absolutely" opposed a pact with the "traditional" parties, denouncing the Liberals and Democrats as *machadistas* and proclaiming that "principles not deals must prevail in defeating *grausismo*."[11] A heated debate ensued in the Ortodoxo Party over the question of allying with the other parties, but Chibás prevailed. With his customary passion, he argued that the party's very survival was at stake. "Independencia o muerte," he proclaimed. "We are alone, yes, but alone with the people."[12] In the end, the problem solved itself when the opposition parties failed to agree on Núñez Portuondo as the unity candidate and the proposed alliance fell apart.

Some suspected that Chibás's real passion was for the presidency and explained his refusal to join the *pactistas*, but Chibás had consistently denounced political pacts "as politics as usual." As further evidence of the sincerity of his position, at one point in the preelection maneuvering he had shown a willingness to support a "Third Front" candidacy in alliance with Suárez Fernández and a further group of disillusioned Auténticos. At the end of February, when Suárez realized that he had no chance for the PRC-A nomination and, like Chibás, of challenging Grau's domination from within, he formed the Auténtico Reaffirmation movement and bolted the party. Chibás agreed to ally with Suárez and support either him or Aurelio Alvarez (a PRC-A senator and president of the Colonos Association) for president and in his February 25 broadcast introduced a new slogan, "Third Front against Third Floor."[13] But Suárez was not content to leave it there and invited the Democrats to join the Front, which was unacceptable to Chibás, and another alliance was stillborn. The Liberals and Democrats finally united behind Núñez Portuondo, and the Auténticos, trumping them all, allied with the Republicans and chose Alonso Pujol as Prío's running mate.

By early April, four candidates had been nominated for the presidency: Prío for the Auténtico-Republican Alliance; Núñez Portuondo for the Liberal-Democratic Coalition; Chibás for the Cuban People's Party (PPC-Ortodoxo); and Juan Marinello for the Popular Socialist Party. The Liberal Party was the only prerevolutionary party in the race. Although purged of *machadista* elements, it was the least attuned to the economic and social reforms of the Constitution of 1940 and the most sympathetic to private sector and foreign interests. It intoned the common litany of the opposition parties in condemning the BAGA, *Inciso* K, the black market, and gangsterism. Its candidate, Núñez Portuondo, was the eldest of the group at age fifty-five, and he had been its standard-bearer before in 1940 and 1944. He was an honorable man and a respected surgeon who had held positions in the medical services of both Machado and Batista. He was not a reactionary but clearly was the only right of center candidate in the running and consequently the principal threat to the Auténticos.

Juan Marinello was typical of Cuba's Communists, being a professor, poet, and essayist. Though he had fought the Machado tyranny and was imprisoned several times, he was more the intellectual than the man of action. Like his comrades of the 1930s and early 1940s, he followed a popular front and opportunistic line, being elected to the Chamber in 1942 and serving in Batista's cabinet, the first Communist in Latin America to participate in a sitting government.[14] In 1948, he was senator from Camagüey and vice president of the upper chamber. With the advent of the Grau presidency and the Cold War, the PSP lost considerable political force, although it still had strength within organized labor and among Cuba's black population. Despite the lowering of the Iron Curtain, the Communists participated freely in the electoral process.

Eddy Chibás represented *autenticismo* without Grau, but the Ortodoxo Party was largely a personalist organ. It was barely a year old in the 1948 election and had not had time to build a political organization. Chibás was immensely popular, and he attracted some of the leading Auténtico politicians to his cause. His running mate, Roberto Agramonte, was Cuba's ambassador to Mexico when he embraced Eddy in August 1947. Chibás enjoyed the energetic support of *Bohemia,* which displayed his picture on the cover of its May 16 issue and filled its pages with article after article extolling him as Cuba's best hope. During the campaign, Chibás had particular success in Oriente, the poorest and most neglected province of Cuba. Fidel Castro, a native of Oriente, spoke at a huge rally in Santiago de Cuba, "the largest in its history," and, predicting that Grau would "suffer a shameful defeat," declared of Chibás, "We are in the presence of a great man!"[15] But in a four-way race, the Auténticos were too strong to overcome, especially since the economy was doing well.

Sugar, of course, was the bellwether of the Cuban economy. Throughout World War II and the Grau administration, thanks to the sugar policy of the United States, Cuba was able to sell its entire sugar harvest at a guaranteed price. This is not to minimize the difficulties and disappointments that Cuba encountered in negotiating its sugar sales to the United States, but, despite the wrangling, the end result was prosperity. According to Ichaso, "Grau's term in office coincided with the era of the greatest bonanza ever known by the Republic."[16] There was a tremendous gulf between the rich and the poor. Per capita income in 1948 was a mere $310. Land ownership remained concentrated. "According to the Agricultural Census of 1946, of a total of 159,958 farms, 2,336 (1.4 percent of the total number) had an extension of over 500 hectares [1 hectare = 2.47 acres] and represented 47 percent of the area of all farms entered in the Census."[17] But the PRC-A had it both ways, being the party of the Revolution, while taking credit for the favorable economy. The opposition parties harped mainly on the issues of corruption and gangsterism. The Auténticos also enjoyed a record of respect for individual liberties. On the eve of the election, Grau published an open letter, proclaiming, "The rule of absolute freedom which characterizes our Government will have one more opportunity to manifest itself in these elections."[18]

As Grau pledged, the presidential election on June 1, 1948, was conducted in an atmosphere of freedom, but there was some question about its honesty. Enrique de la Osa, writing in the "en Cuba" section of *Bohemia,* charged subsequently that Alemán's BAGA had poured money into Prío's campaign and bought votes with promises of teaching positions to unqualified persons. "Cases abound," he asserted, "of teachers of English who scarcely understand the words `yes' and `goodbye.'"[19] José López Vilaboy concurred, affirming that Prío's election was "scandalous" and that "fraud and the buying of votes reached unprecedented levels."[20] Obviously, Prío benefited from the largesse of Alemán, but there was no evidence that the election was rigged or that there was systematic stuffing of ballot boxes, and it is difficult to imagine that Alemán had enough jobs to sell to affect the outcome. Moreover, while *pistolerismo* continued on other fronts, the election was free of acts of violence. Chibás personally telephoned Pérez Dámera to praise him for the "impartial conduct" of the armed forces.[21] He agreed that Prío had won by means of "the most gigantic fraud in our history," but he was philosophical. Four years was a short time, he remarked, being "the time that passed between the battle of Dunkirk and the battle for Berlin."[22]

Prío won the election handily but not overwhelmingly. He received 892,796 votes out of 2,506,554 cast, or 35.74 percent of the registered voters; Núñez Portuondo gained 23.84 percent; Chibás got 12.80 percent; and Marinello trailed with 5.61 percent; 22.01 percent of the registered voters either did not exercise the franchise or cast invalid votes.

The transitional period between Prío's election (June 1) and inauguration (October 10) was no smoother with regard to his relationship with Grau than the time before, when he had to grovel for the nomination. Grau displayed little interest in cooperating with the president-elect and was determined to hold the reins of power up to the last moment. Prío had been a "disciple" of the "Messiah of Cubanidad," but he would no longer be his toady, and *"el Viejo"* sensed it and resented it.[23] The personalities of the two men were distinct: Grau, imperious, funereal, aloof; Prío, younger (he was forty-five) and handsome, "always smiling," of a sunny disposition. Ironically, though Grau retained the "mystique" of the Revolution, Prío was more committed to it. Prío was aware that Grau had failed to meet the expectations of the Cuban people, and he was determined to fulfill the vision of the Generation of '30, but he had no wish to shame Grau. He wanted to be the "cordial president."

Without a true transition taking place, but not wishing to make an issue of it, Prío discreetly "escaped" by traveling abroad.[24] In July, August, and September, he traveled to Mexico, Guatemala, Venezuela, and Costa Rica. Such trips by a president-elect were usually ceremonial in nature, but Prío had a more serious purpose. The Auténticos maintained an informal alliance with other democratic parties in the region, either in power or in exile, and shared with them the goal of getting rid of the dictatorships in the Dominican Republic, Honduras, and Nicaragua. In Guatemala, where Juan Rodríguez, the commander in chief of the Cayo Confites expedition, had established his headquarters, Prío conferred with

President Juan José Arévalo, who was supporting the antidictatorial movement as a means of promoting a Central American Union.[25]

Since leaving Cuba and moving to Guatemala after the Cayo Confites affair, General Rodríguez's Liberation Army had fought in the Costa Rican civil war in March–April 1948, where it was rebaptized the "Caribbean Legion." Before that conflict, and with Arévalo's urging, Rodríguez, José Figueres of Costa Rica, and representatives of various Nicaraguan exile groups signed the Caribbean Pact pledging to liberate Costa Rica, Nicaragua, and the Dominican Republic. With Costa Rica "liberated," the Caribbean Legion began preparations for an invasion of Nicaragua. This was the situation when Prío arrived in Guatemala City on August 20. Two weeks earlier, Juan Bosch came as his "advance agent," presumably on Caribbean Legion business.[26] Bosch, though a Dominican, was one of Prío's "closest associates" and was expected to play an important role in Prío's government "as an idea man."[27]

Truly, Prío's visit to Guatemala was more than a "goodwill" gesture. He came to reassure Arévalo of Cuba's commitment to the antidictatorial struggle. His close relationship with Bosch and his equally close relationship with the Cayo Confites veterans Eufemio Fernández and Enrique (Cotú) Henríquez were clear indications of his intentions. Fernández had been a battalion commander at Cayo Confites, and he was head of the ARG, which had rendered critical assistance to Prío in ousting the Communists from the CTC. He was Prío's personal bodyguard and was slated to be the chief of the Secret Police in the new government. Henríquez was Prío's brother-in-law and one of the most unrelenting foes of Rafael Trujillo. Though Prío did not disclose the nature and extent of his support of the exile revolutionary movement, he and Arévalo pledged secretly to coordinate their efforts.[28] Publicly, the leaders issued a joint communiqué condemning "tropical dictatorships."[29] At the same time, however, Prío's visit to Guatemala had a downside. The more radical elements there condemned his anticommunism and censured him for his role in ousting the PSP from the leadership of the CTC.

Prío traveled next to Venezuela, where he received a warmer reception. In Venezuela, he met with President Rómulo Gallegos and Rómulo Betancourt, the head of Democratic Action (AD), the Auténticos' sister party. Perhaps feeling the sting of the criticism he received in Guatemala, but also in the company of true democratic revolutionaries, Prío spoke more harshly about Grau than he had at any time during his campaign. He said that he would restore effective public administration and would respect the jurisdiction of the courts, especially in carrying out verdicts against "terrorists." He spoke of the special attention he would give to education, health, agriculture, and public works and pledged to create a central bank and enact all the laws necessary to give vitality to the Constitution.[30]

Even as Prío expressed "a feeling of great community with the revolutionary principles of Venezuela,"[31] the AD hosts were in serious trouble. Only two months after Prío's visit, Gallegos was overthrown by a military coup. Betancourt would establish his headquarters in Havana for opposing the military junta in Caracas, stretching to the maximum Prío's involvement in the secret diplomacy of the Caribbean. In the meantime, Prío had traveled to Costa Rica, where he found Figueres facing reality and unable to fulfill his commitment under the Caribbean Pact but trying to find some face-saving way out of his predicament. Because the likelihood of overthrowing Anastasio Somoza appeared remote, the Caribbean Legion turned its attention again to Rafael Trujillo, involving Cuba more directly in the intrigue and further testing the limits of Prío's support. While Prío traveled, another serious matter demanded his attention.

During the presidential campaign, there was no *pistolero*-related violence, but then and during the transition period, the *pistoleros* were tending to other matters and raising the specter of unrestrained gang warfare. On July 16, before Prío's visit to Mexico, Rogelio "Cucú" Hernández Vega, the former deputy chief of the Secret Police, was riddled with bullets in the offices of the Cuban consulate in Mexico City. His murder was related to those of Danilo Alvarez, a former detective of the Secret Police, on May 22, and Oscar Fernández Caral, a university police sergeant, on June 6. All three were MSR, and all three had participated in the Orfila shoot-out. The UIR had proclaimed that all those who took part in "the crime of Orfila" would pay with their lives. With each death, the UIR left its calling card: "All the assassins of Emilio Tró will die! Justice is delayed.... But it will be done!" Prío obviously had these events and others in mind when he spoke in Caracas about his intention to crack down on "terrorists."

In the time between the Orfila shoot-out and Prío's inauguration, six acts of vengeance were carried out by UIR against MSR, resulting in four deaths. The first attack took place on February 22, 1948, outside the Cinema Resumén, against Manolo Castro, one of the masterminds of Cayo Confites. Manolo Castro had no direct part in Orfila; he was in Caracas at the time trying to rally support for the troubled expedition; but "it was said" that a little before his death he was trying to obtain the freedom of

Mario Salabarría, the "assassin" of Orfila.[32] Salabarría had been condemned to thirty years in prison for his role in the Orfila affair, evidence that some regular justice was being done with regard to the *pistoleros*. Among those questioned in the murder of Manolo Castro was Fidel Castro. After being released by the police "for lack of evidence," Fidel Castro issued a statement denying any guilt and asserting that Rolando Masferrer and the MSR had accused him falsely as part of an effort "to take over leadership of the University."[33] Fidel Castro's role has been a matter of speculation. Two contemporaries gave widely divergent opinions. Enrique Ovares, the FEU president and no defender of Fidel Castro, insisted that "Fidel had absolutely nothing to do with the Manolo Castro thing."[34] Cabrera Infante stated matter-of-factly, "Everybody thought at the time that the other Castro [Fidel] did it [murdered Manolo]."[35] Fidel Castro himself felt that it was advisable to leave Havana for the time being and traveled to Bogotá, where he got into more trouble, being swept up into the rioting (the *Bogotazo*) that took place there, April 9–13.

The murder of Manolo Castro was followed by the three killings described above and by two frustrated attempts. (Fidel Castro was accused in one of these slayings also, that of Oscar Fernández Caral, but the charge was dropped.) On July 20, National Police sergeant Luis Miguel Hernández, an intimate of Mario Salabarría, was the target of UIR gunmen, but he escaped unharmed. Then, on August 21, at the very time that Prío was in Guatemala, Julio Salabarría, the younger brother of Mario, was seriously wounded in an assault outside MSR headquarters. His sister Hilda spoke at the hospital: "Julio hasn't harmed anyone. Everyone knows that he was not involved in the events in Marianao [Orfila]. He has devoted himself only to his profession as a veterinarian."[36] The assault on Julio Salabarría, allegedly because he was the brother of Mario, gave rise to concern that the vendetta was spreading beyond the participants of Orfila. Because of the sixty-four *pistolero* murders during the Grau administration, with clear evidence that the situation had grown worse since the Orfila massacre, Prío planned to denounce these outrages in his inaugural address and propose a specific law against gangsterism.

As October 10 approached, Cuba prepared to witness the transfer of power from one democratically elected president to another. Grau would pass the torch, or whatever, to Prío (*Bohemia*'s brilliant political cartoonist and caricaturist, Juan Davíd, depicted Grau as passing his "dirty linen" to Prío). Enjoying absolute freedom, Cubans representing a variety of political and interest groups assessed the work of the outgoing president and expressed their opinions about the nature of his legacy.

Chibás's criticisms of Grau were well known and could be summed up in the charge that he had "betrayed the Revolution." In Eddy's opinion, Grau transformed himself from the "Apostle of honesty" to the "Apostle of the black market, *botellas,* and corruption." Nonetheless, Chibás recognized certain successes, namely, actions taken early on when he was still collaborating with Grau. He cited specifically the removal of Batista's high military command; the return of the armed forces to their barracks to perform their appropriate duties; the recovery of the U.S. air bases in Cuba; the achievement of the sugar differential and policy of *trueques* with Latin America; the maintenance of the salaries of the sugar workers, despite the decline of the price of sugar; the positive public works record; the creation of the ethanol industry, overcoming the oppositon of "the three Ss" (Standard, Shell, and Sinclair); and the absolute respect for the freedom of the press.[37]

Chibás's running mate, Roberto Agramonte, vice rector of the university and dean of the School of Philosophy and Letters, focused his attention on the Ministry of Education. He expressed shock and dismay over Alemán's misappropriation of the funds of *Inciso* K in order to corrupt the political process, provide *botellas,* and support *pistolerismo.* The tragedy in his mind was that there was money to achieve an educated, progressive, and proud public. The erection of "three or four" schoolhouses, he affirmed, did not compensate for the failure to stamp out illiteracy or to open public libraries, create scholarships for advanced study abroad, and establish specialized institutes for scientific, economic, and agricultural research. Agramonte said that many teachers by individual effort "preserved the integrity of learning" but that the educational program of the Grau administration was "bankrupt."[38]

Speaking for the students of the University of Havana, Alfredo Guevara, FEU secretary of foreign relations, condemned Grau for breaking his promise to come to the Escalinata to give an accounting of the work of his government. He did not come, maintained Guevara, because "he feared the just criticism and anger provoked by his perfidious betrayal of the revolutionary principles." The university felt particularly aggrieved, Guevara stated, because it had been the "crucible" of the struggles against Machado and Batista and had sacrificed the martyrs Mella and Guiteras. Grau had destroyed the "auténtico myth," he affirmed, and warned that the students had learned their lesson and would "know how to put it into practice."[39]

Insisting that the criticisms of the Grau government were "unjust and exaggerated," Blas Andrés Orozco, a PRC-A militant and chief legal counsel of the Grau government, admitted that "errors" had occurred but attributed them to elements outside the mainstream of *autenticismo* and not affiliated to the PRC-A. He emphasized that Grau had established a government of civilian authority, ending the times when senators and representatives were summoned to Camp Columbia "to receive their orders." He extolled a regimen of full democracy, marked by the enjoyment of public liberties and a free press, and noted that Grau had received and acted on the petitions ("just demands") of "ordinary people, social groups, towns, and cities." He praised Grau's intervention in labor disputes, in which his government seized and operated businesses (usually foreign owned or controlled), "as a notable step in [Cuba's] economic liberation." In that regard, he referred to international acceptance of the "Grau Doctrine," Grau's declaration that certain economic measures by one country (i.e., Section 202e of the U.S. Sugar Act) might constitute intervention in the affairs of another and be grounds for legitimate grievance. Orozco concluded by asserting that in the history of the republic, the Grau government was outstanding in carrying out an impressive program of public construction without resorting to borrowing abroad.[40]

Segundo Quincosa Valdés, secretary general of the Federation of Workers of Havana Province and representative-elect (PSP), disagreed totally with Orozco's assessment. Referring to the ouster of the PSP from the leadership of the CTC, he accused the Grau administration of "assaults and outrages" against the workers' movement, using public funds to employ *porristas, pistoleros,* and strikebreakers to take over the Workers Palace and create the bogus "CTK" (*Inciso* K Workers Confederation). He challenged the picture of a civilian government adhering to the rule of law, depicting instead a government of force abrogating public liberties and democratic rights and ignoring the Constitution. Contradicting the widely held view that Grau respected individual freedoms, Quincosa Valdés cited the "illegal seizure" of Radio Mil Diez and the use of the army and police to collect dues from the workers in behalf of the CTK, and he alleged that the PSP's correspondence had been intercepted. He concluded with the litany of *Inciso* K, BAGA, *trueques,* and so on contrasting the illicit enrichment of government officials with the "deterioration of the standard of living of the Cuban people."[41]

Among the democratic labor leaders, Ignacio González Tellechea, an officer of the Independent National Workers Committee, judged Grau less harshly. He praised Grau for "recovering" the CTC from the Communists but expressed dismay over the politicization of the labor movement. He foresaw the upcoming struggle between Angel Cofiño and

Eusebio Mujal for control of the CTC and blamed Grau for the division in the ranks of labor. González also felt that the Grau government had hurt workers' wages because its "tolerance" of the black market and "unscrupulous monopolists" prevented wage increases from keeping up with the "urgent necessities of the people."[42]

The most poignant expression of disappointment in the Grau regime emanated from Alfonso González Guerra, a founder of the Cuban Farm Workers Confederation (CCC). Though conceding that four years was a short time in the life of a people, he concluded that from the perspective of the Cuban farmer the Grau government had made poor use of its time in office or simply had squandered it. He affirmed that the *guajiros* (Cuban farmers) had been made "to eat the bitter fruit of deceit." The only compensation the CCC received for its support of Grau in "the popular triumph of 1944" was four decrees that protected the tenants, subtenants, sharecroppers, and squatters of a particular estate against the action of the landowner and one that gave relief to tobacco sharecroppers generally. Otherwise, González Guerra complained, Grau's promises to address the nation's rural problems had been empty. The resources that the government had expended in public works, he noted, did not reflect thoughtful economic planning. Because of the government's failure to build trunk roads and highways to meet the needs of the producing regions, Cuban farmers and farm products were still denied access to markets. The same lack of planning prevailed in education; schools were built next to highways where they could be "showcased" instead of in the interior regions where they were needed. He charged that Grau had done nothing to provide educational opportunity for Cuba's rural children or to improve hygiene and sanitation in the farming areas. Worse yet, Grau had "not even initiated the great task of Agrarian Reform." From the standpoint of the *guajiro*, González Guerra made clear, Grau's was a "do-nothing" government.[43]

This opinion was identical to that of Eddy López, president of the Cuban Association of Theatrical, Cinematic, and Circus Artists, and echoed that of José Rodríguez Feo. "In spite of his constant promises," López charged, "Dr. Grau San Martín has done nothing for Cuban artists." He stated that there was not a single Cuban artist who had a good opinion of Grau and complained that "we are a country without theaters and theatrical enterprises." López seemed to ignore the "cultural awakening" that others, like Cabrera Infante, were sensing, but he concluded, "we are existing thanks [only] to radio, the cabarets, and tent shows."[44]

Judging from this diverse body of opinion, it was evident that the

Grau government respected individual freedoms and asserted civilian authority over the armed forces. Yet it had failed miserably to improve the economic and social condition of ordinary Cubans, largely because it wasted resources through corrupt practices and inefficiency. Despite his haughty nature, Grau displayed a tolerance for free expression and freedom of the press. How else might one explain the vicious attacks made by Chibás, who in a public speech in July 1948 compared Grau to "Cain," accusing him of stealing everything from his brother Francisco, including his widow?[45]

Despite the continued development of democratic practices in the political arena and individual freedoms, Grau's presidency was extremely disappointing. He failed to create the institutional structure foreseen in the Constitution of 1940, as he promised to do in his inaugural address: fundamental budget and accounting laws, tax reform, a civil service, a tribunal of accounts, and a central bank. He had said on October 10, 1944, that the Cuban people wanted "urgently" to correct the "errors, vices, and defects" of public administration that had impeded the achievement of a "better way of life."[46] He also promised a war on illiteracy and illness and to create "thousands of small rural proprietors."[47]

For all the money poured into education, there were actually more illiterate persons ten years of age and over in 1953 (1,032,849) than in 1943 (1,024,584)—the two census years for which figures are available. Admittedly, the overall population had increased in ten years, but the record was shameful nonetheless. Alemán hoodwinked Grau, constructing a few model schoolhouses while misappropriating the bulk of the funds for personal and political gains. The situation with reference to public health was just as bad. Despite greater expenditures for health and sanitation than at any previous time, there were not enough hospitals to tend to the needs of the Cuban population, and those under the control of the Ministry of Public Health lacked even the "most indispensable" facilities.[48] Alemán's ubiquitous BAGA reached into the Health Ministry, siphoning away funds intended for street cleaning and waste collection.[49] As for rural properties, González Guerra said it best: Grau "had not even initiated" an agrarian reform program. The Agricultural Census of 1946 remained substantially unchanged, wherein "one-fifth of all Cuban farmland was divided up among slightly more than 100 farms. Of the total number of farms, 70 percent were 63 acres or less in area, but accounted for only 11 percent of the farmland."[50] Nonproprietors (tenants, subtenants, sharecroppers, and squatters) made up 63.7 percent of all farm operators and occupied somewhat less than one-half of the land under cultivation (42 percent).⁵¹ Moreover, 45.7 percent of *guajiro* families lived in dwellings "sin pagar alquiler," meaning that, being "rent free," they were primitive *bohios* constructed of palm, little more than shelters, "a picture of backwardness and indigence."⁵² In 1953, only 2.3 percent of rural homes had inside running water, and no more than 3 percent had indoor flush toilets; 54 percent "had no sanitary facilities of any kind."⁵³

Grau was a poor administrator and, if not personally corrupt, was an enabler. He tolerated Alemán's thievery and looked the other way when General Pérez Dámera "won" $50,000 as second prize in the National Lottery.⁵⁴ He permitted "First Lady" Paulina de Grau to peddle influence in the Presidential Palace. According to Julio Lobo, one of Cuba's wealthiest *hacendados*, Grau told favor-seekers, "You can't do any dirty business with me, but how about a word with Paulina?"⁵⁵ Guillermo Belt referred to her as "Cuba's Evita Perón."⁵⁶ Equally as serious, owing to Grau's ineptitude, many rural towns lacked essential services such as sewers, paved streets, water, and police protection, forcing private citizens to organize "revolutionary municipalities" to do what "graft-ridden" local governments failed to do.⁵⁷

Finally, Grau's ignoring of the drafting of the U.S. Sugar Act of 1948 was harmful to Cuba's interests. Cuba needed to reduce its dependence on sugar exports and to develop new trading partners. Belt argued that "Cuba should sell its sugar freely and not exclusively to the United States."⁵⁸ In the meantime, however, Grau's failure to press Cuba's legitimate claim to a larger sugar quota in recognition of its contribution to victory over the Axis powers in World War II was irresponsible. José M. Casanova, president of the Hacendados Association, for one, was counting on the United States to express its gratitude in the form of an enhanced sugar quota, which was essential for preventing "a repetition of the experience of 1920."⁵⁹ In his first message to Congress, Grau stated, "True individual liberty cannot exist without economic independence and security."⁶⁰ For the next four years, he failed to live up to those words.

Carlos Prío Socarrás took the oath of office on October 10, 1948, vowing to govern differently. Judging from the fast start he made, he meant to keep his word.

5

The Cordial President

Carlos Prío Socarrás was determined to end the corruption and violence that was scandalizing Cuban society and to revitalize the Auténtico program. With Prío, the Generation of '30 had reached maturity and power. In his inaugural address on October 10, 1948, Prío called for the enactment of a law against gangsterism and for the creation of the National Bank. He achieved both quickly, working with the Congress in a manner that appeared to promise a new era of cooperation between the executive and legislative branches of government. Prío was the "smiling *criollo*," the "cordial" president, whose affable manner seemed strangely out of step with the toughness demanded by the circumstances.

Prío expected much from his cabinet ministers, especially two of his longtime comrades of the 1930 DEU, Tony Varona and Aureliano Sánchez Arango. Varona took on the job of prime minister. He was tough-minded and irascible, thoroughly committed to *autenticismo,* and devoted to the PRC-A. For him, "nationalism, anti-imperialism, and socialism" was more than a motto, it was an all-consuming purpose. He was tactless, and his political acumen "left much to be desired," but he was absolutely honest, "untouched by the scandals of the politics of the times."[1] As the consummate party loyalist, he did not forgive Eddy Chibás for dividing their effort.

Sánchez Arango was equally passionate and honest. He was an educator and a man of action. During the 1930s, he headed the Auténtica Organization (OA), the PRC-A's action arm that harried both Grau and

Batista, albeit for different reasons, and he was a private pilot, flying his own aircraft and likely to turn up anywhere on the island. As minister of education, he assumed the task of cleaning the Augean Stables that Alemán had befouled. He quickly received high praise for getting rid of the gangsters on the payroll and the *botellas* held by unqualified persons and for restoring normal educational services.[2] Because his methods were often rough, after a year in office, a public opinion poll chose him second in the category of "best minister" and first in the category of "worst."[3]

Somewhat senior to the Generation of '30, though a founder of the PRC-A, Carlos Hevia, another honest man, accepted the position of foreign minister. Prío first offered him the treasury office, but he declined when he discovered that he was expected to treat the money embezzled by the Grau administration as a "deficit." Prío was anxious to end the thievery in the treasury, but "he did not wish to wash the dirty linen in public."[4] Hevia had no intention of being party to a cover-up, so he agreed to serve as foreign minister instead. Even in this post he was wary of holdovers from the Grau administration. In his first meeting with the U.S. ambassador Robert Butler on October 14, he showed an interest in resolving outstanding matters between Cuba and the United States but not until he could obtain competent assistants he "could trust." The ambassador understood this to indicate "some distrust of the inheritance from the previous administration."[5] In fact, one of Hevia's principal targets was Guillermo Belt, the Cuban ambassador in Washington, whom he replaced with Oscar Gans y Martínez in April. Belt was not adroit in his handling of the U.S. Sugar Act of 1948 and too often acted as a "lone wolf." He consulted directly with Grau, bypassing Foreign Minister Rafael Pérez y González Muñoz. Hevia, experienced in economic matters himself, did not intend to tolerate such independent behavior.

Not all of Prío's appointments were as wise. When Hevia turned down the treasury position, Prío gave it to his younger brother, Antonio, whose sole qualification for the job was that he was related to the president. Similarly, he appointed Grau's nephew Francisco "Pancho" Grau Alsina (a senator thanks to BAGA) as minister of agriculture. And he retained General Genovevo Pérez Dámera as army chief of staff. None of these persons would enhance Prío's image as a reformer. Pérez especially was living a lavish life, reportedly supplementing his lottery "winnings" with funds stolen from the army retirement fund.[6] But Pérez's retention was motivated by more than simple nepotism. Prío had no wish to stir up trouble with the army. Though Pérez was Grau's man, he at least had no ties with former Batista officers and seemingly posed no threat to democracy, "neither having the figure nor the style to carry out a barracks revolt."[7] Besides, Fulgencio Batista was back in the country, having been elected a senator in the June elections. Batista's presence constituted a threat as always, but Prío wanted no exiles or political prisoners during his time in office. He personally had entrusted Guillermo Alonso Pujol with a mission to New York in 1947 to inform Batista that he could return to Cuba.[8]

Even with senators such as Batista, Prío's relations with the Congress were positive. Miguel "Miguelito" Suárez Fernández was back in the fold as an Auténtico again and as president of the Senate. Exactly one month after Prío's inauguration, the Senate passed the Law against Gangsterism. In his inaugural address, he had called for "energetic measures" to eradicate *pistolerismo*. The law established a special court to try gang-related offenses, with the authority to impose stiff sentences. It provided for the registration of clubs and associations, required individual citizens to have a license to carry a gun, and banned certain weapons. At Varona's insistence, the law did not violate civil liberties, preventing the police from making arrests on suspicion without evidence and proper warrants. It was essentially a gun control law, which led critics to complain that it was not a law against gangsterism but one "to promote" gangsterism.[9] In the beginning, Prío expected it to work, especially with such experienced law enforcement officials as Pérez Dámera, chief of staff of the army; José Manuel Caramés, head of the National Police; and Eufemio Fernández, chief of the Secret Service.

Taking on a matter less controversial and in the end more effective, the Congress quickly heeded Prío's request to establish the National Bank of Cuba. Francisco Ichaso hailed the legislation as an essential step toward "the liberation of the Cuban economy."[10] With Felipe Pazos as its head, Cuba finally had an autonomous central bank empowered to issue and manage a national currency and regulate credit and banking. It was designed further to serve as Cuba's fiscal agent in dealings with the International Monetary Fund.[11] The bank established Cuba as a sovereign nation. Later, revolutionary critics took a dimmer view, charging that the bank "not only placed the nation's financial resources at the service of the domestic bourgeoisie and U.S. investors but also spread the defects of criollo politicking to the economy, opening up new sources of wealth to the ruling circles."[12] There is no evidence that this occurred during the Auténtico era under Pazos's stewardship. Furthermore, the Congress enacted the Organic Law of the Budget, establishing rules for the preparation, editing, implementation, and liquidation of the general and extraordinary budgets of the state.¹³ Even before this measure took effect, Prío submitted an itemized budget to the Congress, the first president since 1937 to make such an accounting before the nation.¹⁴ With such a promising start, Prío departed Cuba for a state visit to the United States, December 8–11, 1948, where President Harry Truman was also savoring an electoral victory.

Prío's visit to the United States appeared to go very well. U.S. officials remarked that "he charmed all by his gracious good humor and vibrant personality."¹⁵ This reaction stood in marked contrast to the report from the U.S. embassy in Guatemala during Prío's visit in August, which described his avowed "revolutionary nationalism" as "violent super nationalism."¹⁶ The terms of Cuban sugar sales to the United States were Prío's main concern during his visit, but he also explored the possibility of obtaining a substantial loan for a program "for the improvement of highways, particularly small rural roads, aqueducts, and sewage systems." U.S. officials indicated that he would have a difficult time attracting foreign capital, raising the long-standing complaint about Cuba's tight labor laws, particularly "the virtual ban on discharging employees regardless of the justification" and "the restrictions governing the employment of aliens."¹⁷ As a suggestion for improving the investment climate, they sought to reopen negotiations for the Treaty of Friendship, Commerce, and Navigation left in limbo by the Grau government, but Hevia, in separate talks, reiterated that such a treaty was "politically impossible."¹⁸ Prío viewed the United States more favorably than Grau, but he could not dare to give the impression that he would be willing to negotiate such an emotionally charged issue that would affect the economic and labor laws inspired by the Revolution of 1933. Hevia suggested that an agreement "by another name," without colonialist baggage, was a possibility and might "accomplish the same objective,"¹⁹ but Prío left Washington with this issue and the matter of the loan unresolved.

When Prío returned to Havana, he encountered the first firestorm of his administration. As hard as he had tried to avoid a run-in with Grau, appointing his nephew to the cabinet and using the euphemism "deficit" to cover up the embezzlement in the treasury, "El Viejo" reacted to Prío's reforms as a personal affront. He viewed Sánchez Arango's mass firings in the Ministry of Education as a "rebuke" because he believed that Alemán had been his most effective and conscientious cabinet minister. Moreover, Grau became enraged over a brief filed before the Criminal Panel of the Supreme Court of Justice on January 18, 1949, by Pelayo Cuervo Navarro charging that Grau, Alemán, and others in his administration had embezzled 174,241,840.14 pesos from the public treasury. Cuervo Navarro was an Ortodoxo, but Grau believed that Prío could have taken measures to quash the charge and prevent an inquiry. At the end of January, *Bohemia* published an interview with Grau in which he expressed regret that he had "made" Prío president.

Grau declared that he had made Prío president of the republic because he believed that he was capable of following the program of *autenticismo* but confessed that he was wrong. He blasted Prío as an "unfaithful disciple" and accused him of abandoning the Auténtico doctrine. He saw no good coming from Prío's heralded "semiparliamentarianism." "The apprentices in the government," he commented, "believe that laws solve everything . . .[when] what is needed is action, executive action. . . . The `law against gangsterism' has served only to encourage what it was supposed to prevent."[20] He went on to assert that Sánchez Arango's so-called cleanup in the Ministry of Education was motivated solely by his presidential ambitions for 1952. He accused Prío and Miguelito Suárez of using lottery tickets to buy votes in the Senate, contrasting his use of lottery revenue "to provide benefits for hospitals, labor unions, charitable works, special constructions, etc." "I hope," he concluded, "that many of those who sit in the `Floridita' will be able to enjoy the benefits, even though they will not admit it, that my government gave to the people."[21]

A split as wide as this was a danger to Cuban democracy. Grau was still the president of the Auténtico Party, and his criticisms could have a destabilizing effect on the Prío administration. Aware of the fragile situation, *Bohemia* applauded Pérez Dámera for the "proper conduct" of the armed forces in the context of the Grau interview.[22] Even Senator Batista appeared to give Prío support, declaring (oddly for him) that Grau's claim that he "made" Prío president was an insult to the nation.[23] But Grau had fired the first shot, and certain Auténticos were pleased to respond. Miguelito Suárez asserted that Grau's remarks "revealed" his ambition to regain power "except by the legitimate means of a popular election." He believed that Grau's statements were "subversive" in nature, "basically disavowing democratic institutions, principally the Congress."[24] Sánchez Arango was harsher, saying simply that Grau was suffering from "old age" and that Prío had been elected president not because of Grau but in spite of him. He insisted that the Auténtico Party nominated Prío because it wanted "to free itself" of Grau's influence and make a new beginning.[25] Prío's reaction was one of disgust.

According to Enrique de la Osa, Prío told his brothers Antonio and "Paco" that he was never Grau's disciple, "unfaithful or otherwise."[26] "In twenty years of revolutionary struggle," he affirmed, "I have always followed my own inclinations, which often have not coincided with those of Grau." He believed that three persons represented the opposition to his government: Chibás, Batista, and Grau. "The most dangerous of all is Grau," he stated, "because he is conspiring against the government. He thinks only of returning to power, but since he knows that he is old and needs to wait eight years in order to regain the presidency legally, he will resort to any means. His statements constitute the best proof."[27] It seemed unlikely that the men could ever be reconciled. Yet the crisis seemed to pass without further acrimony, except for the resignation of "Pancho" Grau Alsina as minister of agriculture, encouraging José Alemán to try to play the role of peacemaker.

He returned to Cuba in June from a self-imposed exile in Miami Beach, where he had used his stolen millions to collect hotels, apartment buildings, prime real estate, and a baseball team. Despite all, he was still an elected senator (BAGA continued to work its wonders) and the consummate political boss. He was looking forward to the midterm elections in 1950 aware, above all else, that party unity was essential for victory. He was hoping also that (with Prío's help) he might derail Cuervo Navarro's demand for an inquiry of embezzlement charges against Grau and himself. He arranged a meeting between the two leaders at Rancho Alegre, the estate of Pérez Dámera, that reportedly went well, causing concern that Prío was going to sell out. The political commentator Francisco Ichaso acknowledged that Grau continued to possess a vote-getting mystique that tempted the Auténtico Party to overlook his wrongdoing, but he urged Prío to continue to steer clear of the "magical caudillo." He stated that *autenticismo* had only two roads to take, either "to free itself from the *grausista* and *alemanista* millstone or to convert itself again into a pernicious and corrupting *grausismo*."[28] Ichaso was correct to point out the possible consequences of Prío's rapprochement with Grau, particularly in the context of other troubles that had arisen since the beginning of the year. Prío's impressive legislative start was being slowed by numerous distractions.

In the first place, there was always Chibás. He launched his barbs against the new administration without missing a turn. During his February 2, 1949, broadcast, he accused three Supreme Court justices of accepting bribes to approve a rate hike for the Cuban Electric Company. Such a charge could not go unchallenged, but Eddy had selected a popular target, a public utility (regulated monopoly) owned by the U.S. company Electric Bond and Share. (Cartoonists had a field day depicting

Chibás in conflict with the corporate symbol, "K-*Listo* [Ready] Kilowatt"). Charged with the crime of defamation, Chibás said he would not retract "a single word" and accused Prío of persecution. He exploited the situation for all it was worth. On April 27, the Urgency Court sentenced him to 180 days in prison. In a scene that appealed perfectly to Eddy's sense of drama, he pacified the outraged crowd in the courtroom, declaring, "It's okay. I repeat that the three judges sold out to the `pulpo eléctrico' [electric octopus]. I shall continue fighting." Taken to the Castillo del Príncipe prison to begin his sentence, he proclaimed, "I have been sentenced to six months in jail for defending the people against the `Anti'-Cuban Electric Company, subsidiary of the international octopus Electric Bond and Share, which, like the Cuban Telephone Company, exploits our homeland in complicity with the venal government in power."[29]

Chibás had great fun in his jail cell. He refused any favors. He told the horde of visitors that came to see him daily, "I'll eat prison food. I've been here before, in 1929 by Machado, in 1935 by Batista, and now [in 1949] by Carlos Prío Socarrás."[30] He mocked Prío from prison, remarking that he did not find any of the thieves of the 174 million pesos there and adding, "in the regime of *cordialidad*, it is a crime to refuse to rob and kill."[31] And he got wind of Prío's intention to obtain a loan from private bankers in the United States to finance his public works program. This effort was not resolved until November, when the Congress approved Prío's loan agreement, but Chibás set the tone of the debate early. "If they had not stolen from the Treasury," he observed, "they would not need a loan." He expressed amazement that a member of the 1930 DEU could consider such an act. He claimed that it "would restore the chains that bind the Republic to Yankee imperialism" and vowed that the Ortodoxo Party would fight against "mortgaging" Cuba again, "especially to the Morgan and Chase banks that made deals with Machado."[32]

Prío was embarrassed by Chibás's imprisonment and realized too late that he had blundered. He had made a martyr of his rival, who was comparing him to past tyrants, diminishing his claim to be a democratic president. In an effort to co-opt Eddy's issue, he announced on May 6 that he was rescinding the electric rate increase and restoring rates to their 1944 level, and his aides floated rumors that he was considering a presidential pardon. Chibás, flushed with victory, said Prío's capitulation did not change the fact that the judges had been bribed and announced that he would not accept a presidential pardon, only a law of amnesty passed by the Senate. He doubted that that would happen, with such senators as Alemán, Batista, Francisco Prío Socarrás, Grau Alsina, and Alonso Pujol.

Finally, the frustrated Prío issued a "conditional" pardon, a form of probation stipulating that Chibás was to be released but would have to serve his full sentence if he was involved in so much as a minor traffic accident. Prío gave Chibás no choice; he had to leave on the grounds that his many visitors were jeopardizing prison security. After serving forty days of his sentence, Chibás scribbled on his cell wall, "Chibás was imprisoned here for fighting the electric octopus," and he emerged from the Castillo del Príncipe at one minute after midnight on June 4, greeted by a cheering crowd of thousands.[33] This episode had exposed ineptness on the part of Prío, but it was a mere distraction in comparison with the renewal of gang warfare that had occurred in the meantime. During the same interim, in March, Prío's wife gave birth to a daughter, nine months after his election, for whom "Victoria" would have been an appropriate name, except that gangsterism was threatening to snatch victory away.

On January 12, not quite two weeks after Prío had proclaimed that the Law against Gangsterism had restored peace to Cuba, National Police sergeant and UIR gunsel Rubén Darío González was gunned down in the Ancla bar in a premeditated assassination. Doctors in the emergency room counted seventeen bullet holes in his body. The police gave chase and managed to apprehend Amado Laura, one of the assailants. Taken to police headquarters and subjected to the "third degree" by Colonel Caramés, Laura gave up the names of his accomplices, Gustavo Massó and Juan Regueiro, and revealed that they were all MSR, acting under the orders of Rolando Masferrer, who supplied them with weapons and an automobile. About seventy-two hours later, the mutilated bodies of Massó and Regueiro were discovered in a lonely spot near the Country Club in Marianao. They were just kids, ages twenty and eighteen, respectively, although they had been expelled from the ARG as "out of control."[34]

According to news reports, Massó and Regueiro had been rivals with Sergeant González for control of the Students Association of Havana Institute Number 1 (a trade and night school). González was also a suspect in the murder of Manolo Castro. Questions arose as to who was responsible for the torture and slayings of Massó and Regueiro, the UIR or the National Police, but it amounted to the same thing because National Police lieutenant Armando Correa, who was in charge of the investigation, was a member of the UIR. In his Sunday evening broadcast on January 16, Eddy Chibás stated that the two youths were arrested on Friday and that their "badly beaten" bodies were found the next morning. "Just as in the time of Machado!"[35] Ernesto de la Fe of *Prensa Libre* predicted that these murders marked the beginning of a new crime wave. He reported that

Orlando León Lemus ("El Colorado"), the MSR chieftain who had fled Cuba after the Orfila massacre, was back in the country and was being sheltered by the Prío brothers. He asserted that the renewed violence was the result of a pact made in Mexico among Lemus, Masferrer, and Eustaquio Soto Carmenatti, the latter representing Mario Salabarría with the objective of forcing Prío to release Salabarría from prison.[36] Masferrer labeled the report as a "fantasy," but the part about securing Salabarría's release was a very sensitive subject.

On April 2, forty-five minutes after the noon hour, as Justo Fuentes, the FEU vice president and UIR militant, crossed the street in front of radio station COCO, two gunmen emerged from their automobile and opened fire on the young man. He had just finished his daily broadcast, "The FEU Speaks," in which two days earlier he had alleged that the Foreign Ministry was preparing a passport to enable Mario Salabarría to leave the country "the minute he received his pardon."[37] In the hospital, before going into surgery, Fuentes said to his friend Fidel Castro, "'*Mulato*,' the police want me to make an identification," and he dictated, "they were 'El Colorado,' Masferrer, [Mario] Aguerreberre, and Soto Carmenatti." Fuentes died on the operating table, but his charges stood. The UIR-MSR feud had claimed another victim. Fuentes had become a marked man following his sensational revelation about Salabarría's possible passport, but he was also tied in with a UIR *bonche* led by Herminio Díaz, the suspected assassin of Rogelio Hernández Vega (MSR) in Mexico City.

In the hospital, Fidel Castro exclaimed openly, "this happened to Justo because he did not have a bodyguard," even though Castro was the one who caused the UIR to withdraw its protection of Fuentes.[38] Castro and Fuentes had a falling-out in September 1948 during demonstrations against Omnibus Aliados (the Allied Bus Company). Grau had decreed a fare hike; in protest, University of Havana students seized eight buses and parked them on the campus. Fuentes objected to the action as the work of "outside elements," and Castro accused him of selling out to the bus company for $2,500.[39] Castro's charge led to the expulsion of Fuentes from the UIR, although subsequently the two youths became reconciled, and Fuentes rejoined the UIR, but with Díaz's splinter group. Given the complex nature of the rivalries and tendencies of the *bonches*, the labels UIR and MSR were usually more general than specific. Nonetheless, the murder of Fuentes touched off bitter acrimony against the Prío government.

Public opinion denounced the government, ridiculing the Law against Gangsterism as ineffective in stopping the "caballeros del gatillo" ("trigger men"). The only persons being arrested, according to word on the street, were innocent citizens who possessed hunting rifles. The strongest reaction occurred on the University of Havana campus. The FEU declared a strike, boycotting classes for forty-eight hours, and issued a defiant manifesto. The FEU proclaimed that the university student body would act on its own to avenge its fallen comrade if the assassins were not punished. It demanded that the parliamentary immunity of Masferrer (who was then a representative in the Chamber) be waived or the students "would take up arms." And it accused Senator Francisco Prío Socarrás of sheltering the "assassin" Orlando León Lemus, a fugitive from justice. The students stopped streetcars below the Escalinata and plastered them with posters denouncing Masferrer, "El Colorado," Caramés, and "Paco" Prío. Prime Minister Tony Varona responded by issuing an order for the arrest of Lemus.[40] But the outbreak of *pistolerismo* did not stop.

On April 19, MSR gunmen struck again, wounding Luis Felipe ("Wichy") Salazar Callicó, a notorious UIR *pistolero* and student activist. At the Emergency Hospital, he refused to divulge the names of his assailants to an officer of the Bureau of Investigation, protesting, "Why should I tell you; everyone knows that the police protect assassins." But before he went into surgery, he whispered the names to a group of friends, among them Fidel Castro, who was delegated to reveal them to the press. "Wichy says," Castro announced, "that those who shot him were Policarpo Soler and `El Colorado' and that a person wearing a police uniform was driving the car."[41] Soler's reappearance (he was a former Batista police official who had been in exile and was considered dangerous) did not bode well for the Prío government. Once again, the student Castro appeared in very rough company, notably of the UIR variety. "Wichy" had been accused of two murders but never tried, as seemed to be the pattern.

The UIR had taken three hits since the beginning of the year, González, Fuentes, and Salazar ("Wichy"), all allegedly involving the Orfila fugitive Lemus ("El Colorado"). Because of Lemus's link with "Paco" Prío, there was speculation that the government was aiding and abetting the MSR *pistoleros*. Masferrer claimed it was just the opposite; he asserted that *pistolerismo* would cease if the government removed the UIR militants from positions in the Bureau of Investigation, the National Police, Secret Police, and other agencies. He blamed all the violence on the UIR and ARG, saying that the government paid ARG leader Jesús González Cartas ("El Extraño") $10,000 a month to eliminate the Communists from the transit workers union. He denied that the MSR used violence, though he admitted that it was actively pursuing the killers of Manolo Castro. Jesús Diéguez, the leader of the UIR, described Masferrer's statements as rubbish and declared that Masferrer was the "central figure" in the unrest. Neither man considered himself a *pistolero* but rather a "revolutionary," fighting on behalf of the workers and peasants.[42]

The Prío administration was caught in the middle of these charges and countercharges. It had given government jobs to both groups, hoping to buy them off, but it could not permit the lawlessness to continue if it wished to preserve the democratic order. While university students demonstrated on the Escalinata and Chibás was agitating from his jail cell, Prío told a press conference that the authors of the crimes would be apprehended and presented to the Urgency Court for punishment. He said that he was "tempted" to send the army into the streets to put an end to the "plague of gangsterism" but that he would do so only as a last resort. Varona stated that he had instructed the attorney general of the Supreme Court "to move heaven and earth" to bring the perpetrators to justice.[43] Prío and Varona may have been sincere, but the astounding revelations by the journalist Néstor Piñango on May 4 damaged their credibility.

Piñango managed to find "El Colorado" in his hideout and tape an interview with him. The interview was broadcast over COCO and excerpts were published in *Pueblo* and *Prensa Libre.* Lemus told Piñango that his ties with Carlos and Antonio Prío went way back, beginning in the Batista era, and continued to the present. For example, he claimed that he "took care of" the voter registration for the PRC-A in Pinar del Río and that he provided the "muscle" for Prío's rivalry with "Miguelito" Suárez Fernández for the Auténtico nomination. Even more sensational was Piñango's assertion that he was taken to the interview in a National Police patrol car and that he observed soldiers guarding the hideout, supposedly a *finca* outside of town.[44] The report created an immediate scandal, which the Prío government made worse by attempting to suppress the interview. Carlos Maristany, the minister of communications, shut down COCO for three days and declared a ban on broadcasts of interviews with fugitives from justice, and the fiery Caramés "detained" Piñango on possible charges of being an "accessory." When a "rather pale" Piñango emerged from police headquarters, he made a statement, "wishing to clarify" the circumstances of his interview of "El Colorado." "Neither the police nor soldiers had any part in it," he affirmed, "and it took place in a friend's house. . . . I am cooperating fully with the authorities."[45] Whether he was fabricating then or before was anyone's guess, but the damage had been done. The public uproar against the failure to apprehend Lemus, coupled with the attacks on the press—Varona said that the newspapers were making heroes of the gangsters—led Prío to use his last resort. "I'm going to put an end to *pistolerismo*! I have a hundred men ready to do what is necessary. I am determined to end this state of affairs."[46]

On May 10, Prío decreed the establishment of a special Group for the Repression of Subversive Activities (GRAS) under his direction, supervised by General Pérez Dámera, the army chief of staff. He intended it as an investigative body to root out gangsterism, a kind of Cuban FBI. It would be the G-men against the gangsters, just as in the American movies. Pérez stated that GRAS was entrusted with "the surveillance, control, restraint, and extermination of all activities of a seditious, extremist, and subversive nature carried out by parties, groups, sects, gangs, or individuals throughout the national territory regardless of their condition, nationality, profession, or purpose."[47] Pérez's statement raised concern that GRAS looked too much like the hated Military Intelligence Service (SIM) under Batista, which had been disbanded in 1944, and a frenzy of protest erupted. Sergio Carbó pointed out that GRAS was no FBI, the latter being a civil not a military agency. Aníbal Escalante declared that GRAS was the first step toward a military dictatorship, and his comrade Blas Roca labeled the new group "Grastapo." The PSP, which had little to do with the *pistolero* violence, perceived the implications in the "overly broad, nebulous, and capricious" charge to deal with "subversive activities." The radio commentator José Pardo Llada castigated Prío. How could he, a revolutionary, restore Batista's despised institution, he asked. Ramón Vasconcelos, the editor of *Alerta*, predicted that GRAS would destroy what it was intended to preserve, just as the cat in the fable that ate both the mouse and the cheese.[48]

Even though GRAS was a military and not a civil agency, Prío had no intention of establishing a military dictatorship. He was desperate to contain the *pistolero* problem, but he did nothing to stem the stream of abuse and even ridicule in reference to his action that appeared in the media. José Agustín Martínez, the former minister of justice, noted that the acronym GRAS was French for *gordo*, implying that the "fat" Pérez Dámera was the man in charge. The satirist Vergara, author of "Picadillo a la Criolla" ("Cuban Hash"), a humor column in *Bohemia*, had great fun publishing "the authentic rules and regulations of GRAS." For example, "ARTICLE 4.—The members of GRAS will submit all their reports to the Chief of the group. The judges and courts of the Republic may, when they deem it necessary, request (not demand) from the Chief of this organization, investigations, provided they do not involve the following: the identification of the thieves of the Capitol diamond . . . and the whereabouts of `El Colorado.'"⁴⁹ Prío even accepted reluctantly the resignation of Eufemio Fernández Ortega as chief of the Secret Police. "I know that I would clash with `el Gordo,'" he explained to the president.⁵⁰ But the resignation may have been a gambit to free him for Caribbean Legion activities (to be discussed in the following chapter). These same activities contributed to the removal of Pérez as army chief of staff in August, further rebutting the idea that Prío ever intended to give Pérez or the military free rein.

Despite the fears raised about GRAS, it comported itself well in its first major test. After two months of relative peace, Roberto Enríquez López, a chauffeur of "El Colorado" and a minor player in the Orfila affair, was machine-gunned as he reached the front door of his home on July 20. The next evening, Manuel Villa Yedra, the former driver of Emilio Tró, was seriously wounded in an assassination attempt as he entered his parked car. On the twenty-second, on a street corner at midday, two men gunned down José Ramón Solís, said to have "fingered" Enríquez López. GRAS went into action. Its agents interviewed witnesses, displaying thoroughness but extreme courtesy. Pérez Dámera, exercising great sensitivity, was determined to allay the public's concerns about the new investigative agency.⁵¹

Working with National Police records, GRAS identified the "trademarks" of the rival groups. Enríquez López and Solís were shot and "finished off" on the ground—a technique used exclusively by UIR. Villa Yerda was killed in a drive-by shooting—the method of operation (MO) of the MSRistas "El Colorado" and Policarpo Soler. Ernest Hemingway, then residing in Cuba, also had identified *pistolero* techniques, describing the "old one-two," whereby a lead auto drove by a gang hideout and opened fire, and as the gangsters came out to shoot at the fleeing car, a second one came up and "wiped them out."⁵² Even *Bohemia*, normally critical of the Prío administration, admired the speed and efficiency of GRAS. After only days of investigation, it announced that it was seeking arrest warrants for Orlando León Lemus, Policarpo Soler, Wilfredo Lara, Leoncio Espinosa Fernández, Eustaquio Soto Carmenatti, and Mario Aguerreberre for the murder of Justo Fuentes and the attempted murder of "Wichy" Salazar. And it named Rubén Díaz and "a certain" Bustamante as the killers of Enríquez López. This was the "first time" that Soler's name was mentioned in an official report, which seemed to indicate that the gloves were off with reference to the top *pistoleros*. GRAS's promising start was disrupted, however, by the removal of Pérez at the end of August for reasons not directly related to the *pistolero* problem.

After a brief hiatus in the gangland slayings, "Wichy" Salazar's luck ran out on September 1. He was riddled with twenty bullets as he drove along Ayestarán Street. In retaliation, Masferrer, the leader of MSR, was the target of a frustrated assassination attempt on September 15, the anniversary of the Orfila shootout. The shocking attempt took place on the very steps of the Capitol building, the nation's Legislative Palace, and consisted of a gun battle that lasted several minutes, taking the life of a companion of Masferrer and wounding two others. It was the fifth attempt against Masferrer; he blamed them all on "the rats of the UIR," including Fidel Castro.[53] Prío himself was outraged that this latest attack took place where it did and against a legislator, even one with whom he had "differences." "Those people," he confided, "are sheltered by politicians; even by senators. Some are put in the police. I believe that the solution, in this last case, would be to take away their blue uniforms."[54]

Prío had finally reached the heart of the matter. He could create as many investigative bodies as he wished, but as long as the Auténtico governments employed the *pistoleros*, they gave them sustenance and legitimacy. The long struggle against tyranny had produced a "culture of violence" that jeopardized the future of the democratic order. Havana in 1949, José Duarte Oropesa observed, was like Chicago in the Al Capone era, complete with gang "trademarks" and gangster "nicknames."[55] "Political violence and extremism," Rolando Bonachea and Nelson Valdés added, "[were] as Cuban as the palm trees."[56] Was there much difference, one might ask, between the rival gang shoot-outs and the duels of Eddy Chibás? He fought with Senator José Manuel Casanova ("the sugar czar") with sabers on June 6 and with René Fiallo (Prío's public relations chief) with pistols on July 24. In August, the Superior Court recommended that "duels of honor be declared a criminal offense."[57] And no institution was affected more deeply by the culture of violence than the University of Havana.

On September 20, the student Gustavo Mejías, who was no *bonchista* but had been protesting the lawlessness on the campus, was shot and killed. A special outrage erupted over his killing; he was a decent young man who had the temerity to denounce the dealing in drugs and contraband that was centered in the popular swimming pool area. Raúl Roa, the dean of the faculty of social sciences and public law, resigned his position in protest, and angry citizens declared, "Gangsterism will not end in Cuba until the university's autonomy is repealed." Why should the university, a place intended for learning and culture, they asked, be a sanctuary for thieves and assassins?[58] On September 23, GRAS raided the School of Agronomy on the university campus, arresting thirty-eight "students" and seizing a formidable arms cache. Prío also followed through with his threat to "take away their blue uniforms," replacing Caramés, whom he held responsible for the attack on Masferrer on the Capitol steps, with General Quirino Uría López. At his swearing-in ceremony, Uría posed with General Ruperto Cabrera (Pérez Dámera's replacement) and Minister of Defense Segundo Curti. A new team for fighting gangsterism was in place, and Curti declared that the scourge would be eliminated "once and for all."[59] By then this was a familiar refrain.

As Prío neared the end of his first year in office, the issue of *pistolerismo* continued to tear at the soul of his administration and at the Auténtico Party. In a public opinion poll assessing Prío's first year, the failure to curb gangsterism and provide for the public safety was listed as the major shortcoming of his government. He appeared inconsistent—cracking down at one time and having a *"mano suave"* (soft touch) at another.[60] Such inconsistency suggested that Prío was not totally impartial in his efforts, tolerating some miscreants more than others.

Pistolero violence contradicted assertions that Cuba enjoyed a functioning democracy, qualified by the lack of evidence of an organized effort on the part of the Prío government to use oppressive tactics against its political opposition. *Pistolero* violence did not follow a clear line of the government against the opposition but was a circumstance of elements within the ruling party or parties competing for influence, power, and spoils, exacerbated by the poison of Orfila. The conflict did not follow a classic right-versus-left dichotomy. The only significant opposition group avowedly favoring insurrection and the use of revolutionary methods was Fidel Castro's faction in the Ortodoxo Party, the Ortodoxo Radical Action, mainly UIR militants, but no battle line had been drawn, at least through 1949.[61] The PSP avoided the use of violence. The powerful concern over *pistolerismo* likely stemmed from the fact that the majority of Cubans were law-abiding and wanted democracy to work and resented the stereotype that they "traditionally"[62] resorted to violence as a means of settling disputes.

Aside from *pistolerismo*, Prío seemed to fare well. The corruption issue had abated, owing largely to the efforts of Sánchez Arango to clean up the Ministry of Education. Prío was credited with eliminating the black market and consequently reducing the cost of living. Cubans, moreover, appreciated Prío's *cordialidad,* his desire "to do good," demonstrated by his working relationship with Congress, specifically the submission of the national budget and the complementary laws of the Constitution for approval.[63] Above all, critics and supporters alike praised the continued enjoyment of "democratic rights and freedoms" (the hoodlums notwithstanding), although the cynical among them said, "We have the freedom to complain, even though no one listens to us."[64]

One of the principal features of the Prío government, its active role in the struggle for democracy in Latin America, which it embraced enthusiastically and proudly, contributed at the same time to its failure to overcome the *pistolero* problem. By 1949, Cuba was one of the few democratic countries left in the Caribbean region. It became a haven for refugees from tyranny and a center for intrigue and paramilitary activities aimed at the overthrow of the area's military regimes. The Auténticos remained a revolutionary party, committed to the forceful overthrow of neighboring dictatorships, a situation that fostered adventurism and kept its *pistoleros* in business. Throughout 1949, Cuban democracy pursued an aggressive foreign policy.

6

The Democratic Bulwark

In November 1948, democracy in Latin America received a severe jolt. A military coup overthrew the democratically elected government of Rómulo Gallegos in Venezuela. Shortly afterward, numerous Venezuelan exiles, mostly members of the Democratic Action Party, took refuge in Cuba. The AD and Auténtico parties were close allies, sharing an ideology and maintaining an uncompromising antidictatorial line. Prío welcomed Gallegos and AD party president Rómulo Betancourt to Havana. He reaffirmed Cuba's adherence to the "Betancourt Doctrine," pledging to withhold diplomatic recognition from governments of force. During the time that Betancourt was provisional president of Venezuela (1945–47), he had proposed a "quarantine" of the dictators of the hemisphere, aimed at creating a "cordón sanitario" to isolate the tyrants Rafael Trujillo and Anastasio Somoza. He hoped now to extend it to the military junta that had usurped power in Venezuela, and Prío willingly obliged, sending a circular message to other democratic governments seeking "to coordinate moral efforts in defense of the democratic unity of the hemisphere."[1]

The Prío government took a large risk in supporting the AD leaders in exile. It was virtually alone in withholding recognition of the military junta in Caracas—only Chile, Costa Rica, Guatemala, and Uruguay responded positively to its plea. The United States, no subscriber to the Betancourt Doctrine, recognized the junta government in January 1949 and urged the American nations to maintain normal diplomatic relations as a requisite for hemispheric solidarity. Cuba, in defying the U.S. position, also permitted the AD exiles to engage in conspiratorial activities on its territory. In a radio broadcast in February, Betancourt outlined the tasks facing the AD, declaring that the party must first arouse hemispheric opinion against the *golpistas* and second show faith in "the ability of the Venezuelan people to recover their lost democracy," serving as the "organized vanguard" of the resistance.[2] The leaders in exile realized that there was no quick solution to their problem, that the road ahead was long and difficult, and that they had to be careful not to endanger their comrades in prison or in hiding in Venezuela. Betancourt remarked that it was impossible "to go to the barricades" in the days of the armored tank and bombing plane.[3]

Betancourt, as party chieftain, assumed the leadership of the AD in exile. He established his headquarters in the Hotel San Luis in Havana. The hotel, owned by Cruz Alonso, a Spanish refugee, had also served as headquarters for Juan Rodríguez during the Cayo Confites affair. In fact, Alberto Bayo, another Spanish Republican exile and a Caribbean Legionnaire, described Cruz Alonso as "the innkeeper for every conspiracy in the Caribbean."[4] Betancourt set up a clandestine radio in the hotel to communicate with his partisans in Venezuela, who went underground and slowly developed the resistance movement. He beamed instructions in cipher daily and provided logistical support in the form of money and supplies through a secret network of smugglers and couriers.

Inside Venezuela, the AD underground engaged in propaganda and psychological warfare, distributing handbills and newsletters that denounced the illegitimate regime and spread rumors designed to create confusion and divide the ruling factions. As an organized center of agitation, it encouraged student, labor, and popular unrest but avoided terrorism as counterproductive. The AD could not afford to alienate its popular base or provide the military junta with justification for acts of repression. The underground also operated a secret radio transmitter to report the actions of the junta and the condition of imprisoned militants, enabling Betancourt to bring specific charges of human rights violations and other outrages to the attention of the United Nations and the Organization of American States. The AD strategy differed from that of the Caribbean Legion, largely because its leaders were civilians without military or filibustering experience.

By mid-1949 the AD militants in Venezuela had regrouped, and Betancourt was doing what he could to encourage and sustain them from the outside. In April, Leonardo Ruiz Pineda took over the direction of the internal struggle. He was the former governor of the state of Táchira and had been Gallegos's minister of communications. He was also a poet. He followed the patient course of mobilizing popular support, seizing every opportunity to remind the nation of its lost liberties, while avoiding violence and fighting "without hatred."[5] Betancourt in Havana used his gifted pen to write a series of articles in *Bohemia* describing the history of military dictatorship in Venezuela and the nature of the military junta in power, exposing its divisions and evils. In an attempt to elicit sympathy and support in the hemispheric community, he appealed to various international organizations such as the Inter-American Press Association (to examine violations of freedom of the press) and the International Labor Organization (to investigate the crushing of trade unions). He likewise disseminated the testimony of victims of torture and other atrocities and listed the names of political prisoners.

The Venezuelan junta denounced Betancourt as a Communist and charged that he was financing his "subversive" activities with funds he had stolen from the public treasury before fleeing Venezuela. It even hired a killer to travel to Havana to make an attempt on his life.[6] Such actions strained Cuban-Venezuelan relations, but since each was violating the other's sovereignty, neither had credible grounds for complaint. The AD exiles did not return home for a decade, and Ruiz Pineda and other leaders of the resistance suffered martyrdom, but as long as the Auténticos exercised power in Cuba, the AD had a base of operations and a place of hope. At the same time, in collaborating with democratic leaders in exile, Prío did not have to deal with the military option with regard to AD, whereas he could not avoid it with reference to the Caribbean Legion.

By the end of 1948, Juan Rodríguez in exile in Guatemala had begun preparations for an invasion of the Dominican Republic. After abandoning plans to invade Nicaragua from Costa Rica, Rodríguez had transferred his headquarters to Guatemala. There, President Arévalo gave him his complete cooperation, permitting him to use the San José Air Force Base for training and as a staging area. Drawing on his experiences in the Cayo Confites and Costa Rican affairs, Rodríguez had developed an elaborate plan for the liberation of his homeland. He envisioned an air, land, and sea invasion in conjunction with an uprising by elements of the Internal Front. From Guatemala, he proposed to airlift a cadre of approximately eighty veteran officers (the Caribbean Legion) and an arsenal of weapons to three sites in the Dominican Republic, where he had arranged to arm and organize volunteers raised by the Internal Front. These revolutionaries would be reinforced by armed groups coming by sea from

Cuba and by land from Haiti. Prío was deeply involved in the execution of this plan.

Prío had agents in all three places of embarkation of the combined operation. Eufemio Fernández, his erstwhile chief of the Secret Police and ever-faithful bodyguard, was with Rodríguez in Guatemala, preparing the air assault. Juan Bosch, his personal secretary and "idea man," was in charge of a force of eight hundred Dominican exiles, prepared to sail from the Cuban port of Baracoa. (Cruz Alonso, with Prío's blessing, had organized the Indo-American Maritime Company and acquired two vessels, the *Alicia* and *Patricia,* for transporting the expeditionary force.) And Enrique Cotubanamá (Cotú) Henríquez, Prío's brother-in-law, was active in Haiti, arranging the land incursion. Rolando Masferrer was there too, plotting.

By June 1949, Rodríguez had assembled a small fleet of airplanes and was ready to launch the attack. On June 18, he and Fernández took off from the San José base with thirty-six men in a C-46, bound for La Vega in the Dominican Republic. Taking off with him in a C-47 with twenty-five men on board, Miguel Angel Ramírez was headed for San Juan de la Maguana, the second landing site. Waiting to join them on signal was Horacio Ornes at Lake Izabal in command of a Catalina seaplane with a company of fifteen warriors, destined for the Bay of Luperón, the third invasion objective. Two other aircraft accompanied Rodríguez, both Guatemalan Air Force planes, laden with arms and ammunition and possibly headed for Cuba, a likely refueling stop and transfer point for the weapons.

The first four planes never reached their destinations. They encountered fierce storms and were forced to make emergency landings in Yucatán, where Mexican authorities interned them. The Catalina, however, was overloaded and could not take off when signaled and did not become airborne until some of its load was discarded the next day. Unaware of the fate of their comrades, after the storm had passed, Ornes and his men flew out over the Caribbean and descended onto the Bay of Luperón without incident. Discovering too late that they alone were invading the Dominican Republic (the Internal Front in their sector had been compromised and wiped out), they tried to withdraw without success. The Catalina ran aground, and a Dominican cutter destroyed the crippled craft. Ornes and the other survivors set out for the Haitian frontier on foot but were quickly rounded up by the Dominican security forces.[7]

Despite the failure, Trujillo was incensed by the attack. He interrogated Ornes personally and forced him to provide the details of the preparations for the invasion and the complicity of the Guatemalan government. Even before Ornes's "confession," Trujillo had learned a great deal about the operation. His spies had furnished him with information about the activities of Eufemio Fernández, "Cotú" Henríquez, and Cruz Alonso in Cuba, and at least one spy, Antonio Jorge Estévez, had penetrated the Internal Front in the Dominican Republic, leading to its destruction. (He was subsequently "executed" in Cuba by Fernández's order.) Claiming that he was the victim of aggression by the "Communist degenerates" Arévalo, Figueres, and Prío, Trujillo sought to invoke the Inter-American Treaty of Reciprocal Assistance (the Rio Treaty) requiring a meeting of consultation by the American nations.

The United States, objecting to this drastic measure and hoping to defuse the issue, proposed instead that the Inter-American Peace Committee (IAPC) investigate the problem of unrest in the Caribbean in general and recommend ways to restore normal relations. Responding to the U.S. initiative, the IAPC addressed a circular message to the American governments on August 4, requesting "information and suggestions" on "the situation prevailing in the Caribbean political areas."[8] The Dominican government was the first to answer with a lengthy brief relating its version of the Cayo Confites and Luperón affairs but reserving its right to seek a meeting of consultation. Among the "accused" governments, Cuba took the strongest stand against the idea that the principle of nonintervention protected tyrants in depriving individuals of their freedom and rights.

"Non-intervention is an American principle," the Prío government conceded, but added, "At the same time, democracy is a basic principle of the American States, and the Bogotá Charter stipulates that `the solidarity of the American States and the high aims which are sought through it require the political organization of those States on the basis of the effective exercise of representative democracy.'"[9] "If we want peace," Cuba observed, "if we hope for harmony without any activities altering it, we should find, together with the means for the fulfillment of the rights and duties of the States, the means to re-establish the guarantee that the will of the peoples, the root of the modern State, should determine, through its free expression, the kind of Government that it should have as its mandatory."[10] Cuba made it clear in its statement that if the American states had an obligation not to interfere in the internal affairs of their neighbors, they had a duty to create effective mechanisms for "the attainment of a more general practice of liberty and right, of justice and democracy." Cuba defended its support of political exiles by stating that they were the symptoms not the illness, and hence it was the latter not the former that had to be treated if the American nations were to live in peace.

The IAPC did not agree with the Cuban position for the most part. It issued "Fourteen Conclusions" on September 14 that set down standards of behavior to assure peace in the Americas. First and foremost, it restated the absolute position of the Buenos Aires Protocol of 1936, that is, "No State or group of States has the right to intervene, directly or indirectly, for any reason whatever, in the internal or external affairs of any other State." It referred further to the Havana Convention of 1928, admonishing the American states to prevent the use of their territory for the preparation of armed expeditions against other states. Moreover, the IAPC recommended that all states adhere to the OAS Resolution of December 1948, whereby Costa Rica and Nicaragua were instructed to "rid" their territories "of groups of nationals or foreigners, organized on a military basis with the deliberate purpose of conspiring against the security of other sister Republics."[11] As a finishing touch to these standards of good conduct, the IAPC advised the American states to refrain from "hostile propaganda" against one another and to maintain "close and cordial diplomatic relations," without exception. The Peace Committee did conclude that the "exercise of democracy" was "a common denominator of American political life" but ignored Cuba's insistence that the American states had a commitment to take affirmative action to promote the "exercise of democracy" in the hemisphere.

In the meantime, while the IAPC's ineffective exercise played out, the Prío administration continued its activist policy. Following the Luperón debacle, the principal leaders of the Caribbean Legion shifted their headquarters to Havana. Miguel Angel Ramírez appeared more visible, substituting for Juan Rodríguez who was deeply depressed after two failures. *Bohemia* interviewed Ramírez in his room in the Hotel San Luis, where the intrepid warrior dismissed the recent setback as merely "bad luck and bad weather." He was ready to try again, remarking that he would not give up until "Santo Domingo, Honduras, and Nicaragua were restored to their place among democratic nations."[12] Eufemio Fernández declared as well that Luperón did not matter and that "they were prepared to lose all the battles that might be necessary."[13] He was busy ferreting out traitors and did in Trujillo's spy, Estévez.

Retaliation may also be a partial explanation for the deaths of the Guatemalan officer, Colonel Francisco Arana, in an ambush slaying on July 18, and Captain Rosales, a "suicide" on August 20. Arana had opposed Arévalo's support of the Caribbean Legion, and Trujillo had broadcast a warning to him the day before his murder. Several days after the Arana slaying, several officers staged a barracks revolt. Fernández flew in from Havana with a load of arms, and he and elements of the Caribbean Legion helped Arévalo suppress the uprising. Succeeding in his purpose, Fernández then returned to Cuba with the rebel Guatemalan officers as exiles and took them to Legion headquarters in the Hotel San Luis, "where they remained under guard for some time."[14] This highly unusual episode provided a small clue to the nature of the secret alliance between Arévalo and Prío. These strange events were repeated in a way in Havana the following month.

Trujillo was no more satisfied with the conclusions of the IAPC than was Cuba, feeling they protected him as much from the intrigues of his enemies as Cuba believed they would promote the "exercise of democracy." He continued a policy of divide and conquer. In the same way that he had broadcast a warning to Arana over "La Voz Dominicana," he warned Pérez Dámera on July 19 (the day after Arana's slaying) that he would be killed at Prío's country estate during an upcoming "nighttime poker session." Ten days later, the Dominican radio beamed a frantic message: "Aló, Aló Habana, Aló, Aló Habana, Aló, Aló Habana, General Pérez Dámera, General Pérez Dámera, be careful, be careful. An attack is being prepared against you. Remember the warning that was sent to Colonel Arana by this same radio station. Be careful General Pérez Dámera."[15] Despite Prío's advice to Pérez to ignore the Dominican dictator, the general sent two trusted aides to Ciudad Trujillo (Santo Domingo) to check out the warnings. The general was sufficiently alarmed by their findings that he surrounded himself with additional bodyguards and sent Colonel Camilio González Chávez, the chief of aviation, to Ciudad Trujillo to meet personally with Trujillo and obtain specific evidence. Although these missions were conducted in secret, spies of the Dominican clandestine movement (Internal Front) learned about them and reported to Prío.[16]

Among the papers that González Chávez brought back with him from Ciudad Trujillo was a letter "to the people of Cuba in general," supposedly written by a dissident member of ARG. It was a spurious document, clearly part of a disinformation campaign concocted by Trujillo to destabilize the Prío government. It repeated the warning that Pérez was a target for assassination and that the would-be killers were Eufemio Fernández and his chief lieutenant Jesús González Cartas ("El Extraño"). It charged that Fernández and González Cartas wanted revenge against

Pérez for his "betrayal" of the Cayo Confites expedition and that they believed he would thwart anew their ongoing conspiracies against the Dominican Republic, "a source of personal enrichment for them."[17] This document began to circulate in Havana shortly after the return of Colonel González from Ciudad Trujillo. It sealed the fate of Pérez Dámera.

Prío had a copy on August 22 and asked Defense Minister Segundo Curti if he thought it was "the work of El Gordo [Pérez]." Curti said he believed it was. The document along with the intelligence report about the secret missions to the Dominican Republic convinced Prío that Pérez "had gone from disobedience to disloyalty." Around midnight on the twenty-third, Prío went out to Camp Columbia and occupied the office of the chief of staff. He assembled the officers on duty and informed them that he was retiring General Pérez as chief of staff and replacing him with General Ruperto Cabrera, who accompanied him. He then telephoned Pérez, who was away at his finca in Camagüey, and informed him that he was being relieved. Pérez wanted to know why, and Prío told him, "You had lost confidence in me, and when a subordinate does not trust in his chief the situation is not good." Pérez responded, "very well," but asked to speak with "someone there." Prío passed the phone to Colonel Pérez Matos.

"What has happened, Colonel?"

"You have been replaced, General, as the President has just informed you."

"What do the officers say?"

"All are at the orders of the President."

"And you?"

"I also, General."[18]

Pérez now knew that he was through, but it was obvious that he had been unwilling to give the president the final say, demonstrating the fragility of Cuban democracy even after five years of constitutional rule. Prío had gone out to the principal army base and carried out a *golpe*, turning the tables on history, whereas in the past the soldiers had rumbled in from Columbia and ousted the civil authority in the Presidential Palace.

Not only had Trujillo's scheme backfired, but it strengthened the position of his fiercest enemies around Prío. One cannot exaggerate the bond between Prío and Fernández. If Prío was implicated in *pistolerismo*, his relationship with Fernández (as head of ARG) was key. Prío's brother-in-law "Cotú" Henríquez was a founder of both the Auténtico and Dominican Revolutionary Parties, a representative from Oriente, and head of the Cuban Farmers Union. He was especially aggrieved over the death of family member Federico ("Gugú") Henríquez in the Luperón raid. He strongly suspected that Gugú had been taken alive and subsequently murdered in cold blood. Reflecting the influence of these confidants, Prío, in his annual message on October 10, 1949, affirmed that he was "not disposed to restrict the activities of political exiles in Cuba." By that time, Cotú Henríquez and his brother Rodolfo were already engaged in the newest plot against Trujillo.

Using the facilities of the Cuban Red Cross (Rodolfo was president of the organization and Cotú was a medical doctor), the brothers set in motion a plan to invade the Dominican Republic by land from Haiti and to attack Trujillo by air from Cuba. Their collaborators included the exiles Juan Bosch, Juan Rodríguez, Miguel Angel Ramírez, and Rómulo Betancourt and the Cubans Eufemio Fernández, Cruz Alonso, and Aureliano Sánchez Arango. Cotú and other Red Cross officials (i.e., Humberto Olguín and Filiberto Ramírez Corría) traveled to Port-au-Prince ostensibly on technical or "goodwill" missions but in reality to consult with sympathetic Haitian officials and to arrange for the shipment to and stockpiling of arms on Haitian territory. In Cuba, the Red Cross acquired equipment more suited to military operations than to humanitarian or relief work and replaced its personnel with veterans of the Cayo Confites affair. Rodolfo leased the "Anacra" airfield, adjacent to Havana's commercial airport, Rancho Boyeros (the same field used for Cayo Confites), and began training Red Cross pilots under the supervision of Cuban army lieutenant Jorge Triana. Triana also accompanied Rodolfo to L'Amelie in Oriente province, in the mountains above Guantánamo, to map out a landing field.[19]

Cotú and Rodolfo Henríquez affirmed that the Red Cross was building a landing strip at L'Amelie to provide emergency medical services to a remote area that was virtually impossible to reach by land vehicles, especially in the rainy season. Héctor Incháustegui, the Dominican chargé in Havana, reported that its real purpose was to serve as a base for an air raid against the Dominican Republic. Paul Giacometti, one of Trujillo's omnipresent spies, provided details that the plan was for the planes to make a bombing run over Trujillo's Estancia Ramfis just after noon, timed to catch the dictator and his family at siesta.[20] In addition to this intelligence, Trujillo learned that Cotú Henríquez had addressed a group of Haitian officers in the Rex Theatre in Port-au-Prince in November, denouncing him and boasting that he had the support of the Haitian government for his enterprise. Certain that Cuba and Haiti were paying no heed to the "Fourteen Conclusions" of the IAPC, Trujillo decided to force the issue.

On December 26, 1949, the Dominican Congress authorized Trujillo to declare war on any Caribbean state that "deliberately granted asylum to the enemies of the Dominican Republic."[21] Trujillo had requested war-making powers on the twelfth, providing him with a phony cover for his next moves. He planned to create a pretext for invading Haiti by setting fire to the Dominican legation in Port-au-Prince and massacring the chargé and first secretary and their families. This diabolical scheme went awry when those marked for death learned about it and fled the country. Before taking flight, Chargé Sebastián Rodríguez Lora called on Haitian foreign secretary Vilfort Beauvoir and told him what Trujillo had planned to do. Without delay, on January 3, 1950, the Haitian government addressed a note to the Council of the Organization of American States (OAS), denouncing Trujillo's plot and requesting the convoking of a meeting of consultation in accordance with the Rio Treaty. The Dominican government reacted to these "fantastic" charges with its own request for a meeting of consultation, citing the repeated aggressive acts against the Dominican Republic by Cuba, Guatemala, and Haiti.

On January 6, the Council of the OAS resolved to convoke a meeting of consultation and, pending the fixing of a time and place for the meeting, constituted itself as the Provisional Organ of Consultation. It immediately created an Investigating Committee to examine the facts and antecedents of the Haitian and Dominican petitions. The committee, with José Mora of Uruguay as president, spent the next two months traveling to Haiti, the Dominican Republic, Cuba, and Guatemala to collect information and interview the officials and individuals involved. In Ciudad Trujillo, it met with the five survivors of Luperón and managed to secure their release and safe conduct from the country; Trujillo was on his best behavior.

The committee arrived in Havana on February 3 and was beset with letters, petitions, and requests for interviews. The open Cuban society was in sharp contrast with the controlled political atmosphere of Ciudad Trujillo. One of the many communications received by the committee was a petition from the Lawn Tennis Club Lyceum of Havana signed by leading political activists and intellectuals. The Lyceum, one of the principal women's clubs in Cuba and an outstanding voice of freedom, defended the right of political exiles to organize for the liberation of their homelands and denounced Trujillo and other dictators as the real disturbers of the peace. There would be no unrest in the Caribbean, they observed, if democracy prevailed throughout the region and there existed universal respect for human rights. The petition advised the OAS to notify dictatorial governments that "they exercised power illegally" and to require them to hold free elections under OAS supervision. If any dictator refused to comply, diplomatic and economic sanctions must be applied and the right of the affected peoples to resist by whatever means necessary, "including armed rebellion," must be recognized. The signatories were not limited to Auténticos but included the Ortodoxos Roberto Agramonte, Manuel Bisbé, and Herminio Portell Vilá, plus such notables as Emilio Roig de Leuchsenring, Maritza Alonso, Raúl Roa, Gloria Jaime de Domingo, Conchita Garzón, and Luis Gómez Wangüemert.[22]

While the committee studied this and other documents and conducted interviews with Prío, Hevia, and other Cuban officials, Alfonso Moscoso, the Ecuadoran member, and Hobart Spalding, a U.S. Foreign Service officer serving as a staff adviser, made an aerial reconnaissance of the L'Amelie airstrip. After studying the aerial photographs, the committee concluded that L'Amelie "could not be used, in any case, for purposes of a military invasion of the Dominican Republic."[23] In making this assessment, the committee overlooked the passion of Cotú Henríquez and the recent history of filibustering in the Caribbean.

After completing its round of the Caribbean, the committee reported its findings and recommendations to the OAS Council acting provisionally as the Organ of Consultation. For purposes of clarity, it divided its report into two parts: Case A, dealing with Haiti's petition, and Case B, treating that of the Dominican Republic. In Case A, it found that Haiti's complaint against the Trujillo regime was just and proper. Case B was more complicated, but none of the parties escaped censure. The committee chastised Cuba for the Cayo Confites affair, citing President Grau, José Alemán, and Manolo Castro, among others, as responsible for aiding and abetting the preparation of the expedition. Concerning Luperón, it came down hardest upon the Arévalo government in Guatemala, writing that Guatemala "expedited and permitted" the operation. It was not certain that there was much to the so-called L'Amelie situation but did observe that the conditions that produced Cayo Confites and Luperón "continued and persisted" and that "a band of elements" (the Caribbean Legion?) was "disposed to cause grave confrontational situations."[24]

About all that the committee had to say about the Dominican Republic, other than the implication that the existence of dictatorial governments was the root cause of unrest, was that certain of its actions were "contrary to the norms of American coexistence."[25]

In its recommendations to the Council, the Investigating Committee proposed five resolutions, which the Council approved on March 13, 1950. Resolution I addressed the Dominican-Haitian dispute and recommended measures to ease tensions between the two states. The matter became moot when Colonel Paul Magloire established a military dictatorship in Haiti in May 1950, replacing the government of President Dumarsais Estimé, Trujillo's enemy. Regardless, Resolution II contained the heart of the OAS action, designed to put an end to filibustering activity in the Caribbean. It admonished the governments of Cuba and Guatemala "not to permit the existence on their territory of armed groups of nationals or foreigners with the deliberate intention of conspiring against the security of other countries." As a corollary, it advised the governments of Cuba, Guatemala, and the Dominican Republic "to take adequate measures to assure the absolute respect for the principle of non-intervention." It requested the governments of Cuba and Guatemala to confiscate any weapons "in possession of revolutionary elements" and to prevent the illegal trafficking in arms. Finally, it encouraged the governments of Cuba, Guatemala, Haiti, and the Dominican Republic, within the limits of their respective constitutional powers, to avoid "systematic and hostile propaganda" against other American countries, to support the "conclusions" of the IAPC, and, once the current crisis had passed, to resume normal diplomatic relations. To ensure compliance with the resolution, the Council created a Special Commission for the Caribbean to oversee the relevant efforts of the parties and render periodic reports.[26]

In taking the sternest measures yet to control the activities of political exiles in the Caribbean, the OAS did not overlook completely Cuba's position that the American political system required the effective exercise of representative democracy. In resolutions IV and V, the OAS recognized the "confusion" that existed between the principle of nonintervention and the commitment to promote the exercise of democracy. It resolved to order a series of studies by the juridical organs of the OAS to "harmonize" the two concepts and recommend ways to achieve democracy throughout the hemisphere without violating the principle of nonintervention. Nonetheless, Cuba's efforts to topple Caribbean dictators, at a time when the United States wanted stability in the region above all else, belies the suggestion that Cuba "toed the line" of U.S. Cold War policy. Denied the option of armed action, Cuba and the democratic exile community found other ways to oppose the dictators of the Caribbean and penalize them.

In September 1949, the Inter-American Confederation of Labor held its Second Congress in Havana and moved its headquarters to the Cuban capital. This was the second move of CIT since its First Congress in Lima in January 1948. The establishment of military dictatorships in Peru and Venezuela during 1948 shifted the emphasis of the CIT's activity from trade union organization to an aggressive advocacy of human rights and workers' freedoms. Moreover, these new dictatorships swelled the CIT's ranks with exiled labor leaders such as Arturo Jáuregui of Peru and Augusto Malavé Villalba of Venezuela. The Havana Congress, noting the "crisis of democracy in America," approved several resolutions that targeted dictatorial governments, including the Betancourt Doctrine that withheld recognition from governments of force and a proposal for a labor boycott of goods and products of Peru, Venezuela, and the Dominican Republic.[27] President Prío addressed the Havana Congress and received its endorsement of his proposal to hold a meeting of democratic forces in Havana in May 1950. The congress also elected Auténtico labor leader Francisco Aguirre as secretary general, placing Cuba at the very center of free labor's struggle against dictators in the hemisphere and making it a "safety island" in the midst of tyranny. In this instance, Cuba displayed a parallel or common interest with the United States in opposing Communist-sponsored international labor organizations.

At the same time, the Congress put into place the machinery for the transformation of CIT into ORIT (the Inter-American Regional Organization of Workers), accomplished in January 1951. CIT became ORIT to enable it to affiliate with the International Confederation of Free Trade Unions (ICFTU), with headquarters in Brussels, providing it with greater resources and support for the free trade union movement and advocacy of human rights in the hemisphere. When ORIT was established, it kept its headquarters in Havana and stayed there for as long as the Auténticos remained in power. With Betancourt and Malavé Villalba in exile in Havana, ORIT became a strong voice for denouncing abuses against workers in Venezuela, seriously affecting relations between Venezuela and Cuba, but Prío did not seem to mind. The pressure was strong enough on the junta in Venezuela to force it to permit labor to hold its traditional May Day parade in 1951.[28] At its founding congress, ORIT resolved furthermore to send a workers' committee to the Dominican Republic to investigate the status of labor, but Trujillo, put to the test, would not let it in. In Havana, PRD exile Angel Miolán organized the Dominican Democratic Workers Committee in Exile (CODDE) and worked closely with ORIT to continue embarrassing Trujillo in this way. Meanwhile, free labor honored its pledge to assist Prío in holding a conference to mobilize the democratic forces of the Western Hemisphere.

The founding conference of the Inter-American Association for Democracy and Freedom (IADF) took place in Havana, May 12–14, 1950. It had its genesis in the idea of Víctor Raúl Haya de la Torre for the creation of an American human rights tribunal to protect individuals against state abuses and the proposal of Rómulo Betancourt for a formal alliance of democratic governments in opposition to dictatorships. Both men were deprived of power before they could implement their ideas, but Prío perceived the need to unify democratic individuals and organizations in defense of democracy before it was too late. When the conference convened, Argentina, Bolivia, Colombia, the Dominican Republic, Haiti, Honduras, Nicaragua, Paraguay, Peru, and Venezuela were all under the heels of tyrants. Although Prío denied that the Cuban government was an official sponsor of the conference, the plenary meetings took place in the Capitolio, and Education Minister Aureliano Sánchez Arango served on the organizing committee.

A galaxy of democratic leaders and activists from Latin America and the United States attended the conference. They included Betancourt, Raúl Leoni, Figueres, Roa, Bosch, Miolán, Sánchez Arango, and Guilermo Toriello from the Caribbean region and Roger Baldwin, Frances Grant, Pearl Buck, Walter White, Serafino Romualdi, Robert Alexander, Arthur Schlesinger Jr., Chester Bowles, Clifford Case, and Norman Thomas from the United States. In all, over two hundred individuals from twenty countries took part. The large number of North Americans present reflected the anxiety of the times that the U.S. government's preoccupation with communism was affecting its role as a defender of democracy. It indicated, moreover, that the IADF would be active principally in the United States, alerting American leaders and the public to abuses of human rights in Latin America. In fact, in the years ahead, the IADF relied heavily upon the leadership of Frances Grant, its secretary general, working from her office in Freedom House in New York. Nonetheless, the Prío administration had taken the initiative to rally the democratic forces of Latin America and succeeded in establishing liaisons for propaganda and lobbying purposes with organized labor and liberal political and civil and human rights groups in the United States.

Concurrent with the founding conference of the IADF, on June 30, 1950, the OAS watchdog group, the Special Commission for the Caribbean, rendered its first report. It concluded that the parties to the unrest in the Caribbean were complying with the OAS resolutions and were taking "concrete measures" to establish "an atmosphere of understanding and good will."[29] This rosy picture did not comport fully with the facts but reflected the reality that filibustering activity was in abeyance. Prío, the Auténticos, and other Cubans continued to collaborate with Dominican and Venezuelan exiles, especially, in their propaganda and clandestine efforts, but Cuban leaders abstained from sponsoring further armed expeditions. Still, they kept the Caribbean's dictators off balance.

On May 12, 1951, Luis Thomen, the Dominican ambassador to the OAS, reported to the Special Commission for the Caribbean that Figueres, Betancourt, Arévalo, and Cotú Henríquez had met in Havana at the end of April under the auspices of President Prío. Their purpose was "to plot a new interventionist conspiracy" against the Dominican Republic, "consisting of an expedition probably embarking from a Cuban port." He provided details involving the acquisition of large quantities of arms and ammunition by the "conspirators" and the commitment by Prío to make available the *Aurora* and *Fantasma,* the vessels of Cayo Confites.[30] Actually, this meeting had been reported in *Bohemia* on May 6, without reference to any intrigue, and had been hosted by the magazine's editor and publisher, Miguel Angel Quevedo. But such was the state of nerves in the Caribbean, a year after the OAS had "resolved" the crisis.

The United States disapproved generally of Cuba's interventionist policy but was upset specifically over its sympathy toward the Puerto Rican Nationalists. Nationalist "exiles" were active in Havana, and Cuba supported their effort in the United Nations to place Puerto Rico under the jurisdiction of the UN Trusteeship Council. Cuba's attitude, the State Department complained, reflected the "crusading `democratic' zeal" of officials and politicians associated with the Auténtico Party, "to give sympathetic assistance to peoples in other countries whom they consider to be repressed and struggling for democratic expression."[31] Although the issue of Puerto Rico's status strained U.S.-Cuban relations, the United States tended to tolerate Cuba's antidictatorial policy, within limits, especially in light of Prío's strong anti-Communist stance and vigorous support of the United States in the Korean War. The United States was aware that the Auténticos despised dictators as a "carryover" from the struggle against Machado.[32]

As long as there were dictators in the Caribbean there would be refugees, and as long as the Auténticos governed in Cuba there was a place for them to agitate and plot. But there were risks involved. During the first two years of Prío's presidency, the governments of Peru, Venezuela, and Haiti were overthrown by military coups; Prío should have paid heed.

7

New Directions

Carlos Prío took some hard hits during his first fifteen months in office. The *pistoleros* continued their mayhem, and the OAS criticized his government sternly for its support of revolutionary activity in the Caribbean. As Prío got further into the second year of his presidency, the situation seemed to improve. *Pistolerismo,* in particular, abated. The peace would not last, but Francisco Ichaso, writing in *Bohemia* in May 1950, declared that "the government of Prío has eradicated gangsterism."[1] It had done so, he affirmed, by depriving the *pistoleros* of government funding, largely by Aureliano Sánchez Arango's having "cleansed" the Ministry of Education of gangsters. He concluded that Prío needed to keep up the good work and not revert to "the interminable *grausista* night."[2]

There were indications that Prío intended to do just that. Early in his second year, he spoke of "nuevos rumbos" ("new directions"), signaling a definite break with the politics of *grausismo*. This meant a commitment to fiscal accountability and a likely end to the Auténtico pact with the Republican Party. Never mind that the popular press changed "nuevos rumbos" to "nuevas rumbas." Even when he was serious, the "cordial president" had difficulty overcoming the image of his "happy smile" and "mano suave." He looked too much like a "good-time Charlie" to be taken seriously as a revolutionary, and his generally lavish lifestyle added to the impression.

Although there were no serious charges of corruption against Prío in the first year of his presidency, the problem of perception appeared in his battle for approval of a foreign loan in November 1949. Prío was aware that the World War II sugar bonanza was nearing its end. The sugar crop experienced an 18 percent reduction in 1949 and was expected to drop an additional 20 percent in 1950. At the time, he did not foresee that the outbreak of the Korean War in June would reverse this unhappy trend and actually produce a shortage. Consequently, he sought a loan to finance a major public works program to offset the anticipated rise in unemployment.[3] Moreover, he hoped to participate in the Point Four Program of President Harry Truman (as outlined in the Inaugural Address of the U.S. president on January 20, 1949), to undertake "a comprehensive program for the development of Cuba" and reduce the island's dependence on sugar.[4] In November, the Congress approved negotiations for a $200 million loan with the First National Bank of Boston and other private foreign banks, but not before overcoming powerful opposition laced with emotion.

Eddy Chibás led the opposition. Noting that one of the projects to be financed by the loan was the construction of a tunnel beneath the entrance to Havana Harbor, Chibás declared that Prío was seeking a loan to build "not a tunnel but rather the famous cave of Ali Baba." In an open letter to Prío, he wrote, "You know very well that loans constitute the instrument of imperialist penetration, the favorite arm of `dollar diplomacy' for the economic subjugation of the peoples of our America."[5] *Bohemia* editorialized that the objections to the loan were more "moral" than "technical" and complained that it would "mortgage the Republic."[6] On October 31, Chibás led a demonstration of forty thousand people before the Capitolio, protesting the loan and carrying anti-Prío and anti-Yankee placards. He was joined by a diversity of protesters, including the PSP, Batista, and Grau. Prío stuck to his guns, showing a determination to put Cuba on a firmer economic path.

To that end, the National Bank of Cuba began operations in April 1950 under Felipe Pazos y Roque. The bank was considered the most important initiative of the Prío presidency. *Bohemia* hailed it as "an historic event" and "a decisive step toward [Cuba's] economic liberation."[7] The National Bank of Cuba, an autonomous credit institution, was established "to centralize monetary reserves, supervise and regulate credit, create and retain means of payment, act as fiduciary agent and economic advisor to the Government, fulfill the functions prescribed by the law, and act as a clearing house."[8] The bank also served to keep money out of the hands of would-be grafters. During 1950, Prío continued the trend toward fiscal responsibility.

In June, at his request, Price, Waterhouse & Company of New York made a special investigation of the financial position of the Cuban treasury. The accounting firm reported that in the last five years alone (since 1945) Cuba had accumulated a deficit in excess of $104 million.[9] To prevent further deficits, particularly through waste and mismanagement (as implied in the report), he finally secured legislation in December creating the Tribunal of Accounts, to act as the comptroller general of the nation to audit the application of public funds. This was another of the long-delayed complementary laws of the 1940 Constitution. Congress also enacted the General Accounting Law for the State, Provinces, Municipalities, and Autonomous Institutions, "an accounting law for the national government that introduced the double entry feature into national accounting and an improved distribution of budget expenses."[10] Finally, in December 1950, Congress created the Agricultural and Industrial Development Bank of Cuba (BANFAIC).

BANFAIC, an autonomous institution, was designed to provide credit to farmers of little means or to those cultivating products commercial banks considered too risky and to assist entrepreneurs starting up new industries. The bank's purpose clearly was to promote the diversification of the Cuban economy. To facilitate that goal, the law authorized Rural Credit Associations to operate in various parts of the island as affiliates of BANFAIC.[11] Justo Carrillo Hernández served as the bank's president, bringing another member of the 1930 DEU into government service. Too few of his comrades took part in the politics of the Auténtico years. As Prío undertook these measures to institutionalize money and banking and economic development, he also acted to remove the last vestiges of Grau's influence in his administration. This meant, above all, the dissolution of the Auténtico-Republican alliance.

As the midterm elections set for June 1950 approached, the Auténticos and Republicans were at odds over selecting candidates for the various offices. The Republicans boasted that they were instrumental in the victories of Grau and Prío in 1944 and 1948, respectively, but the Auténticos were not so sure that they needed them in 1950. Moreover, the hard-line Auténticos—the Generation of '30 Auténticos—objected to political pacts in principle, believing that they diluted the revolutionary program of the PRC-A. They asserted that the presence of Republicans in the cabinet and Congress accounted for the failure of the Auténticos (especially under Grau) to live up to the people's expectations. They affirmed furthermore that the Republican leader and vice president Guillermo Alonso Pujol undermined Cuban foreign policy, being too sympathetic toward Trujillo and other dictators of the Caribbean. Alonso Pujol rejected these assertions, pointing out that the Republicans in Congress unanimously supported the Auténticos' legislative program, including the National Bank, the budgetary laws, and the Law Against Gangsterism. They even supported, Alonso Pujol added with a touch of sarcasm, the foreign loan authorization, "despite being aware that it infringed upon an aspect of Auténtico doctrine."[12] The real cause of the split between the two parties, Alonso Pujol claimed, was the Republican insistence on nominating Nicolás Castellanos (a treasury official) for mayor of Havana, instead of supporting the Auténtico favorite, Antonio Prío Socarrás, the president's brother.

Both sides presented valid arguments. There was truth to the Auténtico claim that the alliance with the Republicans was a holdover from the Grau era, and Alonso Pujol was correct that Prío wanted his brother on the ballot for mayor of Havana. Prío knew as well as anyone that he owed his election to José Alemán's political machine (BAGA) and deals made with Alonso Pujol and the Republicans, but he had already taken steps to free himself from the corrupt bargain. The midterm elections gave him the opportunity to make it final. In February, the breakup of the Auténtico-Republican alliance became official when Alonso Pujol (still the vice president of the republic) entered into a formal pact with his old friend Grau. They formed the Cubanidad Alliance, known commonly as "la Coincidencia" ("the concurrence"), and endorsed Castellanos for mayor of Havana, although they all had their eyes on the presidency in 1952. The race for mayor of Havana, the second most powerful office in Cuba, was on. In this and all other midterm elections, the Auténticos were now competing on their own. For mayor of Havana, the PRC-A nominated Antonio Prío to oppose Castellanos (Cubanidad), Manuel Bisbé (Ortodoxo), and Aníbal Escalante (PSP).

The election of 1950 marked a high point in Cuban democracy. By all accounts, the election was free and fair; there were no complaints by any of the parties. Not only did Castellanos defeat Antonio Prío for mayor of Havana, but Roberto Varona, the brother of Prime Minister Tony Varona, lost his bid for mayor of Camagüey. The brothers of the two most powerful men in Cuba lost their electoral contests. Francisco Ichaso, exuberant, wondered aloud, "It would be interesting to know the reactions of public opinion in our America, so inclined to Caesarism, to the exemplary democratic fact that a brother of the President has been defeated in an election."[13] Carlos Márquez Sterling, an Ortodoxo, echoed these sentiments, addressing Prío with a backhanded compliment: "The few words that you pronounced recognizing your defeat honor you as a democrat, as a member of a revolution that up to now has only succeeded in holding honest elections."[14] Prío could afford to be magnanimous; the Auténticos lost a few marquee races but won more than 100 of the 126 mayoralty contests and gained substantially in the 475-seat Chamber of Representatives. But they lost one seat in the Senate that had a particular sting.

Eddy Chibás won the Senate seat from Havana province, replacing José Alemán, who had died on March 24. Chibás himself was in poor health during most of 1950 and his senatorial campaign was not as spirited as usual. He had surgery for a diaphragmatic hernia in February and did not respond well, causing him some concern that he had stomach cancer. He persisted in campaigning against his doctor's orders. Although he lacked his characteristic vigor, he still had bite, referring to his rival candidates Virgilio Pérez as a "ladrón" ("bandit") and Guillermo Belt as "William," and won his race easily. He had surgery again in August and spent the next two months recuperating in the United States, giving the Prío administration a respite, though only briefly, from his nagging opposition.[15] In this context, the death of Alemán removed one of the most powerful figures from the political scene.

Alemán was the consummate politician right up to his death. He represented the concept that the democratic process could be finessed by a generous slush fund, which may explain one of the contradictions of the Auténtico era, wherein respect for individual freedoms was not matched by honest administration. Even though Alemán was in failing health (he suffered from Hodgkin's disease) and he found it discreet to live in Miami Beach, he continued to use his vast fortune to play the role of kingmaker in the Auténtico Party. For him, party unity was critical for victory in 1952, and he kept his lines open to Prío, Grau, and Alonso Pujol. The last person he summoned before his death was the vice president, "to whom he entrusted not only his last political plans but also documents of inestimable value for enhancing the Republican leader's position."[16] For one described as Cuba's "strong man" during the Grau presidency, the press treated "El Bicho" ("the Beast"), as his friends called him "endearingly," with scant respect. *Bohemia* for one described him as the "symbolic figure" of a regime that had "no precedent" with regard to the embezzlement and squandering of public funds. It reported that Alemán supposedly replied, "in suitcases," when asked how he had "taken" money from the treasury.[17] The attacks continued for months after his death. When it was revealed that Alemán had bequeathed five million pesos for a children's tuberculosis hospital, a critic wrote, "First he causes tuberculosis in children, and then he funds the Anti-tuberculosis Hospital with five percent of what he robbed."[18] About the only thing that Alemán escaped was going to trial for the theft of public monies.

The investigation of Grau and his ministers for the alleged misappropriation of 174 million pesos of public funds was still dragging on at the beginning of 1950. Pelayo Cuervo Navarro, who made the charge initially on January 18, 1949, complained a year later that nothing was being done, except for a cover-up. Though justice was slow, it had not stalled. In June 1950, Judge Federico Justiniani y de los Santos issued indictments in "Case 82," charging Grau San Martín, Miguel La Guardia, Isauro Valdés, Florentino Martínez, Eduardo Sánchez Alfonso, and Armando Da'Lama with embezzling 174 million pesos from the state. (The deceased Alemán was not charged.) *Bohemia* was almost poetic: "We are now before the august, respected justice of a civilized country, of a democratic republic, inspired by the defense of society and enthroned in the granite seat of the Law."[19] Justiniani had compiled a mountain of evidence showing that the misappropriation of the income of *Inciso* K alone amounted to 65 million pesos, attributed to Alemán, his top aide Isauro Valdés, and Grau's treasury minister Florentino Martínez. No sooner had Cuba celebrated this triumph of justice than it was rocked by one of the most scandalous affronts ever to its democratic order.

On the fourth of July, in the early morning hours, six masked men armed with machine guns entered Judge Justiniani's chamber and walked off with the precise 6,032 file folders containing the investigative findings of Case 82. There were only two guards on duty and, despite Justiniani's warning not to open the door off hours to anyone, even to him, they opened it when the men knocked. The theft appeared to be an inside job. One of the assailants directed the other five, knowing exactly where to look, ignoring all other documents in the filing cabinets. "Without hesitation, they took the package with the evidence of the scandal, in spite of the fact that there was nothing on the outer wrapper to indicate what was within."[20] Who had done such a thing? Chibás believed the answer was easy. "Always, whenever a crime is committed," he observed, "the police go in search of those who will benefit the most from it."[21] With the finger thus pointed at Grau, his onetime cabinet minister Humberto Becerra proclaimed that the guilty one was none other than Prío, engaged in a maneuver to force Grau to leave the country. He asked why, though bail for those charged in the indictment was set at ten million pesos, indicating the seriousness of the matter, the government assigned only two men to guard the documents.[22] Moreover, one of the guards was assigned just two days before and was with the Radio Patrol, a unit not usually given such duty. Carlos Márquez Sterling believed, indeed, that Prío was the "intellectual author" of the theft.[23]

Though incensed over the outrage, Justiniani affirmed that he would be able to replace the stolen documents. "We will not be delayed a second," added Pelayo Cuervo, "those who carried out this assault have done so in vain, since there are copies available in each of the State archives or departments that produced the originals. This lamentable event, far from detaining the process, will make us more determined to pursue it."[24] Justiniani did try to pick up the pieces, but Case 82 never regained the momentum it had before the theft of the evidence; the thieves were never identified, and the case never came to trial. Case 82 symbolized Prío's "new directions" in a strange way, that is, the familiar one step forward and two steps backward. There was an ambiguity in Prío's relationship with Grau. He took positive steps to clean up after "*el Viejo*" but seemed disposed to cover up for him. It was characteristic of the Auténtico administrations that there were spectacular examples of the exercise of democracy and equally spectacular examples of the breaching of the democratic order.

Despite the controversy over Case 82, rumors persisted that Grau aspired to the presidency in 1952, even though the Constitution mandated that he wait eight years after his previous term. He was not alone in his ambition. After the midterm elections, campaigning for the presidency began in earnest, displaying the vibrancy of Cuban democracy. The polls showed that Chibás was the front-runner, preferred by 26 percent of those asked, followed by Batista with 18 percent and Miguel Suárez Fernández with 14; Grau and Alonso Pujol were far behind in single digits. Miguelito Suárez's poll number was higher than all other Auténticos combined, but there was no shortage of challengers in the party, namely, Sánchez Arango, Varona, Hevia, Pepe San Martín, Felix Lancís, Rubén de León, Eusebio Mujal, Luis Pérez Espinós, Oscar Gans, and Pepin Bosch. The latter was a dark horse coming on strong. He had taken over as minister of the treasury when Antonio Prío resigned to run for mayor of Havana, and he was widely credited with throwing the rascals out of treasury, as Sánchez Arango had done in the Ministry of Education. Ichaso wrote that he, along with Varona, Hevia, Sánchez Arango, and others, gave Prío "one of the best Cabinets of any President ever."[25] It was no surprise, then, that the Auténticos had so many good candidates in the running.

The maneuvering within the PRC-A was intense, and Suárez's rivals tried to slow him down. Sánchez Arango complained that by starting his campaign so early he was obstructing the work of the administration. But Suárez pointed out that Chibás and Batista were already "cleared for action," exploiting the Auténtico's defeat in the Havana mayor's race, and that "it would be suicide for the PRC to go to sleep now."[26] He was a shrewd politician and perceived that Sánchez's thesis of "administration first and politics later" was a ploy, "to play politics *in* the administration, while he was put on the shelf on the pretext that his campaign was premature." He pointed out that neither he nor any of his supporters were members of the cabinet and that he was "disposed" to assist the administration from his position as president of the Senate. He realized that his rivals hoped to make up for their lack of support by inducing Prío to assume the role of kingmaker, leading him to declare that he was certain the president would remain above politics and fulfill his constitutional role as the nation's guide and "moderating force." Outside the party, too, the consensus was that Suárez was the PRC-A's most formidable candidate, resulting in efforts to drive a wedge between Suárez and Prío. Chibás suggested slyly that Suárez would do to Prío what Prío was doing to Grau.[27] The Auténticos would not nominate their candidate until November 1951, and for the time being the maverick senator from Las Villas was out in front.

Simultaneous with the initial jockeying for the presidential race in 1952, the Korean War broke out in June 1950. The war had a significant impact upon the Cuban economy. By 1950, the Cuban sugar-based economy was showing signs of stagnation. It appeared that the guaranteed sale of Cuban sugar in the United States that enabled the country to prosper in the decade of the 1940s would not extend into the 1950s. In 1950, Prío had begun exploring new ways to develop and diversify the economy and had invited the International Bank for Reconstruction and Development (IBRD), the World Bank, to send a mission to Cuba to study the economy and make recommendations. Suddenly, with the advent of the Korean War, an anticipated sugar surplus of a million and a half tons was transformed into a shortage and a new bonanza. The sugar sale of $511.5 million in 1949 climbed to $572.3 million in 1950 and soared to $672.1 million in 1951, beating the postwar peak year of 1947. The "Island of Cork" was afloat again. The World Bank's report, which will be discussed in the next chapter, noted that Cuba suffered from a "lottery mentality," that is, relying on the lucky strike or big payoff instead of the patient incremental way of investment and savings.

The Korean War also had a profound political effect on Cuba. Prío's reaction to the war was extraordinary. He was known to be more friendly toward the United States than Grau and than many of his comrades of the Generation of '30, but his support of the United States in the Korean conflict surprised even the Yankees. He appeared to go out of his way to tell President Truman, "we're on your side," and he even considered sending troops to Korea.[28] At the same time, his policy had a dark side. He cracked down hard on the PSP (the Communist party), proclaiming he wanted no "Communist bridgehead" in Cuba. In the event of a "crisis," he contemplated measures against the PSP, including mass arrests and the establishment of detention camps. On August 24, he ordered the seizure of the Communist newspaper *Hoy*, accusing it of "attacking the national interests and undermining Cuban international policy." The same month, he forced the cancellation of the fifteen-minute radio broadcast "Workers Unity" over COCO, charging it with broadcasting Communist propaganda and material "offensive to the United States and United Nations with respect to the Korean War."[29] As if to vindicate the government's crackdown on the Communists, Prime Minister Varona "displayed a number of envelopes, bearing the letterhead of *Prensa Continental* and addressed to Communist agents in all the countries of the Western Hemisphere." He explained that they were discovered in a search of the offices of *Hoy* and served as "proof" that the PSP was the "center of Russian espionage in America."[30] The intervention in *Hoy* was enough to raise a public outcry, but at the end of June Prío issued Decree 2273, which also affected the Cuban media and had it up in arms. Decree 2273 provided for free, equal radio time for any government official to answer "slanders" by radio commentators.

Ramón Vasconcelos, editor of *Alerta* and minister without portfolio in the Prío cabinet, was among the most outspoken in protesting the closing of *Hoy*. He had opposed the action when it was proposed in the Council of Ministers, arguing that it would restrict freedom of thought and that the proper way to proceed was through the courts. "In the United States," he observed, "in spite of the war in Korea, the *Daily Worker* circulates freely." When Prío acted anyway, Vasconcelos exploded, resigning his position and accusing the government of acting illegally, thus placing every newspaper under threat of government seizure. "In Cuba the worst thing is the precedent," he noted; "above the head of every newspaper there will always be a pretext for decapitation at any given moment."[31] He was especially harsh toward Tony Varona, who was Prío's point man in the takeover, wondering how a "revolutionary" could "trample under foot" the very ideals that led him into revolution in the first place. "The *dernier*—because he has never known how to be *premier*—who they say acted to protect individual rights, does not know what rights are, and ignores the fact that without public freedoms democracy is impossible."[32] Vasconcelos was not defending the Communists, but he was arguing that with the arbitrary closing of even one newspaper, "there was no effective freedom of the press." It was apparent, however, that he was exercising it then. *Bohemia* weighed in with an equally strong attack on Decree 2273.

The popular magazine editorialized that Decree 2273 was a "decreto-mordaza" ("gag order") that would serve as a "point of attack" for silencing all forms of public criticism. Today it is radio, *Bohemia* said, tomorrow it will be the print media or something else. "The concept of freedom is indivisible," it affirmed, "and no one can be indifferent, because the infringement of one right will be followed by another and another, in succession."[33] Moreover, the editorial continued, the so-called "right of reply" was merely a "smoke screen" to silence certain popular political "hours," specifically those of Eddy Chibás and José Pardo Llada. It noted that these two very popular Ortodoxo radio commentators had been elected to the Senate and Chamber, respectively, in the June elections. It believed, therefore, that the purpose of the decree was not to seek redress for alleged injuries (which could be obtained in the courts in any event) but was politically motivated. The piece stated sarcastically that when Prío proclaimed his "nuevos rumbos," there was widespread anticipation that he was going to depart from "certain practices" of the past but that no one expected him to abandon "the one great virtue" of Cubanidad. "One may blame Grau for many things, but not for even the slightest attack on civil liberties."[34] The "authoritarian mask" did not become the "smiling leader," the "cordial President," it concluded, asserting that the Prío who signed Decree 2273 was not the same Prío the people had elected on June 1, 1948. And it asked, finally, "Can it be that the Generation of '30 has not learned the lessons of History?" Prío's "new directions" appeared to be progressing well through the first half of 1950, but after the midterm elections the situation changed drastically. First, there was the theft of the Case 82 documents, followed by the uproar over the attacks on freedom of expression, and then a renewal of *pistolerismo*.

There were only a couple of MSR-UIR-related shootings during the year, one in January and another in July, but the murder of Dr. Tulio Paniagua Recalt at the end of September was the spark that touched off the feuding anew. The murder had all the earmarks of an MSR killing. Paniagua was the deputy minister of the treasury and a close friend and collaborator of Miguelito Suárez. Suárez had publicly acknowledged his links to UIR leaders and several weeks before the Paniagua assassination had received reports of a plot to kill him or someone allied to him. Witnesses to the crime identified MSRistas Leoncio Espinosa and Sergio Acebal Betancourt as the assailants, the latter a driver and bodyguard of Representatives Gilberto Leyva and Rolando Masferrer.[35] Armed with this information, Suárez was certain that the crime was politically motivated, and he accused "the Government" of failing to arrest the suspects so it could cover up the possible complicity of "high governmental figures." Expressing outrage over the suggestion that he was "playing politics over the corpse of [his] slain friend," Suárez resigned as president of the Senate, hoping thereby to facilitate "an effective and speedy police investigation of the motive and nature of the murder."[36] Here was *pistolerismo* at its highest level, an intrusion into the political process but still seemingly "intramural" in nature. Suárez perceived it as an effort to eliminate him from the presidential race. Suárez's resignation, indeed, diminished his chances for the Auténtico nomination and caused Prío to make significant changes in the makeup of his government toward the end of his second year in office.

Tony Varona assumed the position of president of the Senate, and Félix Lancís succeeded him as prime minister. "En Cuba" was critical of Varona's performance as prime minister, claiming that his notorious ill temper made it difficult for him to establish an effective working relationship between the executive and legislative branches. His relationship with Suárez was particularly strained, it reported, and almost scuttled the approval of the National Bank legislation.[37] There was little question that Varona was not easy to get along with, but he was honest and dedicated and much of the successful legislative record of Prío's first two years could be attributed to him. The defeat of his brother for mayor of Camagüey was perceived as a serious blow to his presidential ambitions, although he was rumored to be Prío's personal choice.[38] His revolutionary credentials went back to the 1930 DEU, but his conduct in the closing of *Hoy* was considered authoritarian and further harmed his chances for the PRC-A nomination in 1952. Lancís, in contrast, was often cited as a likely compromise candidate. He was unimaginative though loyal. As prime minister he saw himself playing a "coordinating" role and expressed a strong desire "to have the Revolution take a juridical form."[39]

In addition to Varona and Lancís, Prío made other cabinet changes. He had pledged that he would make cabinet appointments on the basis of merit alone, but when certain provincial Auténtico leaders complained that there were not enough party members in the cabinet, Prío became more partisan in his new appointments. *Bohemia* observed that the new cabinet was not as distinguished as the old.[40] Nonetheless, two of the new appointees, Luis Casero Guillén (public works) and Lomberto Díaz (government) proved to be exceptionally capable and served "nuevos rumbos" well. As mayor of Santiago de Cuba Casero had compiled an impressive record for civic improvement and personal integrity. A new public market was one of his most notable achievements. Díaz, for his part, undertook to clean up the vice-ridden barrio of Colón.

The barrio of Colón, in the "very heart" of Havana (along the streets Virtudes and Industrial; Trocadero and Amistad), was the center of organized vice. Díaz launched a "campaign of moralization," carrying out drug busts and closing the infamous brothels of the red light district. Prío and Díaz confronted "powerful interests" in their crackdown, but both wished to clean up the area in an effort to stimulate a healthy tourism. They were tired of the image of Old Havana as a "raunchy liberty town" for sailors. In March 1949, there had been a disgusting incident in which several drunken sailors (U.S. Navy) urinated from atop the statue of José Martí. Fidel Castro led a protest demonstration before the U.S. embassy. The American ambassador Robert Butler apologized, and Prío hoped to avoid a repeat performance. Díaz took a great deal of criticism from the "powerful interests," who slandered him with the charge that he wanted to seize valuable real estate for personal speculative purposes. The charge was rooted in "an old complaint" that the district "was too valuable to be left to 'red light' activities."[41] Regardless, his campaign was spectacularly successful, *Bohemia* noting the empty streets of the barrio and remarking that Díaz had converted "the oasis of sin into a desert of virtue."[42] Despite this success, there was another "oasis" in the barrio that probably resented the encroachment of the desert.

The notorious tenderloin was home to Havana's Bohemian colony, living on the margin of conforming society. The "commune" maintained by José Lezama Lima, the editor and publisher of *Orígenes,* was located on Trocadero, and Antonio Ortega, the fiction editor of *Bohemia,* lived at the corner of Amistad and Trocadero, in the "navel" of the Colón barrio.[43] Mid-century was an exciting time for Cuban letters. Lezama Lima's "stable" of writers was beginning to produce a Cuban literature. In the search for the means to express "Cubanidad," they turned to the abstract, undoubtedly an attitude of alienation toward the current political and social scene. "In this way, the works evolved among nostalgia for an idealized past (Eliseo Diego), a deformed and grotesque vision of an absurd present (Virgilio Piñera), and the delirium of the imagination (José Lezama Lima)."[44] At the same time, Cuban arts extended beyond the limits of the

Colón barrio. Though they published in *Orígenes,* the authors Nicolás Guillén, Alejo Carpentier, and Fernando Ortiz were important voices beyond Lezama Lima's circle. Ortiz, like Ramiro Guerra, was an "ideologist of the *colonos,*" making a cultural argument as much as an economic case, seeking to preserve a way of life against the spread of latifundium.[45] And Ernest Hemingway, on the other side of the Prado, in his room in the hotel Ambos Mundos or at his finca, Vigía, was writing his masterpiece, *The Old Man and the Sea.* Whatever the Auténticos' shortcomings, they presided over a period of cultural awakening and unprecedented freedom of expression.

The 1950 season of the performing arts further demonstrated this phenomenon. Two new theaters opened that year: Las Máscaras for drama and the Blanquita, a huge auditorium on the edge of the sea in Miramar, with a seating capacity of sixty-six hundred (larger than Radio City Music Hall), for reviews and spectaculars.[46] Cabrera Infante noted, "Cuba, poor in arts, mediocre in architecture and babbling in theatre, becomes a realized people in its music."[47] Lisandro Otero echoed this sentiment, writing that Havana had become one of the "music capitals" of America. He listed the famous foreign artists who had performed there in 1950: Herbert von Karajan, Bruno Walter, Eugene Ormandy, Vladimir Horowitz, Arthur Rubinstein, Artur Schnabel, Claudio Arrau, Yehudi Menuhin, and Isaac Stern. He cited also native musicians who were creating a Cuban music, such as Marcel Quillévéré, who composed symphonies and ballets with African resonances, and José Ardévol, who put Martí's "Versos sencillos" to music.[48] Yet popular music was "the truly great Cuban creation."[49] One of the most outstanding popular artists was Beny Moré, a singer and big band leader, who performed in Sloppy Joe's and popularized the mambo. He fashioned a Cuban national music, combining "the *guajiro's* capacity for verbal improvisation with the rich rhythm of the Blacks."[50] Amid this cultural flowering, television came to Cuba in 1950.

Prío inaugurated Cuba's first telecast on October 24. Initially only Havana and Pinar del Río provinces were affected, but, in time, TV stations CMQ and RHC (Cadena Azul) brought television to the entire island. Cubans responded enthusiastically, buying TV sets in large numbers. "Sales are expected to be very heavy," the *Hispanic American World* reported, "since many Cubans have plenty of money and sugar prospects promise much more."[51] The purchase of TV sets emphasized the disparity within Cuba, primarily between the cities (especially Havana) and the rural sections that did not even have electricity. There were many contradictions in Prío's Cuba in 1950, as exemplified by Cuba's relations with the United States.

Prío's thought of sending troops to Korea in support of the United States and the United Nations contrasted sharply with his reaction to the abortive uprising in October by the Puerto Rican Nationalists, who simultaneously tried to assassinate President Truman. Demonstrating the long-standing empathy of Cubans toward their Puerto Rican brethren, particularly over the issue of independence, the Congress approved a letter from Prío to Governor Luis Muñoz Marín expressing concern for the well-being of the imprisoned Nationalist leader Pedro Albizu Campos. Both Muñoz and the U.S. government considered Albizu Campos to be a terrorist and consequently resented Cuba's "interference."[52] Yet this episode did not seem to affect the overall nature of U.S.-Cuban relations during 1950. With the Cold War "dominating hemisphere politics," the United States applauded Prío's "anti-Communist crackdowns."[53] The American embassy reported that "the Cuban people and their Government are basically friendly to the United States and have indicated that they generally approve our position on international problems. These circumstances appear to offer us a favorable opportunity to seek the fuller realization of our objectives to the mutual benefit of both countries and the free world."[54] The United States considered Cuba's defense of political exiles a "nuisance" but one that appeared to be contained within reasonable limits.

In many respects, 1950 was a turning point in the Auténticos' exercise of power. The year started out well, marked by the oft-heard expression, "!no hay problema, hermano, no hay problema!"[55] ("There's no problem, brother, no problem!"). GRAS appeared to be winning the "war against gangsterism," the National Bank began operations in April, and the Price, Waterhouse study showed a determination to be fiscally accountable. Though *Bohemia* labeled Prío a "do-nothing" president in October, after two years in office, the passage of legislation in December for the creation of the Tribunal of Accounts and the Agricultural and Industrial Development Bank maintained hope that "new directions" was still on track. Aside from the theft of the Case 82 documents, there were no major scandals involving corrupt practices. The voice of Eddy Chibás was unusually quiet, which may be attributed more to his ill health than to his lack of anything to say. In the midst of these favorable signs, the exemplary nature of the midterm elections and the reprieve granted Cuban sugar production by the Korean War gave the Auténticos a tremendous boost politically and economically. Deep down, Prío must have sensed that the

Auténticos had reached a critical point in the history of Cuba, but he proved too weak intellectually and morally to take advantage of his instincts.

Prío sensed that the economy was living on borrowed time. Before the Korean War began, he had realized that sugar alone could not sustain the Cuban nation. To that end, he invited the World Bank to send a mission to Cuba to study its economy and resources and make recommendations for its future growth and development. The mission's report provided an excellent overview of the Cuban economy and a means for assessing the economic and social policy of the Auténticos. Though clothed in diplomatic language, the verdict on the state of the Cuban economy was not favorable.

8

Sugar and Vinegar

At the request of President Prío, the World Bank sent a mission to Cuba in the summer of 1950 to make "an independent study of the economy of Cuba and, on the basis of such study, to prepare a report of its conclusions as to the more important economic problems and feasible development possibilities in Cuba."[1] Francis Adams Truslow, a prominent New York attorney and president of the New York Curb Exchange, served as chief of mission. During World War II, he had been in charge of the program for stockpiling natural rubber for the U.S. government and, to that end, had traveled extensively in Peru. The mission spent the months of August, September, and part of October in Cuba carrying out its study, before returning to Washington to assemble its findings and present its report in July 1951. The report consisted of 1,052 pages—ten books and a total of fifty chapters. The study touched on every aspect of the Cuban economy, including "human problems" and even the prickly issues of public administration and policy along with economic and social consequences. Prío got more than he bargained for, particularly in the sense of a Wall Street assessment of a political economy beholden to social democratic philosophy.

The mission concluded the obvious, that the sugar industry dominated the Cuban economy. But it gave substance to the notion, providing statistics, tables, and charts. The data showed that more than 50 percent of the cultivated land was devoted to cane, that nearly one-third of the five hundred thousand gainfully employed workers were directly involved in the *zafra* (sugar harvest), and that 31 percent of the total national income for 1949 (507 million pesos out of 1,657 million) came from sugar production.[2] Such domination created problems, particularly since all but 5 percent of sugar production was exported. Moreover, 90 percent of Cuba's total exports consisted of sugar products, making the country dependent on foreign markets and the international price of sugar for its well-being. The mission put this reality into historical perspective.

It noted that throughout its history Cuba had experienced good times and bad as the result of events in "the outside world over which it [had] little or no control."[3] Among these was the "dance of the millions," the period after World War I when sugar prices soared on the international market. This phenomenal rise stemmed from the combination of the lifting of wartime price controls and the fact that European sugar beet production had not yet recovered from the war's devastation. From 5.5 cents per pound in 1918, the price of sugar rose to 9 cents in February 1920, to 18 cents in April, and topped off at 22.5 cents on May 19, 1920. The island was swept by "a mania." Slowly a decline started, picking up speed through the summer, until the price dropped to 8 cents in September and to 3.75 cents before Christmas. Cuba had hardly recovered from this disaster when the worldwide depression of the 1930s dropped per capita income to a low of $98 in 1932 (compared with over $250 in 1920). But once again, the "outside world" came to the rescue of Cuban sugar, with World War II providing rising prices and an insatiable market. Finally, just as the postwar recovery of Cuba's competitors threatened its sugar production anew, the Korean War broke out to create another bonanza. Cuban sugar production had a record year in 1947, and per capita income reached $341, placing the island nation near the top in that category in Latin America and ahead of Italy and Spain.[4] These experiences, the mission concluded, induced Cubans to believe that nothing they could "do at home" was "nearly so important" to the economy "as a variation of a cent or two in the price of sugar."[5] Elaborating, the mission observed, "Assuming exports of three million tons, a one-cent variation up or down in the average price received for its sugar can make a difference of 60 million dollars in Cuba's receipts."

Operating under this general premise, successive Cuban governments pursued policies designed to control and regulate the sugar industry as much as possible and to make certain that Cubans were the industry's principal beneficiary. These policies affected every element involved in sugar production, which became rigidly organized. The core element was the *central* (sugar mill), which ground the cane. In colonial times, there were as many as 1,500 *centrales,* but these were primitive units. Improved technology and modern machinery required substantial investment and had greater capacity, but the inevitable result was concentration, and the number of mills shrank to 161 in 1950. Moreover, Cuban ownership of mills expanded from 56 in 1939 to 108 in 1950, whereas during the same period the number of U.S.-owned mills fell from 68 to 44. Eight of the ten largest sugar companies in Cuba at the time, however, were U.S.-owned.[6] Though the *hacendados* (mill owners) owned approximately 70 percent of the land planted in cane, they grew very little of it themselves. In 1950, the mills grew only about 10 percent of the cane, known as "administration cane"; the rest was grown by *colonos* (sugar farmers), who leased land from the mill.[7]

Though *colonos* was the generic term for sugar farmers, the term *colonos libres* (free sugar farmers) applied to *colonos* who owned their land. Whether owners or tenants, about 15 percent of the *colonos* were well off, and another 70 percent made up a "middle class." Descending the ladder from the *colonos* were various other sugar growers classified by their relationship to the land, that is, subtenants, sharecroppers, squatters, and hired labor (mainly for administration cane). The forty thousand *colonos* in 1950 exhibited a land settlement pattern similar to that in the rural United States, that is, dispersed farmsteads (*bohios*) on individual parcels of land. Located around each of the mills in European-style farm villages were *bateyes,* in effect, company towns, populated by mill workers and hired farm labor. In addition to the farmers and laborers directly related to sugar production, scores of workers were employed in transportation and port services. As successive governments sought to protect Cuban sugar production from the vicissitudes of the international market, they also endeavored to defend the interests of the various elements in the production cycle, particularly small and medium-size growers, against the large estates (latifundia).

The dominant philosophy of all government controls over the sugar industry was to protect the price of sugar by limiting production. In 1926 Gerardo Machado had imposed legal restrictions on sugar production through the Verdeja Act that set production quotas for individual mills and prohibited opening new lands to cane. In 1931, Machado created the Cuban Sugar Stabilization Institute (ICEA), which was destined to be the linchpin of the Cuban sugar industry. Influenced also by the argument of Ramiro Guerra y Sánchez that the policy of latifundium threatened to convert Cuba into a vast plantation, the 1933 revolutionary government of Grau San Martín issued a spate of decrees directly related to the sugar industry. Though scarcity economics still prevailed, the purpose was to redistribute earnings to preserve the existence of Cuban farmers and workers. The "nationalization of labor," for example, required 50 percent of workers in each enterprise to be Cuban natives. It sought to end the importation of Jamaicans and Haitians to work in the cane fields. Guerra was careful to insist that the ban on the importation of labor was not "race-based" but precluded "undesirable immigration—not of a given race but of foreign workers of any nationality who would force down the wages of native Cuban workers."[8] Other labor decrees, such as the eight-hour day, minimum wage, and right to organize and bargain collectively, affected the sugar industry as the major employer on the island. More directly related, Grau created the National Association of Colonos, which gave sugar farmers a corporate voice in the ICEA in competition with that of the *hacendados*. Finally, he established the right of *tanteo* (preemptive bid), enabling the government to acquire foreign-owned properties at auction, with land redistribution and Cubanization of land ownership the ultimate goal.[9] Ironically, the effort to defend and even enhance the proportional share of the small grower (*colono*) in the sugar industry received its biggest boost from Fulgencio Batista.

The Sugar Coordination Law of 1937 virtually created a straitjacket for the sugar industry. In particular, it guaranteed the small grower (*colono*) a privileged place in the production cycle. "It provided that, so long as a *colono* kept his land cultivated with cane and delivered the right quantity to the appropriate *central* (mill), he should never have to give it up: this meant that, if he were a lessee, his lease was underwritten by the state."[10] In this context, the *colono* was guaranteed access to a mill for grinding his cane and a controlled price on a sliding scale determined by the mill's average yield of sugar. At the same time, the individual mills ceased to be competitors, each operating in a specified zone as a sanctioned monopoly. In March 1941, the various laws for controlling sugar production were codified by Law No. 21. Under this omnibus measure, the sugar industry ceased to exist as a free enterprise system. The Cuban president, with the ICEA serving as adviser and agent, in effect ran the sugar industry. The law enabled him to set "legal dates for commencement of grinding; marketing quotas for U.S., world, and domestic outlets; sugar production quotas for individual mills; cane production quotas for individual *colonos*; and minimum quotas for small mills and *colonos*."[11] Thus, several years before the Auténticos assumed power, the sugar industry was already operating under Aprista and mixed economy concepts.

During his presidency beginning in 1944, Grau did not tinker with the system, content to continue a process that reduced foreign ownership and redistributed income from upper-class Cubans to workers and small farmers.[12] But he shifted the emphasis from internal controls to Cuba's relationship with its major sugar market, the United States. Grau strove not merely to defend the price of sugar but to enhance it and to link improved prices with wage increases.

The Reciprocity Treaty of 1902 between Cuba and the United States had provided the "economic motive" for the growth of the Cuban sugar industry, and all subsequent U.S. tariff actions had similar effects on Cuban sugar production. In 1934, the Jones-Costigan Act initiated a quota system to replace the tariff preference as the means for determining Cuban sugar sales in the United States. When the United States entered World War II, however, President Franklin Roosevelt suspended the Jones-Costigan Act and its sister Sugar Act of 1937, and the United States sanctioned the "free *zafras*" (unrestricted harvests), agreeing to purchase Cuba's entire sugar crop through 1947. The terms of purchase were arranged initially through the Defense Supplies Corporation and beginning in 1943 by the Commodity Credit Corporation. In negotiations for the sale contracts of 1945–46 and 1947, the Grau administration succeeded in introducing an "escalator" clause "that provided for increases in the sugar price in conformity with higher commodity prices in the United States."[13] Because Cuba obtained 80 percent of its imports from the United States, this was a necessary protection from the anticipated postwar inflation. Moreover, in 1945, Grau decreed an increase in wages for workers in the sugar industry when the price of sugar rose above 3 cents (the 1945 sale price was set at 3.10 cents per pound).[14] In 1947, when the price of sugar sold to the United States peaked at 4.97 cents per pound, Grau issued a decree fixing 1947 wages as the minimum rate for 1948, reflecting his administration's consistent pro-labor stance and meaning that coordination was largely "one way." This situation existed at the time of the Truslow mission.[15]

With the end of World War II, and the U.S. commitment to purchase Cuba's entire sugar crop due to expire in 1947, Grau initiated another plan to have sugar underwrite broad economic and social programs. By decree in February 1946, he introduced the concept of the sugar differential, whereby Cuba reserved a portion of the sugar harvest to pay for commodities imported from countries other than the United States. This so-called free sugar sold for a higher price on the world market than that set for the guaranteed U.S. sale. Rather than passing along what amounted to a windfall profit to the *hacendados*, the government, through the ICEA acting as exclusive agent, "captured" the differential and made a commitment to use it to build rural schools and an experimental farm station and to purchase machinery and seeds for peasant farmers. Eduardo Suárez Rivas described this as Grau's "most important revolutionary act."[16] Recalling the Inocente Alvarez affair, Grau also traded (bartered—*los trueques*) free sugar for needed commodities on the world market, especially with other Latin American countries. Ideally, this exchange provided scarce foodstuffs to consumers at bargain prices.

When the anticipated postwar recession did not materialize, Prío accelerated the pace at which these policies were carried out. Although the Sugar Workers Retirement Fund had been established in 1941, the Prío administration made significant changes in 1948, augmenting the share contributed from sugar revenues, increasing the size of individual pensions, and dedicating a portion of the fund to discountable loans and a housing program for workers. He also extended the guarantees of land tenure enjoyed by *colonos* to growers classified as tenants and sharecroppers. One of his most important measures was a 1951 law affecting the *bateyes,* providing for free commerce and urban planning. It was designed to end the monopolistic practice of the company store and to tear down the "miserable colonial barracoons" (barrackslike structures, holdovers from slave quarters), replacing them with real towns, that is, decent housing, medical facilities, schools, paved streets, electricity, water, and sewers.[17] Also, in conjunction with BANFAIC, Prío secured legislation creating the Land Distribution Fund and the Agrarian Development Fund for the purpose of acquiring and breaking up fincas and dividing the land among small farmers. Finally, Prío decreed the suspension of farm evictions, making it extremely difficult to dispossess a tenant of his land.[18]

Despite the good intentions of the Auténticos, the Truslow mission concluded that the Cuban sugar industry was overregulated, stifling growth, innovation, and productivity. The twin concerns of overproduction and social justice created an inefficient economic system, in its judgment. The system was "static," with all groups concentrating on the distribution of existing wealth and employment rather than creating "new wealth and more work."[19] There was a disposition to "freeze or rigidify economic relationships."[20] The sugar industry was "irrational," governed by "economic baronies" (cartels), each seeking to preserve its place in the status quo and thwarting dynamic change. These included such private groups as the Hacendados Association, the National Association of Colonos, and the Sugar Workers Federation and such public agencies as the Cuban Sugar Stabilization Institute.[21]

According to the mission, the Cuban sugar industry was regulated "hand and foot," depriving management of any freedom of action. "The inefficient are being protected," it affirmed. "The *colono* who delivers inferior cane to the mill receives the same price as his neighbor, and wages have been frozen at the high level of 1947."[22] Using the quantitative ability of a farmer or mill to fulfill a quota as the standard for staying on the land or in business resulted in, among other things, "technological stagnation." The mission reported that 60 percent of Cuban cane was a variety developed in Java in the late 1920s and that the last mill constructed in Cuba was built in 1925. While other cane-growing countries were actively engaged in scientific development and mechanization to improve yields and reduce costs, the Cuban sugar structure provided little incentive for research and development. The mission pointed out that the sugar industry, "with gross sales of well over $500 million a year in recent years," had been spending only $50,000 a year on research—a mere 0.01 percent—ignoring the opportunity for "increased efficiency and the development of new by-products."[23] There was an appalling lack of "continuity" in research efforts; projects would be abandoned over the years owing to the lack of trained personnel or adequate funding. During the entire republican period, the functioning of institutions dedicated to basic research for economic development was "precarious" and "ineffective."[24] The Truslow mission thus deplored what it described as "apathy" toward by-products, even though successful by-product research could "reduce the economy's vulnerability to fluctuations in the market price of sugar alone" and help overcome seasonal unemployment imposed by the *zafra* pattern.[25] It also criticized the opposition of organized labor to the mechanization of sugar cane production, out of fear that the introduction of modern farm machinery would replace workers.

The mission neglected to state that the Cuban system of production quotas operated within the master quota of what the United States was willing to buy, determined by the U.S. Congress. Moreover, the U.S. quota was more restrictive for refined sugar and by-products, in effect stifling the development of an integrated sugar industry. The positive trend in the acquisition of sugar mills by Cubans—by 1949, Cubans owned 100 of the 161 mills in operation, producing 45 percent of raw sugar—was partially the result of the unloading by American companies of obsolete plant. "By the end of the Auténtico era, U.S. sugar men believed that Cuban sugar was in its declining stage."[26] Auténtico labor policies may have contributed to their withdrawal.

The Truslow mission was particularly critical of organized labor. It stated bluntly that "conflicts in labor-management relations in Cuba today are undoubtedly among the chief obstacles to economic progress."[27] Its assessment applied to the economy as a whole, not just to the sugar industry. Labor in Cuba had been "badly exploited" in the past. "Not so long ago," a labor leader told the mission, "the mill owner had power almost of life and death over the workers." But the mission concluded that since the 1933 Revolution, the pendulum had swung "too far" toward the other extreme, developing into "irresponsible" behavior on labor's part and amounting to "a pyramid of excesses."[28] The mission placed much of the responsibility for this circumstance on the commitment in the Constitution of 1940 that work was "the inalienable *right* of the individual," that the nation must assure "employment to all" and guarantee every worker "acceptable economic conditions." It itemized what amounted to one of the most labor-friendly set of laws in existence in any country at the time.

The laws included the more common guarantees: the eight-hour day, minimum wage, equal pay for equal work, wages in legal tender, paid vacations, protection of women and children, pregnancy leave, right to form unions and to strike, and social security provisions (attending to the exigencies of life). At the same time, they contained provisions that were fiercely Cuban, such as limiting the right to work to native-born Cubans (with no distinction as to race or color); prohibiting the discharge of workers without just cause (burden on the employer); prohibiting relocation of factories for the purpose of hiring a lower-cost labor force elsewhere; requiring that a replacement worker be hired while an employee was on vacation; setting a maximum workweek of forty-four hours with forty-eight hours' pay; tying wages to a cost-of-living index or a commodity price (with adjustments only upward); and stating that if a company was unable to pay the legal wage, "it should not be in business."[29]

Though the Truslow mission recognized the "reasonableness" of the Auténticos' progressive labor policy, it concluded that it was "somewhat arbitrarily administered" and that many aspects of it were counterproductive and actually discouraged economic expansion. It stated, for example, that labor contracts were determined by reference to the laws and decrees on the books rather than by "genuine" collective bargaining. Negotiations began, it affirmed, with labor's claim "to know its rights" and ended with wage settlements and prescribed working conditions bearing little relationship to productivity or the profitability of the enterprise. Nor did this practice of labor's invoking "legal" rights end with the signing of the contract.

The mission charged that labor either resisted the introduction of new machinery and methods into an industry or permitted it to occur under stipulations that no workers be displaced and that "the new equipment turn out no more products than the old." The cigar makers and port workers were among the most obstinate in this regard. As a result, the mission noted, "featherbedding" was rampant throughout Cuban industry.[30] The situation was bad enough but made worse, the mission reported, by the worker's "virtual immunity from discharge." It cited the grounds for dismissal, which it considered "ample," but discovered that in Cuba it was "easier, quicker and cheaper to divorce a wife than to fire a worker."[31] The mission believed that knowing he could not be fired had a "ruinous psychological effect" on a worker. "It destroys his initiative and incentive, and makes him feel irresponsible."[32] In this connection, a theme ran throughout the report that "unconstructive attitudes" were "among the chief obstacles to economic progress."[33] Nowhere was this problem more serious, it opined, than among the leadership of organized labor.

After a review of the history of organized labor in Cuba, the mission concluded that the Cuban Workers Confederation was more a political organization than a "legitimate" collective bargaining agent. Referring to the anarcho-syndicalist foundations of the Cuban labor movement, it traced the CTC's origin to its founding in 1939 under the auspices of Batista and the Communists, remarking that the Communists retained control until 1947 through "superior industriousness, devotion, training, and tactical skill." It noted that the takeover of the CTC in 1947 by Eusebio Mujal and other Auténtico labor leaders was a political move, with the consequent politicization of the labor movement. Mujal was as much a politician as a labor leader, holding a seat in the national Senate. The ability of the CTC to "deliver" for its rank and file always had been tied to its relationship with the governing party, but once Auténticos were installed in the leadership they felt the need to show they could be tougher than ever to prevent a Communist "comeback."[34] Mujal was given "free rein."[35]

Concerned that the CTC was becoming a "tool" of the state (Auténtico Party) and vice versa, the mission warned that "healthy growth" was impossible in the absence of "voluntary" cooperation among labor, management, and government. It was convinced that organized labor had to change its attitude, stop acting with a spirit of "revenge" against past abuses, and adapt "to its new position of power and responsibility."[36] One way of achieving this, it suggested, was by making the union more "democratic" through better grassroots organization and improved education of the members. "It must be remembered," the report stated, "that nearly all the popular education of working people on how an economic system works and what might be done to improve it came first from the anarcho-syndicalists, and most recently—and most effectively—from the Communists."[37] This theory contradicted Samuel Farber's contention that the Communists failed to educate the workers in defense of their interests or to achieve a "working class consciousness."[38]

The Truslow mission's criticisms of labor had all the characteristics of the rejected Treaty of Friendship (1947), which expected labor to make all the concessions. Writing in 1987, the Cuban historians Oscar Zanetti and Alejandro García accused the mission of being "obsessed" with the "labor situation" and of "hammering away at it." "For the World Bank experts, the wage and legal advances by the Cuban proletariat were far above what the country could afford and constituted the main obstacle to the mobilization of investment capital."[39] Carlos del Toro, a University of Havana colleague, went further, denouncing the mission's report as "a reactionary formula against the rights of workers achieved in the Revolution of 1933."[40] Implicitly, he acknowledged that the Auténticos ignored the mission's suggestions, writing that Batista applied them later (1952–58).[41] Del Toro and the mission were more in agreement regarding education in the Auténtico era. The former wrote that "illiteracy and low educational levels prevented the rational use of the nation's natural resources,"[42] and the latter stated that education was the "principal tool" for developing human resources.

Though the Truslow mission emphasized the vital importance of education for the economic progress of Cuba, its findings with regard to the educational system were "disquieting." It was particularly disturbed that all statistics showed that Cuba was falling backward from the high ranking it once enjoyed. According to its observations, literacy rates, enrollments, and hours of instruction had been declining under the Auténticos. Moreover, it affirmed that the "deterioration" of Cuba's educational system did not stem from the lack of expenditure. Rather, the Cuban people were not getting their money's worth. The slippage was the result of "unstable administration, poor planning, political patronage, and maladministration of funds."[43] The mission, of course, had come across the corruption by José Alemán. It hastened to add that there had been "a distinct improvement" over the past two years, thereby lending praise to Prío and Aureliano Sánchez Arango. It even quoted Sánchez Arango, who admitted: "The Ministry of Education was an opprobrium and a shame and, in addition, a dangerous menace to the Cuban nation. It was a cave of entrenched bandits and of gunmen and an asylum of professional highway robbers."[44] The mission recognized that proper administration was the key to Cuba's educational system and, hence, to the development of human resources for the future of the economy but noted that certain systemic defects needed to be corrected first to enable any administrator to be effective.

Among the defects, it cited, first, "over-centralization of administration." Lowry Nelson stressed this point repeatedly in his book *Rural Cuba*, which the mission duly noted. Everything "depended" on Havana, from teacher appointments to textbooks and supplies to paychecks. This situation was particularly harmful to rural schools, weakening local responsibility and initiative and promoting neglect. The historian Emilio Roig de Leuchsenring stated the problem in stark terms: "The cities monopolize the government and administration of the nation, centralizing it, with complete neglect of the countryside and rural dweller. . . . [Many *guajiros*] live at the edge of civilization and the law. For them, there are no doctors, medicines, or hospitals; and their children are deprived completely of teachers and schools and grow up in the most absolute illiteracy."[45] The situation served only Alemán, providing him with access to all the money and a huge pool of jobs. Overcentralization contributed to the second structural weakness, "discontinuity of administration." Because everything depended on the ministry in Havana, a change in minister disrupted the entire system. During Grau's four years, there were five ministers of education, "each averaging less than one year," affording little time to learn the needs, much less to develop a plan and carry it out. Although Alemán had been employed in the ministry for twenty years before taking charge, there was a general "lack of professional administration" in the school system, constituting a third weakness. As was the case in the public sector in general, there was no career civil service system to ensure professional development, job security, and pay based on merit.[46] Finally, the mission listed "a demoralizing heritage of political patronage and graft" as the linchpin of all the ills cited.

Ironically, the Ministry of Education became a center of patronage and graft because the Cuban people showered it with money to make it the best. Alemán exploited this "laudable" goal to enrich himself and build a political machine. The effects of patronage and graft permeated the entire educational system. Political appointees, whether teaching or not, enjoyed lifetime tenure and good salaries, tearing down standards and teachers' morale. The mission confirmed the reports that teachers of certain subjects had no knowledge of the subject, plus the cases of those "too incompetent" to be teachers being kicked upstairs to be "inspectors."[47] Sánchez Arango informed the mission that the Grau administration had constructed 628 schoolhouses but that only 37 were "located according to need." The rest were so-called show-window schools, built along the Central Highway, "to impress the superficial."[48] The condition of school buildings in general, not just those in rural areas, was described as "deplorable." The mission heard from one teacher, "When a building is no longer fit for people to live in, it is turned into a school."[49] Although much of the anecdotal information reported by the mission applied to the Grau administration, it concluded that unless the Prío government improved the public educational system "within a short time," its chances for successful economic development were bleak. "Better fundamental education is needed to prepare for the initiative, vocational skills and social cooperation required by a modern economy."[50] Del Toro added another dimension to these depressing findings—as a shortcoming of the entire republican era—stating that the defects in public education contributed to juvenile delinquency. In 1956, at one juvenile rehabilitation center (the *finca* Torrens), 48.26 percent of the 690 residents were illiterate. Only 18 (2.61 percent) had a sixth grade education.[51]

The Truslow mission repeated much of its criticism of the public educational system in discussing government administration in general. Alemán may have pushed the practice of *botellas* and sinecures in his ministry beyond the limit, but the mission found that in many other government ministries most jobs were held by political appointees, persons selected for reasons "other than for the good of the public service." This circumstance, coupled with Cuba's lack of alternate employment opportunities and the fact that 80 percent of government budgetary expenses were salary payments, convinced the mission that government service had become a form of "social assistance," taking the place of an "official unemployment insurance or unemployment relief."[52] Government was Cuba's second largest employer (after the sugar industry), and too much of its workforce was incompetent or irresponsible. Since government performed many services necessary for sound economic growth (relating to health and human services, public works, and money and banking), the mission declared that Cuba had to reform its personnel practices without delay.

It pointed out that the Constitution of 1940 addressed the issue of public service, setting out sound principles for a civil service system, but that essential legislation was lacking. It noted that Prío had proposed legislation to provide for "the administrative career" in government that included competitive examinations for selection and merit for promotion and pay, and it urged speedy adoption.[53] Recognizing that such reform required time, the mission suggested that the Prío administration begin immediately with the newer agencies, the National Bank and BANFAIC, to serve as models for revamping the entire system. This indeed was done, and both the National Bank and BANFAIC earned reputations for effective administration and efficient service. Despite the importance of competent and honest civil servants and efficient government operations for overcoming Cuba's economic problems, the mission affirmed that until Cuba reduced its dependence on sugar nothing else was going to work. It stressed, "Unless it is realized to what extent the island is a one-crop export economy, it is impossible to understand the basic problems of further economic development."[54]

In response to its admonition, the mission turned its attention to the diversification of the Cuban economy. It compiled an inventory of Cuba's resources for development, concluding that Cuba had "ample, unused human and material resources" for broadening its economic base. Lowry Nelson had informed the mission that a high proportion of Cuba's land was flat and fertile; he waxed enthusiastically that Cuba was "without question one of the most favorable spots for human existence on the earth's surface."[55] The mission was not as sanguine about mineral resources, claiming that the development of such resources had been "retarded by official and public ignorance and lack of interest." It was the old story of "the diabetic dangers of the dominance of sugar in [Cuba's] economic blood stream."[56] In any event, the development of nonsugar agriculture and industrial enterprises was subject to the same sorts of corporate entities (producer associations, government stabilization agencies, and trade unions) that controlled sugar production. As in the case of sugar, "output restrictions, pegged prices, and other monopolistic practices blanketed the livestock industry, and tobacco, rice, potato, and coffee farming."[57] What the mission referred to as attitudes that needed changing was fundamentally a criticism of economic nationalism and the mixed economy approach of social democracy. This criticism was noticeable throughout the report, although the mission's negative appraisal of the possibilities for developing the tourist industry was particularly blunt.

As in the case of the mission's complaints about the Cuban economy in general, it criticized the "wrong attitude" of labor as the main obstacle to the development of tourism. It cited substandard accommodations and poor travel facilities on the island as factors discouraging tourists but blamed principally labor intransigence, especially the difficulty in firing employees. "Since it is difficult for hotel proprietors to dismiss inefficient, lazy or discourteous staff, standards of service suffer. Sometimes the guest is insulted and the manager can do nothing."[58] Moreover, the mission observed, the unions opposed reductions in staff during the off-season, refusing to acknowledge that tourism was seasonal in nature. The effect was high rates year-round, harming competitiveness. The mission reported that excessive charges (by customs officers, baggage handlers, taxi drivers, and others) and gouging of tourists were more the rule than the exception. It asserted that some taxi drivers were in cahoots with "undesirable establishments of various kinds in which the tourists [were] cheated."[59]

According to the mission, Cuba was "living in the past" and had done little to upgrade its tourist facilities since the Prohibition era, when Americans flocked to Sloppy Joe's and other drinking and gambling joints. "Ron y sol" ("rum and sun") were no longer enough to attract tourists; Cuba needed to develop roads, hotels, beaches, and recreational facilities if it was to have a modern tourist industry. The mission concluded that the situation was so bad that Cuba had to "start from scratch" but insisted that it go slow and not make "great expenditures" right away. "Tourism can only be developed efficiently and economically by stages, as the country as a whole is developed," it advised.[60]

This assessment of Cuba's tourist industry contrasted sharply with that of the author Adolphe Roberts. He declared that "the influx of pleasure seekers from the United States has swelled yearly, reaching a figure that makes Havana the principal tourist resort of the Western World. Nothing apparently can halt its growth."[61] Even though his book was published in 1953, its text pertains more to the Auténtico years than to the hotel-building boom of the mid to late 1950s. He described tourism as a $50 million business annually and asserted that the Cuban government "coddled" tourists. Far from perceiving tourists as "victims," he insisted that they were "protected as guests." There was a special tourist police force that extricated even the "most obnoxious" tourist from a jam. Except for major crimes, it generally regarded visitors as "above the law."[62] The distinction between the findings of Roberts and those of the Truslow mission may stem from reliance on different sources.

The mission stated that opinions about the tourist industry differed greatly between the "official" Tourist Commission and those engaged in the tourist business. In disputing reports by the Cuban Tourist Commission concerning the tourist count and revenues, travel professionals claimed that estimates of revenue from tourism were too optimistic and that the numbers of tourists included "many short-term or transient visitors,"[63] that is, persons who came for a one-or two-day "fling" but had no desire "to stay long." It was another manifestation of the fast-money syndrome, an attitude that the mission ascribed to many sectors of the economy.

In drawing up its report, the mission commented generally that Cuba was enjoying prosperity in 1950 and had the opportunity to reduce its dependence on sugar, "not by producing less sugar, but by developing additional enterprises."[64] It cited history as proof that the sugar bonanza would not last and pointed out that even in this prosperous period there continued to be "serious permanent as well as great seasonal under-employment." It stressed that there was no magic bullet for Cuba's economic progress, advising that Cuba could achieve diversification "only by concerted effort in many spheres, by diligent improvement of its institutions and by new attitudes in many people." Above all, in the mission's opinion, Cuba had to escape the "vicious circle" imposed by sugar's dominance. In good times (rising sugar prices) no activity was as rewarding as sugar, and in bad times (falling sugar prices) investment in other activities was considered just as risky as staying with sugar. The result was a "static" economy, with the development of defensive positions, a sort of hunkering down, an uncooperative, negative mood. "Unconstructive attitudes," to which the mission referred repeatedly, were "among the chief obstacles to economic progress."

In recommending diversification, the mission overlooked Cuba's trade reciprocity with the United States as among these obstacles. Under the terms of the 1934 Reciprocal Trade Treaty, Cuba received preferential treatment for its sugar and thirty-four other articles in return for tariff reductions for four hundred U.S-produced articles. In 1946, 77.7 percent of Cuba's exports were destined for the United States, and its imports from the United States constituted 86.9 percent of all goods purchased abroad. Moreover, in that same year, sugar and sugar by-products made up 74 percent of all exports. In 1950, the figure had soared to 89 percent.[65]

During the war years, the scarcity of imported goods led to the development of certain "new" or "war" industries and efforts to protect them in the aftermath. In 1948, Grau issued Decree 530, designed to protect the incipient textile industry from foreign competition, but the sugar interests, fearful that the United States would retaliate against the sugar quota, invoking Section 202e, forced the president to issue a new, more moderate decree. José M. Casanova, speaking for the Hacendados Association, questioned the wisdom of any measure that placed the sugar industry in jeopardy—"our natural production"—for the benefit of a weak or "artificial" one.⁶⁶ Given the attitude of the *hacendados*—"without sugar, there is no country"—the proponents of protectionism as a means of diversifying the economy fought a losing battle. U.S. trade policy endorsed this concept, willing to provide Cuba with the fig leaf of a sugar quota to fulfill its larger purpose of selling American products to Cuba. Nor should one overlook the influence of the Colonos Association in the effort to defend sugar's dominance. Contrary to those who argued that Cuba lacked a fundamental class consciousness, "the *colonos* considered themselves to be middle-class businessmen and nationalists."⁶⁷ In their summer meetings they resolved to wear the *guayabera* shirt, shunning jacket and tie, as a "symbol of *criollismo*."⁶⁸

Taking advantage of U.S. efforts to promote free trade in the post–World War II era, Cuba had an opportunity to alter its trade relationship with the United States by becoming a party to the General Agreements on Tariffs and Trade (GATT) which, among other goals, sought to eliminate preferential trade practices. Neither Cuba nor the United States wanted to lose the preferences based on the sugar quota, however, and both nations negotiated an Exclusive Supplementary Agreement, preserving for the most part earlier reciprocal trade arrangements. In a subsequent GATT conference in Torquay, England (1950–51), Cuba won approval for a modest tariff increase in defense of its textile industry and obtained some relief from reciprocity with the United States, causing Prío to proclaim "the economic independence of Cuba."⁶⁹ In accordance with GATT, Cuba made progress in diversifying its export markets, negotiating trade treaties with England, Canada, and Germany.⁷⁰ Nonetheless, imports from the United States remained high, reaching 79.04 percent in 1950 and 76.88 percent in 1951 (not significantly different from the previous five years). In the effort to overcome the geographic concentration of Cuba's foreign trade, the Prío administration walked a tightrope, keeping its sugar "safety net" in place.

According to Zanetti, the tensions between the sugar interests and the nonsugar sector were reduced by shifting the emphasis from tariff protection to labor relations. He asserted that the two elements reached a consensus that salary reductions were essential to enable Cuba to produce and export competitively and that this new attack was reflected in the Truslow report, urging "a reduction of salary levels in Cuba."⁷¹

Nonetheless, the mission cited other obstacles to economic progress, among them "insufficient confidence in Cuba." It affirmed that the historic "insecurity" of the sugar economy caused Cubans to lack confidence in Cuba, accounting for the get-rich-quick style of investing or the preference for investing abroad (capital flight). Low confidence, the mission declared, resulting in reluctance to invest in Cuba, discouraged "the research and technical initiative needed for a more diversified economy." Management was demonstrating a "quick profit" mind-set, and labor likewise was out to get as much as it could as quickly as it could. None of the players thought about new enterprises or new jobs but rather about ways to preserve their particular niche and of exploiting it for all it was worth.[72] This no-growth mentality was compounded by a "lack of confidence in others." Though the mission was careful to avoid the corruption issue directly, its inference was clear in observing a consensus among Cubans of the lack of integrity in public life. "Apparently great numbers of Cubans believe, rightly or wrongly, that for many years the misuse of public funds has been extensive and that public administration still leaves much to be desired." The mission reported that this lack of faith in the integrity of leaders extended to business enterprises and labor organizations. Without using the specific word, the mission suggested strongly that the presence of corruption discouraged investment in Cuba and retarded economic development.[73]

These low confidence indexes inspired negative "attitudes toward the law" that further "checked individual initiative." A widespread belief that the law and its administration were neither fair nor impartial distracted business and led to such practices as tax evasion. The mission affirmed that government decrees, appearing politically motivated and capricious, reinforced these circumstances, "promoting uncertainty." It affirmed that the "basic unpredictability" of decree laws raised "vast areas of doubt in plans for investment."[74] The mission did not make a distinction between the Grau and Prío administrations in the matter of issuing decrees or enacting laws. Finally, when speaking in general of attitudes, the mission criticized successive Cuban governments for "a lack of continuity and consistency of purpose and policy." Traveling across the island, the mission encountered numerous "unfinished and abandoned projects such as roads and public buildings." Graft and corruption contributed to this state of affairs, but poor planning and insufficient funding also played a role, even under Pepe San Martín, who generally received high marks as minister of public works. The tendency of governments to support the "extreme demands" of organized labor, wiping out tax incentives and customs exemptions intended to attract new industries, was also cited as an example of inconsistency and lack of continuity.[75]

The mission stated that Cubans tended to blame the incompetence or avarice of successive governments for their problems but observed that such an explanation was too easy. It suggested that the fault rested with the attitudes it had described, "which governments have reflected." It concluded, "The choice before the people of Cuba is clear-cut. They may take advantage of their present opportunity to start to substitute a growing, dynamic and diversified economy for their present static one, with its single crop dependence."[76] To assist Cubans in their choice, the mission completed its report with a series of recommendations.

In setting out "a course of action to foster development," the mission emphasized the importance of applied research. It advised the establishment of a Cuban Foundation for Technological Research as an immediate step "to find the products, production methods and processes most suitable to Cuban conditions and problems."[77] It added that education needed to be decentralized and removed from political influence by reviving local boards of education and creating a nonpolitical National Board of Education. It put labor-management relations squarely in its cross-hairs, "hammering away" at the need to end government paternalism of labor and urging the substitution of free collective bargaining. It was particularly harsh with reference to port labor, deploring what it described as its "low efficiency and make-work" practices. Referring to work stoppages imposed by port workers in opposition to the Seatrain enterprise, as well as to other forms of bulk handling, the mission declared that the situation was intolerable. It permitted "an organized group of no more than perhaps 1% to 2% of the working population to use its strategic position to impede Cuban commerce in order to exploit the other 98% to 99%, of whom the overwhelming majority are also wage earners."[78]

In recommendations concerning "government policies and development," the mission touched on three areas. In the area of general policies, it listed broad objectives in monetary and fiscal policy, commercial policy, wage policy, and price and production control policies. Generally, its suggestions were not friendly to Auténtico philosophy, declaring, for example, that existing price and output controls were the result of "historical accident" or political action. "Their cumulative effect in certain instances has been extremely harmful to further diversification and development."[79] The mission suggested a reappraisal of controls, "with the object of removing them as rapidly as possible." A second area involved government action to improve the nation's infrastructure. The mission considered the "reorganization and rehabilitation" of Cuba's railroads as the most urgent project in this area. It recommended specifically the combination of the nation's two major railroad systems, Ferrocarriles Unidos (United Railways) and Ferrocarriles Consolidados (Consolidated Railways), "into a new company and operated as a single railway system."[80] "Any breakdown in the railroads would imperil the entire economy. A part of Cuba's railroad system has deteriorated to a dangerous degree," it intoned.[81] Roads were not far behind. The mission stated that Cuba's roads were in terrible shape. It pointed out the need for a Highway Advisory Committee to work closely with the National Development Commission, removing the planning of road construction from the authority of the politicians running the Ministry of Public Works. In the third area, the mission referred to government action to improve human resources through education, health services, and the dissemination of technical information, among other measures. The mission had reported that disease was not a problem in Cuba but that health was, mainly problems caused by parasites and malnutrition.[82] It added that Cuba had "some of the best physicians and surgeons in the world" but that "the administration of public health measures and of public hospitals left much to be desired." The mission turned next to the subject of "government reforms."

"Virtually all spheres" of Cuban administration needed "urgent" reform, in the opinion of the mission. It placed civil service at the top of the list, in order to eliminate political patronage and *botellas*. It urged more fact-finding before making decisions, recommending, for example, the creation of an economic unit in the Ministry of Finance to compile data and statistics to inform policy formulation. The National Bank should be consulted before taking economic action. With regard to financial policy in general, it emphasized "the need for a much greater sense of fiscal responsibility and for further improvement in the handling of public funds."[83] The mission stressed the strengthening of tax enforcement and collection, commending the Prío administration for commissioning a study in this matter by Price, Waterhouse & Co.; the mission endorsed the accounting firm's report. In addition to the technical problems of tax administration, the mission cited the issue of tax evasion, proposing that the government publish the names of offenders and impose stiff penalties. It observed that tax cheats frequently excused their conduct by pointing to government corruption and the misuse of public funds, thus providing the mission with another opportunity to scold, declaring that this attitude indicated "the effect of maladministration on the morale of taxpayers."[84] The lack of moral authority on the part of the Grau and Prío administrations affected the political dynamic generally, encouraging malfeasance and lawlessness. Finally, the mission reiterated its suggestions concerning public works administration, particularly the need to establish the authority of the National Development Commission for planning, noting that in the past public funds spent on public works had been "wasted."

The mission also recommended "actions to increase agricultural and industrial production." With reference to "king" sugar, it urged "increased expenditures" on research, encouraged mechanization, and argued that wages ought to have a downward as well as an upward flexibility. Concerning nonsugar agriculture and minerals and forests, the mission's recommendations were similar, that is, research and more research. It advised specifically the expansion of the Agricultural Inspectors Service and improvement of provincial agricultural schools and of government agricultural experimental stations. It suggested the establishment of a Ministry of Mines, Water, and Forests, "to be responsible for the development not only of minerals and forests but also of irrigation and of water resources of Cuba."[85] The mission's advisories implied strongly that Cuba was an undeveloped country, with untapped and underused resources, and that even sugar production was in danger of falling behind foreign competitors. The mission provided a long list of opportunities for industrial development, including a bag mill, food processing, and furniture. It warned, however, that before any of these enterprises could be successful, problems retarding development must be solved, revealing again its negative attitude toward labor: "wages and port costs may be prohibitive," "labor opposition to modern methods," and "insufficient technical research."[86]

The mission concluded with commentary on "aids to production" and with a listing of "five specific projects" that should be undertaken immediately. It described railroads, roads, and water supplies as "essential" aids to production and urged improvements in public power, telephones, and telegraph. It skirted the issue of rates for public power and telephone but acknowledged that they were kept low as a matter of policy and implied that this discouraged investment. Rates ought to be reviewed and, "if necessary," revised, "to make these services profitable and attractive to capital."[87] The dilapidated railroad system was first among the mission's priority projects, followed closely by road construction and maintenance. Next came the "rescue and overhaul" of government and nongovernment pension funds, those "cash cows" for venal civil and military officials. Looming large among all projects was the mission's repeated call for research, insisting that Cuba "urgently" needed empirical data "applied to Cuban conditions and problems" before it could move ahead with any of its programs. It urged the establishment of a Cuban Foundation for Technological Research and a special project to solve the problem of the water supply for the city of Santiago de Cuba.[88]

For its parting words, the Truslow mission explained that it had not tried to make a detailed examination of the Cuban economy or to provide "an exact" blueprint for development. Rather, it stated, it sought to make an impartial assessment of the "more outstanding facts in Cuba's economic life" and to reach "broad conclusions" within the limits of its collective "knowledge and experience."[89]

Despite the Truslow mission's claim of impartiality, its "obsession" with the "labor situation" has already been cited. A more specific question about the mission's objectivity arose over its recommendations concerning Cuba's railroads, stated as the number one priority of the report. R. G. Mills, the president of United Railways, met with Truslow during the mission's time in Cuba and later wrote, "Mr. Truslow was a very good friend of this company."[90] United was a British-owned company, operating in the western provinces. Owing to a labor dispute, the Cuban government intervened in (took over) the railroad in April 1949. The line was run-down and mismanaged, financially and otherwise. The company had been shortsighted, extracting revenues without reinvesting in equipment and rolling stock. Its tracks were in urgent need of repair, and "the average age of its locomotives was between thirty and thirty-six years."[91] The English were anxious to unload an enterprise that was dependent on a sugar industry possibly in decline (sugar products accounted for 80 percent of all railroad traffic). Railroads in Cuba were a creature of the sugar industry. They were originally built on a north-south axis, "to take sugar to the ports"; only later (at the beginning of the twentieth century) were east-west lines constructed to "link all parts of the country."[92] Added to United's woes, truck traffic was restored in the post–World War II era. "Between 1946 and 1950, the number of registered trucks increased by 93 percent, reaching a total of 29,638 vehicles."[93]

The U.S.-owned Consolidated Railways, operating in eastern Cuba, was in better condition. It did well during the war years and had "three more good years," 1949 through 1952. Using this time to good advantage, Consolidated devised a plan to reduce its debt (the line was highly overcapitalized) and restore credit. It undertook a modernization program, replacing its old steam locomotives with modern diesel-electric engines, and in 1949 began an effort to acquire United Railways. The Truslow mission's recommendation that United and Consolidated be combined "fit in perfectly" with such designs. According to Zanetti and García, it fit in too perfectly:

> The implications of such a program are easy to see. With the government taking over Ferrocarriles Unidos and its British owners withdrawing, the fusion of the two companies would, in fact, mean giving Ferrocarriles Consolidados control of the country's entire railroad service. In essence, implementation of the proposal would create a gigantic railroad monopoly under U.S. control. The World Bank's recommendations entirely coincided—by chance?—with Ferrocarriles Consolidados's interests.[94]

Despite this suspicion, these historians acknowledged that, in analyzing Cuba's railroad situation, the Truslow mission "had observed details objectively," with the caveat that "it credulously ignored the key fact that the problems of Cuba's railroads were deeply rooted in the general crisis of the country's economic structure" (i.e., "its single-crop economy, dependence on trade, and poor use of its natural and human resources").[95] Depending on one's point of view, the IBRD *Report on Cuba* may be judged in different ways, but it remains a valuable contemporary document for understanding the state of the Cuban economy during the Auténtico era. It revealed the sharp contrast between the promise of the PRC-A as a social democratic party and its lack of fulfillment. It revealed specifically the gross disparity between the urban standard of living (Havana especially) and the ignorance and poverty afflicting the rural population.

Though valuable as a contemporary document, the Truslow report had little practical effect at the time. It was not released until July 1951, when there was little opportunity left for Prío to act on it. Supposedly, "the Prío administration fell all over itself praising the work,"[96] but by the time Prío received it he was struggling to survive, much less plan ahead. He promised "to study it." The free market analysis of the Truslow mission was not attuned to the mixed economy philosophy of most Auténticos. They were thinking of more socialism, not less. Even as strong a critic of the Cuban sugar industry as James O'Connor observed, "No Cuban politician dared to tamper with the quota system and the cartelization of the industry."[97] Politics was at the root of economic decisions, and the economic system was encased in the emotionalism of Cubanidad. The very soul of the Generation of '30 bore the scar of the Platt Amendment, and the Auténticos regarded sugar as a national treasure for the exclusive benefit of as many Cubans as possible. Francisco Ichaso wrote in 1950 that *"Autenticismo"* (not limited to the official brand of the

PRC-A) had replaced "Liberalism" as the "collective state of mind" of Cubans. "The majority of our people are `auténtica' today as they were `liberal' yesterday, with a passion that shows no reason, with a zeal that is somewhat blind, and with a fanaticism similar to a sports team partisan."[98] The report failed to address the contemporary liberal philosophy of the responsibility of democratic government to guarantee its citizens freedom from want, as sanctified in the Constitution of 1940.

The report's harsh criticism, for example, of the close relationship between the Cuban government and labor tended to reflect the complaints of the American Chamber of Commerce of Cuba. As desirable as better labor-management relations may have been, the reality was that Mujal as secretary general of the CTC was a creature of the Auténticos, and he followed a philosophy that his continued success was dependent on favors from the government in power. Moreover, he learned how to blackmail Prío, using the specter of a Communist comeback. Add the Guiteras Revolutionary Action, as a militant syndicalist group, to the mix, and the prospect for any change in the "labor situation" was severely diminished. The Auténticos had struggled too long and hard to rid themselves of the dominance of Spanish *hacendados* and Yankee bankers to permit them to return on anything less than the terms of the "Authentic Revolution." The Truslow mission was correct in describing the Cuban economy as stagnant and underdeveloped, and O'Connor was right in saying it was irrational, but their analysis included solutions that ignored the Auténticos' overriding quest for economic independence. No reform (no matter how wise) was acceptable that required the PRC-A to abandon its revolutionary principles. Nonetheless, there were many valuable lessons in the Truslow mission's report that were compatible with the goals of the Auténticos, but Prío and the Auténticos needed time to absorb them, and they were in danger of losing that opportunity. Eddy Chibás was seeing to that.

9

"Crazy Eddy"

Eddy Chibás was the defining figure of 1951 in Cuba. Impeded by illness for much of 1950, Chibás was at full cry the following year, a persistent critic of Prío and the Auténticos. A "brave" and "excitable" man, Eddy was driven by two powerful obsessions: to rid Cuba of thieves and to become president. Sitting atop the presidential preference polls in 1951, he seemed to revel in one exposé after another, almost as if he needed to outdo himself each time. He played his Sunday evening radio broadcasts over CMQ like a set of bongos, arousing his listeners and being energized in return. There was reason enough to criticize Prío and the Auténticos, but Chibás got carried away in his attacks, tending to exaggerate and even fabricate charges. Called a demagogue and "el loco" ("crazy man") by his critics, he was "el adalid" ("the leader") to the Ortodoxos and to the thousands of humble Cubans who during 1951 expected him to be the next president of the republic.[1]

Chibás ended 1950 with an open letter to Prío, accusing the president of stealing from the National Lottery revenues and comparing him to "Raffles."[2] He continued in the same vein in the new year, charging that Prío and his "gang" had taken money from the "foreign loan" to purchase "skyscrapers" in New York. "Do the bankers of the government of *cordialidad* believe," he asked, "that the Cuban people are so idiotic that they are going to spend years paying them the money they loaned to Carlos Prío so that he could buy *rascacielos* in New York?"[3] The bombast was an example of Eddy's irresponsibility; he had no proof that Prío was buying skyscrapers in New York, much less that he was misappropriating the loan funds. He received inspiration for the allegations from an article in the real estate section of the *New York Times* of Sunday, November 12, 1950, that reported the purchase of the twenty-five-story Heckscher Building on Fifth Avenue for more than $5 million by "Havana interests" acting through a Florida broker. The report noted that it was the fourth such purchase in recent months. "While the identity of the buyers was not revealed," it stated, "in nearly all of these cases Cuban plantation money was reported to be involved." Chibás may have received further inspiration from his visit to the observation deck of the Empire State Building during his convalescence in the United States the previous October. Given Chibás's fertile imagination, it did not take much to link the alleged purchases with the foreign loan that he had denounced strenuously.

Prío was convinced that Chibás had gone too far this time. Addressing the nation by radio on January 17, 1951, Prío lashed out in strong language against Chibás's accusation and particularly against his threat to disavow the debt. He declared that he was accustomed to Chibás's "campaign of defamation and slander" against him personally but that in this instance Chibás had impugned the "honor and credit of Cuba" and wounded the "very heart of the Republic." He challenged the "responsible organs" of the Ortodoxo Party to declare whether they endorsed Chibás's threat to repudiate "a legal commitment undertaken by the nation," or if they would honor "an act constitutionally voted upon and ratified by Congress."[4] Prío's unusual public offensive against Chibás was quickly taken up by other elements of his administration and party. After all, under the Constitution, a president was expected to act as the "moderating power and protector of national solidarity," placing himself above sectarian passions and political interests.

Orlando Puente, the secretary of the presidency, was among those leading the charge. He stated that the president was reviewing his constitutional obligations in the face of Chibás's threat to the banking institutions and bondholders of Cuba. Furthermore, he exhibited a notarized affidavit on television denying that Carlos Prío, any member of his family, any official of the Cuban government, or anyone representing them had a direct or indirect interest in the properties described in the *New York Times* article. He went on to accuse Chibás of trying to undermine the enactments of the present government and Congress whenever it suited his personal ambition. "He seeks to attain power," Puente proclaimed, "on the ruins of the nation."[5] No sooner had Puente made his remarks on

January 20 than the Auténtico leaders in Congress released a lengthy statement in which they described Chibás's "repudiation" of the loan agreement as a "parliamentary *golpe de Estado*." They wrote that he was guilty of "subversive and illegitimate pronouncements and of wanting to divide the nation." In reading the statement over Unión Radio, Senate president Tony Varona affirmed that Chibás was one of those "delinquents who abuse the attributes of democracy in order to destroy the Republic; they are outside the law."[6]

Chibás delighted in the controversy. He declared over radio that the government had mobilized its immense propaganda resources against him, "undertaking the most intensive campaign of defamation against any political leader in the history of Cuba." He accused the government leaders of wanting to expel him from the Senate and of wanting to destroy the Ortodoxo Party and put him in jail. None of these threats would force him to change his stand, he declared. The slogan of the Ortodoxos, "Honor before Money," was never more effective, he concluded.[7] Eddy's rhetoric lacked substance, and an appearance on television by Ortodoxo representative Luis Orlando Rodríguez revealed why. "What is important to the country," he said, "is not to know from a North American affidavit that Prío has or does not have buildings on Fifth Avenue in New York, but to know if it is true that he has them in general, whether in New York or Havana." He affirmed that one did not have to travel to New York to find buildings owned by Prío and his brothers. While admitting that the buildings in New York did not belong to the president, he proclaimed, "Travel down Fifth Avenue in Miramar and you will find a huge mass of reddish granite, an enormous apartment building worth 300,000 pesos belonging to Francisco Prío Socarrás."[8] Chibás had lied about the skyscrapers in New York; nonetheless, the Ortodoxo Party rallied to his defense.

With hundreds of partisans gathered around the home of Roberto Agramonte in Vedado, the leaders of the PPC (Ortodoxo) met on January 18 to draft a reply to Prío's challenge. The Ortodoxo leaders engaged in a lengthy and serious debate. Chibás began by claiming that he had knowledge of a "vast plan" concocted by Prío, Sánchez Arango, and others to "destroy" him as a presidential candidate and to "divide" the Ortodoxo Party. Carlos Márquez Sterling, charged with drawing up a working paper, accused Prío of "using all the resources of power" to install his brothers "Paco" and Antonio in the Senate and of aspiring to place his sister Mireya there as well. Luis Orlando Rodríguez and Herminio Portell Vilá, however, objected to using the document to make personal attacks. Rodríguez said it ought to stress "fundamentals of a juridical and moral nature." Portell Vilá agreed, pointing out the need to keep the reply on a "high plane" and adding, "Chibás has hit the administration where it hurts." He was referring to the loan and the rumor that the loan was to be used to finance the presidential candidacy of Carlos Hevia. The *pepeceístas* (PPCístas) had arrived at a consensus, as summarized by Jorge Mañach: avoid personal attacks and stress the "political character" of the loan.[9]

On Sunday, January 21, Eddy Chibás went before the microphones of CMQ to read the Ortodoxo statement. It declared that the Cuban people had the right whenever they wished, in accordance with international law, to reexamine and repudiate the loan agreement if they found that, "besides having been unnecessary, the loan funds were wasted or dishonestly managed." These were Chibás's precise words, the statement affirmed. It concluded that at the proper time the PPC would adopt a position regarding the foreign loan, "that public opinion might declare through its legitimate organs of expression and representation."[10] Prío's attack on Chibás had backfired; Chibás's skyscraper lie got lost in the fray, and Prío found himself on the defensive again over the foreign loan. *Bohemia* selected Chibás as its "Figure of the Week" (January 28, 1951), declaring that he had withstood "all the forces available" to the Presidential Palace and had emerged with the "unanimous" support of his party. The uproar over Eddy's first fight in 1951 had barely settled down when he picked another. This time he went after Rolando Masferrer, the Auténtico representative from Holguín, MSR chieftain, and one of the most violent men in Cuban public life at the time.

Masferrer had been in the headlines himself in January, when he was involved in another outbreak of gang warfare. On January 10, Antonio Bayer, the editor of the political page of *Tiempo en Cuba*, Masferrer's newsmagazine, was riddled with twenty-nine bullets as he sat drinking beer in the Corbón bar, after completing his day's work. Bayer was a former ARGista and was preparing an exposé of the ARG action chief, Jesús González Cartas ("El Extraño"), for his new boss Masferrer. Commentators expressed surprise that the attack was carried out in a bar in the Colón barrio in light of the extraordinary police surveillance there in connection with the crackdown on vice by Minister of Government Lomberto Díaz and National Police chief General Quirino Uría. Nonetheless, Masferrer exploded when he heard of the murder and took matters into his own hands. He first abducted Humberto Huguet Domínguez, an ARG member, and, threatening to kill him, forced him to reveal the names of the assailants. He next abducted Salvador Hernández Garriga and Luis Díaz Duque and, taking them to an isolated spot in Jaimanitas, was in the process of having them dig their own graves when police arrived on the scene.

Masferrer assured the police that he had been authorized to carry out an "investigation" by GRAS and that his method of threatening death was "more effective" than physical violence.[11] He claimed to have learned that González Cartas had ordered the murder of Bayer in revenge for his reports attacking the "scandalous depredations" of the ARG. Upon hearing Masferrer's accusation, González Cartas accused Masferrer in turn of making false allegations, calling him "a spy and agent provocateur in the service of Cuban reaction and imperialism." Demonstrating that *pistolerismo* was not fully devoid of ideology, he declared that the attempt to associate the ARG with "such reprehensible acts" was an effort by the "reactionary elements misgoverning the country to crush the social gains of the working class." "They know," he affirmed, "that the Guiteras Revolutionary Action constitutes the most powerful obstacle toward that end within the CTC."[12] Soon after this exchange, Chibás made his attack on Masferrer.

On February 8, Ortodoxo leader Roberto Agramonte discovered a bomb in the driveway of his home. He had received a call earlier in the day inquiring about a meeting of the leadership scheduled for that evening. Wasting little time, and with less proof, Chibás took to the airwaves on the eleventh and accused Masferrer of planting the bomb. "El Tigre" (Masferrer) just as quickly invoked Decree 2273, demanding his "right of reply." It was the first major test of the so-called gag decree, and Minister of Communications Rubén León authorized Masferrer to take over Eddy's radio hour on February 18 to answer the charge. Chibás was outraged, describing the action as a blow to free speech and enlisting his supporters to block Masferrer's access to the CMQ studios. On the appointed Sunday, the police attempted to cordon off a five-block area surrounding the radio station, but events got out of hand, and a riot ensued. Masferrer managed to get inside and exercise his right of reply, though at the cost of "Bloody Sunday" and the life of one young man. At the funeral of the victim, José Otero y Ben, two days later, Chibás excoriated the "gangster" Masferrer, the president, the ministers Rubén León and Lomberto Díaz, and General Uría, proclaiming that they would "have to answer for their crimes before the Tribunals of Justice."[13] For good measure, he challenged Masferrer to a duel. In reaction to this turmoil and quoted in *El Mundo,* Senator Fulgencio Batista stated that it was necessary "to cut off" Chibás's road to power "at all costs."[14]

Chibás was unstoppable, taking advantage of every opportunity to blast Prío and the Auténticos. He got another chance in March, when the Auténticos made a pact with the Liberals for the 1952 elections. Chibás acted dumbfounded. Describing the agreement as "shameful" and as a "pact of renegades," he wondered how the PRC-A could ally with the party of Machado. It was "the final betrayal of *autenticismo,*" he exclaimed.[15] Even though no party had ever won the presidency without forming a coalition, Chibás reiterated the position of the PPC that it would not enter into pacts, that it would not make deals. Actually, he was demagoging the issue; the Liberals had long since purged their ranks of *machadistas*. The Liberal leader, Senator Eduardo Suárez Rivas, was highly respected and had sponsored two significant pieces of economic and social legislation: the law protecting tenants and sharecroppers and the law of the *bateyes*. Fault could be found with the pact, however, on the basis of a report that the Liberals had demanded the liberalization of gambling as a condition of their participation.

The Liberals, according to a report in *Bohemia,* sought to ease the restrictions on gambling as a means of diverting public attention from political problems and of establishing better relations between the gambling public and the authorities responsible for monitoring the activity. *Bohemia* noted that the Liberal Party "had always been the principal protector of illegal gambling in Cuba." Emilio Roig de Leuchsenring considered gambling one of the great evils of the entire republican era, along with illiteracy, racial discrimination, and corruption.[16] At the time that this matter was being debated in the preliminary meetings between the Auténticos and Liberals, the participants observed that National Police chief General Uría would be an obstacle, given his powerful opposition to gambling. "Well," said an Auténtico senator, "we're not going to lose the elections by keeping Uría. We'll ask for his relief and we'll get it."[17]

Prío, indeed, removed Uría on April 8, but the Liberals' wishes may not have been the only factor. *Bohemia* implied that he was also fired because he was too efficient and honest. Uría had been doing a good job, which meant that he was stepping on the toes of many powerful politicians. Antonio Prío complained that he "didn't get out the vote" for him in the Havana mayoralty race in 1950. In his raids against illegal gambling and prostitution in the Colón barrio, he ignored warnings not to arrest "certain gangsters . . . who were useful as electoral agents." He was particularly vigorous in his crackdown against the "numbers racket," to the extent of posting policemen at the windows where National Lottery tickets were sold, which apparently was a sore point of the Liberals. Most of all, he had been trying to wipe out *pistolerismo*.

In the aftermath of the failure to capture Orlando León Lemus ("El Colorado") and Policarpo Soler in November 1949, Uría removed several police officers with ties to the action groups. Many complained that "never before" had they been reprimanded for letting fugitives escape! Uría was "between two fires," the public, which demanded the arrest and punishment of the gangsters, and the "senators, representatives, or ministers," who had "sufficient power to invalidate the action of the authorities."[18] It was noted that whenever Uría traveled abroad there was a "resurgence" of *pistolero* activity. Indeed, while Uría was in Washington during March, Mario Carrillo Lima and Tomás Cabrera Flores were victims of two separate gangland-style slayings. Nonetheless, when Prío removed Uría, with the excuse that it was too much to ask him to serve as both police chief and inspector general of the army, he seemed to imply that he was ineffective, that too many crimes remained unsolved. It was another example of Prío's indecisiveness, first declaring war on gangsterism and then betraying his own orders by thwarting enforcement.

It was the lack of enforcement, above all, that angered the Cuban people about the *pistolero* issue. There had been only three gang-related killings during the first half of 1951, but the arrogance of gunsels like Masferrer and Soler and the failure to punish any of the miscreants was a "social cancer" afflicting the Prío administration. Moreover, the media tended to dramatize and even glamorize the *pistolero* shoot-outs in pulp fiction style. For example, the March 11 issue of *Bohemia* reported the murder of Mario Carrillo Lima on the second in the following way:

> The automobile was parked a short distance from the intersection of Laguna and Escobar. A young man could be seen seated within, in casual conversation with the driver. The attitude of both men seemed to indicate that they had nothing to fear from anybody. Everything was normal on the peaceful street corner of Havana. Ordinary citizens were walking by, engaged in their usual occupations. Those two, for example, who were coming along from Escobar street—one a mestizo, the other white—could not appear more innocuous. They did not even catch the attention of the men in the car. Besides, there were two policemen nearby.
>
> But scarcely having gone a few steps beyond the vehicle, the pair turned around and separated. Each man—with his hand eloquently

placed inside the left side of his jacket—approached from opposite sides. Rapidly, with perfect synchronization, a burst of shots in crossfire fell upon the defenseless occupant of the auto, while the driver, terrified, crouched down to escape.

The last shot, fired point-blank at the body of the already lifeless victim, was accompanied by this phrase: "Just so you know that justice takes time, but it comes."[19]

The coup de grace and watchword were the modi operandi of the UIR. Orfila had claimed another victim. Carrillo Lima had been a driver for Rogelio "Cucu" Hernández Vega, the notorious MSRista, killed in exile in Mexico City in 1948. The fact that the shooters fled the scene "without much haste" (the policemen on the scene preferring to attend to the victim rather than pursuing the assassins) caused as much indignation as the deed itself. Nonetheless, this latest episode may have led to an effort to end the gang warfare.

After two months of negotiations, the leaders of the "action groups" announced an agreement in early May to end the bloodshed. After seven years of feuding and a toll of 150 deaths, the *pistoleros* agreed "to bury their old hatreds and dedicate themselves to constructive political and social activities."[20] Presidential Secretary Orlando Puente and Eufemio Fernández of the ARG brokered the deal, acquiring the assent of "Pepe" Jesús Ginjaume of the UIR and of Pedro Suárez, representing Policarpo Soler and Orlando León Lemus ("El Colorado"). Other persons who declared their approval of the "peace plan" and taking part in the negotiations were Jesús González Cartas ("El Extraño"), Auténtico representatives Rolando Masferrer (MSR) and Gilberto Leyva (UIR), and Miguel Suárez Fernández. (Incidentally, "Miguelito" was back in the Auténtico camp and was serving in the cabinet as minister of foreign relations.)

The armistice agreement was simple. It declared, first, the immediate end to the "war of the groups"; second, that the members of the groups were to be provided the means to reenter normal civic activities (in effect, be put on the public payroll); and, third, that those who wished to leave the country could do so, pending arrangements for their residency abroad.[21] *Bohemia* hailed the restoration of peace "to the hundreds of Cuban homes affected by the excesses of political passions." Chibás, however, perceived a darker purpose. He believed that the intention was to enable certain *pistoleros* to run for political office and achieve the "ultimate amnesty." His suspicions had substance; the "fugitives" Orlando León Lemus and Policarpo Soler announced their candidacies for representative to the

Chamber from Pinar del Río and Matanzas, respectively. Upon hearing that Soler was putting up campaign posters, Chibás observed that they should be "wanted" posters instead. He had a point. Soler's campaign in Matanzas deteriorated into violence and led to his arrest. On June 19, a group of armed men "freed" Soler from his jail cell, and *Bohemia* declared that the action groups constituted a "state within a state" and that the "gangster pact" was null and void.[22] As will be seen, Fidel Castro gathered evidence that Prío's effort "to buy peace" ended up intensifying the "war."[23]

Chibás denounced these events with equal scorn, claiming that Prío was ineffective and unable to guarantee the public safety, but he did not confine his criticisms to *pistolerismo* alone. For example, in March Judge Federico Justiniani had managed to reconstruct the documents of Case 82 and announced that he intended to bring Grau and his ministers to trial. Grau retained the distinguished attorneys José Miró Cardona and Carlos Rafael Menció Hernández to defend him. Miró insisted that Justiniani was incompetent to handle the case and that, because it involved a president, only the Supreme Court could sit in judgment.[24] "Miguelito" Suárez Fernández, the new foreign minister, back in the hunt for the Auténtico presidential nomination, pointed out that most of the persons charged did not belong to the "historic PRC-A" but joined the party after Grau assumed power.[25] Chibás entered the fray, giving no quarter, not even to his onetime mentor, exclaiming, "Send the thieves to jail!" The Court of the Havana *Audiencia* removed Justiniani from the case, however, charging him with being a Chibás partisan, and the thieves did not go to jail. At the same time, Chibás, not content to rehash old crimes, looked for new ones.

On the Senate floor and over the radio, Eddy kept up his steady barrage against the Prío administration. In the Senate on April 27, in a debate over a tax increase to guarantee the public employees' retirement fund, he accused the government of thievery, making it necessary for other senators to restrain Lomberto Díaz and Eduardo Suárez Rivas. "Retirement Fund! How many thefts have been committed in your name!"[26] Even when Prío achieved a success, such as the passage of the Tribunal of Accounts in May 1951, Chibás chastised him for taking overly long to propose the laws necessary for cleaning up the government. He claimed, besides, that much of the credit belonged to Ortodoxo congressmen, such as Pelayo Cuervo Navarro and Dorta Duque.[27] As might be expected, on occasions Eddy's intemperate language backfired. In a broadcast on May 27, he accused Prío of ignoring Cuba's hospitals, asserting that his "corruption" had converted them "into morgues." The reaction of Eddy's faithful audience was one of panic, causing him to apologize to Cuba's doctors and to declare that they were not responsible for the conditions in the hospitals. He reminded everyone that he had refused to go abroad for his surgery the previous year, proclaiming that Cuba had "the best doctors in the world."[28] Despite his excesses, or maybe because of them, Chibás remained atop the presidential preference polls at midyear.

The latest poll, taken on May 17, placed Chibás first with 29.70 percent, followed by Batista with 19.03 percent; Pepe San Martín, 7.73 percent; and the four Auténtico candidates (Hevia, Suárez Fernández, Sánchez Arango, and Varona) with a combined total of 13.64 percent. Chibás led in all six provinces, and José Pardo Llada, studying the data, noted that Chibás was actually the front-runner among the rank and file of Auténticos, obtaining 21 percent of their vote to 17 percent for Miguelito Suárez, his nearest competitor.[29] As Francisco Ichaso had said, *autenticismo* extended beyond the Auténticos. At the same time, Andrés Rivero Agüero, a spokesman for Batista, claimed that the former president was closing the gap, pointing out that in four months Chibás's percentages in the polls had dropped from 35 to 29, whereas Batista had risen from 15 to 19. That constituted a 100 percent gain, he boasted, and added that the polls showed that Chibás was the candidate of the rich and Batista the favorite of the poor.[30] The claim was not accurate, given Chibás's strong support among black Cubans. For example, when Kid Gavilán (Geraldo González) won the world's welterweight title from Johnny Bratton in Madison Square Garden on May 18 and returned to Cuba a national hero, Chibás was among the welcoming throng. Accusing Prío of snubbing the champion, Eddy and the "Kid" from Camagüey had lunch together. Defenders of Prío denied that he harbored racial prejudice, pointing to his ending of the "whites-only" hiring practices of the Cuban Telephone Company and Compañía Cubana de Electricidad and the retail establishments Ten-Cent, Fin del Siglo, and El Encanto.[31] Nonetheless, Chibás moved on, seeking something sensational for his followers to bolster his poll numbers.

In his zeal to find a major scandal in the Prío administration, Chibás seized on a rumor involving Sánchez Arango, the minister of education. In his June 1 broadcast, Chibás accused Sánchez Arango of stealing money appropriated for school supplies and the "school lunches of Cuban children" so he could invest in a real estate development in Guatemala.[32] It was an attack on *Inciso* K all over again, a recycling of the most egregious scandal of the Grau government, but Sánchez Arango was not José Alemán, either in character or temperament. For the next two months, all of Cuba was absorbed by the clash between these two combative personalities. Sánchez challenged Chibás to a debate in Parque Central, but Eddy declined, saying that such an event would "desecrate" the statue of Martí. He proposed instead to face his antagonist on the floor of the Senate, offering to relinquish his parliamentary immunity in bringing charges of graft and corruption against him. Sánchez retorted, "no way." "That evil crazy man wants to throw me to the wolves." He had no intention of permitting Chibás to demonize him in the Senate.[33] Finally, after a prolonged exchange of insults, the two men agreed to a debate on July 21 in the auditorium of the Ministry of Education. At the last minute, Chibás called off the encounter.

Chibás's cancellation of the debate was the beginning of the end for him. He affirmed that he withdrew in objection to conditions imposed by Sánchez Arango that they limit their remarks to the specific charge, refraining from attacks on the president and his family or on the government "as an entity."[34] Chibás claimed that he insisted on only one condition: "absolute freedom of speech, without restrictions or *mordazas* [gags] of any kind." Regardless, public opinion turned against him, believing he had been unwilling "to meet his accused face to face in open debate solely on the issue at stake."[35] As a result, Chibás became more reckless than usual. During his radio broadcast the next evening, he announced that the following week he would open his "suitcase" and furnish the nation with "evidence of the misapplication of school supplies and lunches, the land deal in Guatemala, and other matters even worse, in order to demonstrate that the Government of Carlos Prío [was] the most corrupt in the history of the Republic."[36] The next week came and went, with nothing more than rhetoric; even *Bohemia,* Chibás's staunch supporter, asked, "Where's the proof?" and political cartoonists had a field day with Eddy's "suitcase." Cubans mockingly danced a conga to the beat of *"la maleta"* (the suitcase) and *"el loco."*[37] Chibás faced the gravest crisis of his political career.

On Sunday, August 5, faced with the challenge to "present the proof," Chibás could not. Comparing his inability to provide evidence of Sánchez Arango's peculation with Galileo's inability to persuade doubters that the earth orbited the sun, he ranted on. He repeated his charges that the Prío government was the most corrupt of any Cuban government and that Sánchez Arango had stolen funds from his ministry intended for school supplies and student lunches (the mantra ad nauseam), but he produced no documentary evidence. Instead, he dug up some old dirt alleging that Sánchez Arango had been a "botellero" (patronage job holder) in the government of Batista puppet Federico Laredo Bru (1936–40) and that he had been reprimanded by the Havana Bar Association for "unethical conduct."[38] Exhorting his listeners to "take a broom and sweep away the thieves in the government,"[39] he concluded his broadcast, "Forward! People of Cuba, goodbye! This is my last call!"[40] Then he took his pistol and shot himself in the abdomen. It was intended to be Eddy's most dramatic gesture ever, except that he miscalculated. He had run overtime. His audience did not hear his last words; instead, it heard a commercial for Café Pilón, informing ironically, "the coffee tasty to the last drop."[41] Chibás lingered on for eleven days; he did not die until August 16. Sánchez Arango believed he did not intend to kill himself, only to end the debate and elicit sympathy, asserting that the wound was "anatomically calculated."[42] Cabrera Infante disagreed, insisting that Eddy had committed "hara-kiri," for which a stomach wound was traditional. Be that as it may, the wound was not immediately fatal.

Fidel Castro drove the wounded Chibás to the Medical Center and stood watch over him for the next eleven days.[43] Eddy seemed to improve before suffering a relapse and succumbing. Castro opposed having Chibás's body lie in state in the Capitolio (a political place), arguing that instead it should be placed in the Aula Magna of the University of Havana (an academic site). As a member of the guard of honor, he chased away "degenerates" and burned the wreaths of "corrupt politicians."[44] Eddy's funeral touched off "an unprecedented national mourning,"[45] reported to be the "greatest demonstration in the history of the island."[46] An estimated crowd of two to three hundred thousand Cubans escorted Chibás's body from the university to Colón Cemetery. Reportedly, Castro wanted to march to the Presidential Palace, "with the body as a flag," in an attempt to depose President Prío. Pardo Llada supposedly vetoed the idea.[47] According to Cabrera Infante, Castro might have succeeded if he had tried. "If they had wanted to," he wrote, "the Ortodoxo Party could have taken power that day."[48] Georgie Anne Geyer reported that Prío actually "had his bags packed" and was ready to flee, "in case the burial resulted in a popular insurrection."[49] Prío was not deposed, but he was badly shaken by the events of the day.

The aftershock of the suicide of Chibás threatened to bring down the Prío administration. Rafael Estenger, writing in *Bohemia,* claimed that Eddy's enemies celebrated his death with "French cognac and Peruvian cocaine" and predicted that their rejoicing would be short-lived. The people were now aroused. Essentially admitting that Chibás had libeled

Sánchez Arango, Estenger declared, "so what?" It did not matter where the stolen money was invested (and he even repeated the discredited Manhattan skyscraper story). Nor did it matter that the Guatemalan Register of Deeds had certified that Sánchez Arango had "no properties registered there in his name."[50] He was a pariah, blamed for the death of the man who had falsely accused him. The important point, according to Estenger, was for the Cuban people to be aware that Prío and his ministers were "living under the pirate flag." That was the only reason Chibás had sacrificed his life, "to wake up the sleeping."[51] Faced now with the prospect that his critics did not even have to prove charges against him and his government, Prío appeared despondent and reportedly prepared to resign. If August had been bad for Prío, September was a disaster. Prío contributed to his waning popularity by making all the wrong moves.

Cuba had been experiencing a series of labor strikes and protest demonstrations. The Seatrain controversy had erupted again in May, pitting dock workers against railway employees, and the cigar makers in Las Villas went out on strike in July over plans to permit partial mechanization of the industry. In all, there had been 120 strikes and 151 demands for salary increases in less than a year,[52] and Prío was at wit's end. On September 5, when the University Students Federation (FEU) proposed to march down San Lorenzo to the Presidential Palace to protest a bus fare hike, Prío ordered the police to stop them at Infanta, the traditional place of police-student encounters, "regardless of the consequences." He confided to a small group of legislators that he was aware he had "committed errors" but nothing so grave, he insisted, to justify the rancor and aggressiveness of the attacks on him. He said that he never expected to have to use force to maintain respect for the law. "If that doesn't work," he went on, "there's nothing left for me to do but to leave before the end of my term, turning over the government to the military authorities."[53]

A bombshell of this nature, even if it was the private musing of a man overwhelmed by self-pity, was bound to leak out. Ramón Vasconcelos, the editor of *Alerta,* was the first to react. Under banner headlines, "Don't Resign, Mr. President! Resignation Will Cause Chaos!" he implored Prío not to commit the "unpardonable sin" of resigning and going into exile, leaving the country under the control of the military. Foreseeing dire consequences, he wrote, "We will revert to the days of insecurity, uncertainty, bloodshed, and anarchy." He begged Prío to rethink his plans. "Retrace your steps," Vasconcelos exhorted, "reflect, steel your courage, and, as a Cuban, as a man, fulfill your constitutional mandate as President of the Republic."[54] Such extraordinary language provoked an extraordinary response.

On the evening of September 19, Prío addressed the nation over radio and television. He denied the story that he intended to resign and pledged to put a stop to the "climate of anarchy and confusion" being manufactured as a means of "unleashing civil war in Cuba." In a wide-ranging speech, he criticized virtually every sector of society: political parties, labor unions, the press, intellectuals, and business groups. He faulted them for spreading criminal rumors and vicious lies. He came down especially hard on labor, accusing its leaders of following "a permanent policy of work stoppages and strikes." Was the Truslow report having an impact? But in the end, he excused them all as mere dupes. Cubans were not behind the "sinister purpose" to destroy the constitutional order, Prío avowed. No, he charged, releasing a lightning bolt, "the Communist Party [was] responsible for the dangerous situation in which Cuba found itself." Having made the Communist Party (PSP) the scapegoat for the agitated state of the nation, Prío gave assurances that he had no intention of restricting public liberties. What he was going to eradicate, "without any hesitation," he stated, were "insults, coarse behavior, hidden or open inciting to rebellion, [and] lack of respect for [Cuban] institutions and the level of political culture [Cubans] have attained."[55] He concluded by appealing to all Cubans to exercise "sufficient responsibility" to avoid the "weight of the law."[56] It was a remarkable statement for a democratic president.

For a short time, owing to Prío's demagoguery, Cuba's democratic order seemed in jeopardy. *Bohemia* described Prío's speech as "one of the most offensive and inopportune pronouncements ever made by a President."[57] It noted that he did not flash his "famous" smile once during his address. Sánchez Arango, however, described the speech as "a model of decorum and good sense," emphasizing once again that "international communism" was behind the effort to "confuse and mislead" public opinion. Prío did not say how he intended to carry out his determination to eradicate this "seditious behavior," but the events of the next few days provided certain clues. On September 21, he created a special commission composed of the ministers of government, defense, education, and communications to oversee the effort to end the agitation "threatening the stability of the Republic" and placed Lomberto Díaz in charge. Díaz immediately announced that he had met with the heads of the security forces to put a plan into effect to "restore the moral peace." He had provided them, he said, with information and background data about the "plot" designed to undermine the institutional order and incite acts of violence that "the government will not tolerate."[58] Simultaneously, whether related or not, disturbing incidents started occurring in the capital's cinemas. Toughs carrying blackjacks beat moviegoers when they whistled (the Havana equivalent of the Bronx cheer) at the images of government officials projected on the screen during the newsreel. Cubans wondered if the *porra* (Machado's storm troopers) had been resurrected to deprive Cubans of "the sacred right to whistle."[59]

Next, on September 24, agents of GRAS showed up at Masferrer's door and took him into custody. Although he was released with apologies that it was all a mistake, Masferrer was furious. He believed that the agents would have killed him had he resisted arrest. He went immediately to the offices of *Tiempo en Cuba* and drafted an open letter accusing Prío of planning to assassinate him. If Prío had complained about disrespectful behavior before, Masferrer's letter exceeded all bounds of civility. "President Prío," he stated, "you have ordered my assassination. And this afternoon your agents were on the verge of carrying it out. You and the friends that you still have will have to fight me from this point on. There is no alternative. . . . Carlos Prío, you would not dare to confront me face-to-face, because you are not noble."[60] The police and GRAS quickly confiscated the copies of *Tiempo en Cuba* bearing the offensive letter, and Lomberto Díaz ordered the closing of the periodical and the seizure of the presses. After he calmed down, Masferrer was less inclined to blame Prío for the state of affairs, naming the "rabid dogs" Díaz and Sánchez Arango instead. But the day's events had not concluded.

At two in the morning, several automobiles pulled up in front of the offices of the PSP newspaper *Hoy*, and a group of masked men armed with machine guns and pistols got out and forced their entry into the building. For the next hour and a half, they methodically destroyed everything in sight: rotary presses, linotypes, engravers, typewriters, tables, and chairs—everything. When the editor Aníbal Escalante was called to survey the devastation, he did not hesitate to hold Díaz responsible. "[Díaz] had said," Escalante affirmed, "that he could not take legal measures against the newspaper *Hoy*, implying that he would adopt extralegal means."[61]

The turbulent events of September 24 provoked outrage on the part of opposition leaders and groups. Grau San Martín, who had received his share of criticism for many things but never for suppressing freedom, stated that "a worse act than criticizing the government is a government that cannot accept criticism, resorting to the persecution of its opposition."[62] Roberto Agramonte, Chibás's successor for the Ortodoxo presidential nomination, citing with disgust the events just described, observed that the government had said it had a plan it intended to put into effect immediately, "and now everyone knows what it is: that plan is in progress."[63] His fellow *pepeceísta*, Pardo Llada, who had taken over Eddy's Sunday evening radio hour, affirmed that the government was following the road to dictatorship. "What it has started today with *Hoy*, with Masferrer, and with *Tiempo en Cuba*, it will continue tomorrow with any journalist or politician opposed to its ambition to remain in power."[64] Finally, the National Association of Journalists, protesting the Prío administration's "attacks on the free press," staged a twenty-four-hour walkout, leaving Havana without newspapers or newscasts on October 3.[65] Suggesting that Prío's actions were merely a vain effort to salvage "a third Auténtico victory," Ramón Vasconcelos admonished the president "to preside over the party's inevitable defeat with dignity and patriotic grandeur, restoring your role as the moderating power."[66] Prío had appeared to replace a *mano suave* with a *mano fuerte*, but it was not in keeping with the "cordial president."

Prío's get-tough stance "scarcely lasted any time at all." Certain party leaders persuaded him that the policy was wrong, and he yielded.[67] In this instance, Prío, who was frequently criticized for vacillation and indecisiveness, took the appropriate course. He attempted to put the September crisis behind him by reshuffling his Cabinet. The major changes affected the two most controversial ministers in the crisis. Lomberto Díaz was replaced by Segundo Curti, and Sánchez Arango was shifted from education to foreign relations. Díaz was bitter, complaining that this was what he got for cleaning up the Colón barrio, for debating with Chibás in the Congress, and for risking his life arresting Masferrer, "all under orders from Carlos."[68] Sánchez Arango had been widely praised for restoring the Ministry of Education to respectability after the looting by José Alemán, but his fight with Chibás caused his approval ratings in the polls to plummet and ended his chances for the presidency. Prío moved him over to foreign relations, a less significant post, to fill the vacancy created by the resignation of Suárez Fernández. Yes, "Miguelito" was gone again. He had bolted the Auténticos this time, either because he knew he was not going the get the party's presidential nomination or because he resented being censured by "party leaders" for visiting the wounded Chibás in the hospital.[69] Suárez Fernández would show up again as the presidential candidate of Grau's Cubanidad Party.

The other cabinet changes were more cosmetic than substantial, not what were expected given the gravity of the crisis. They were not much more, commented *Bohemia*, than "the same persons in different suits."[70] Félix Lancís took over in education, and Oscar Gans replaced him as prime minister. Lancís continued to be respected, but "en Cuba" described Gans as an "old *machadista*" and as "a mere echo of the President."[71] It was generally concluded that the parliamentary system was not very effective and that the president still exercised vast authority. Rafael Estenger, writing in *Alerta*, claimed that the shake-up was a product of "governmental defeatism." He asserted that the Auténticos, aware that they had no chance of carrying Camagüey and Oriente provinces, reorganized the cabinet to favor the three provinces where they had a better chance: Havana, Las Villas, and Matanzas. In his analysis, Estenger ignored Pinar del Río and overlooked Luis Casero, the honest former mayor of Santiago, the provincial capital of Oriente, who remained at his post in public works. Nonetheless, Estenger may have been correct that the September crisis and cabinet reshuffle were desperate efforts on the part of Prío and the Auténticos to recover from the devastating effects of the suicide of Eddy Chibás.

Thus, as Prío ended his third year in office, the Auténticos were on the defensive and seemed unable to stop their declining popularity. "The governmental propaganda could not be worse," observed Francisco Ichaso. He pointed out that the accomplishments of the Prío administration, such as the impressive record in public works and the creation of the National Bank, BANFAIC, and the Tribunal of Accounts, did not elicit popular enthusiasm. The opposition got all the attention, he noted, with sensational charges of government corruption and accounts of the lawlessness of Policarpo Soler and León Lemus (El Colorado).[72] Ichaso's observations had merit. In assessing Prío's record after three years in office, *Bohemia* criticized the president as weak and indecisive and affirmed that the only consistency of his administration was its "persistent venality." But the discussion of such "venality" was more general than substantive.

Up to that time, other than the general observation that speculators in commodities were doing well in the booming economy and that the black market persisted, no specific money scandal of the nature of BAGA or *los trueques* had been exposed. Whereas specific charges of corruption were brought against Grau's minister of the treasury, Florentino Martínez, nothing of the sort had been raised against the three men who held the position under Prío: Antonio Prío Socarrás, Pepín Bosch, and José

Alvarez Díaz. Brother Antonio was criticized as inefficient and for attempting to cover up the theft from the treasury by the Grau government, but he appeared to be clear of corruption charges as of October 1951. The following month, however, Cuervo Navarro (Grau's accuser) accused him of failing to burn thirty-nine million pesos of old bills supposedly withdrawn from circulation, a harbinger of scandals to come. As for Bosch and Alvarez Díaz, their records were spotless, as were those of other key figures with access to large amounts of public monies: Felipe Pasos, president of the National Bank; Justo Carrillo, president of BANFAIC; and Carlos Hevia, president of the National Development Council. Sánchez Arango, another effective cabinet minister, had cleaned up the mess in the Ministry of Education, though he was criticized for neglecting his job in his third year out of a "burning desire" to be president.[73] And Eduardo Suárez Rivas, the Liberal Party leader brought into the cabinet to satisfy the terms of the Auténtico-Liberal pact, served as minister of agriculture with distinction. He was responsible for the law protecting tenants and sharecroppers and for the reform of the *bateyes*. Prío had indeed surrounded himself with capable individuals, but he also associated with some very questionable characters.

Prío's collaboration with the ARG and certain labor leaders in the struggle for control of the CTC in 1947 held over into his presidency and probably accounted for his incredible tolerance of the activities of Policarpo Soler and Orlando León Lemus. Though the number of gangland killings had diminished by late 1951, these two scoundrels continued to escape punishment for their crimes. In fact, both were candidates for Congress in the 1952 elections, running on the Auténtico ticket. Soler gave himself up in October 1951 but continued his political campaign from his jail cell in the Castillo del Principe in Havana. Prío's relationship with Eusebio Mujal, the CTC chieftain, was no less disturbing.

The labor minister Arturo Hernández Tellaheche endeavored to exercise an even hand in labor disputes, but Mujal, with direct access to the Presidential Palace, was able to prevail every time. Frequent strikes, leading to government "interventions" in the affected industries, placed business owners at a distinct disadvantage. Under the practice, the government continued to operate a strike-bound business, keeping the workers employed (as noted earlier with reference to United Railways). Under such circumstances, Orange Crush of Cuba closed down its operations permanently in October 1951. *Bohemia* complained that organized labor was a "privileged" class that inconvenienced the public for parochial and partisan interests. It charged that Mujal did not represent the will of the workers, having been imposed by the Auténtico governments, noting that he sat in the Senate as a government representative. Zanetti and García agreed with this notion, claiming that it restrained Prío from carrying out the Truslow mission's recommendations for the reorganization of the railroads, fearing a labor backlash. "Installed in their [Mujal and others] positions by means of government support and gangster-style procedures, they were having a hard enough time as it was, trying to `represent' the workers."[74] Moreover, according to Conrado Rodríguez, a sugar worker, Mujal and the CTC leadership had raided the workers' retirement fund to pay for their political campaigns.[75] Though Prío was a victim of the excesses of the *pistoleros* and the CTC "caciques" (bosses), he was, nonetheless, identified with them, and his public standing and that of the Auténticos suffered as a result.

With the national elections in June 1952 only eight months away, the Auténticos' chances of capturing a third presidency appeared diminished. Though the party continued to lead in voter registration, the commentator Ichaso observed that the PRC-A had "lost the street." The voter registration for 1952 placed the Auténticos in the lead with 621,000 affiliates. The other parties trailed in the following fashion: PPC-Ortodoxo, 330,000; Unitary Action (Batista), 204,000; Democrat, 195,000; Cuban National (a hybrid formed by Vice President Guillermo Alonso Pujol and Havana Mayor Nicolás Castellanos), 189,000; Liberal, 185,000; Cubanidad (Grau's splinter group), 94,000; PSP (Communist), 53,000; and Republican (having lost Alonso Pujol), 40,000.[76] The registration figures showed that Ichaso was right, the Cuban people still embraced *autenticismo*, but he warned that the PRC-A would have to "galvanize" the spirit of its affiliates and restore their lost faith.[77] Moreover, the rifts in the Auténtico Party caused by the defections of Grau and Suárez Fernández had to be overcome. To this end, the Auténticos met in a national convention in the Teatro Nacional (Havana) beginning on November 18 to draft a program and nominate a presidential candidate. Prío and Carlos Hevia were principal speakers.

Hevia, the eventual nominee, addressed the convention presenting a nineteen-point program for the development of the Cuban economy. His remarks were strongly influenced by the Truslow mission report of the World Bank. The report was made public in July and had been analyzed in a six-part series in *Bohemia* by Herminio Portell Vilá. No effort had been made to suppress it. Hevia called for the application of technology to agriculture and industry, a central point of the IBRD report. He echoed its recommendations for improved labor-management relations and for priority attention to transportation facilities as essential for the rescue of the sugar industry and the expansion of nonsugar agriculture and diversification of the economy.[78] Prío likewise demonstrated that he had read the report.

He toned down Auténtico rhetoric, calling for greater ideological tolerance within the PRC-A. Speaking to an assembly that had "socialist" in its motto, he affirmed, "We are not a socialist country, nor can we be at the present time." "We are constituted as a democratic nation," he stated, "the formulas that we seek and that we apply must be in accord with the general will, not imposed by force." Taking a swipe at organized labor, Prío said that he was not concerned with better conditions for those who had jobs, but in expanding employment. "We have to multiply the number of those who earn money in daily toil." Nor did he dodge the issue of corruption, warning, "If we do not change our internal conduct, we are going to lose the popular aura that surrounds us."[79] One aspect of the party's stand that was helping to maintain its mystique, Prío expressed proudly, was its opposition to all forms of tyranny. He criticized as "immoral and dangerous" the position that condemned Communist dictatorships but tolerated the military dictatorships of the hemisphere. Prío concluded by recalling that, when he assumed power, the nation was plagued by three "evils": the black market, peculation, and gangsterism. He claimed to have brought down prices and to have "decapitated the hydra of peculation." Gangsterism "has ceased," he proclaimed, "but its roots may still be alive," he conceded.[80] As will be seen, the PRC-A drafted a program more in keeping with its social democratic philosophy than with Prío's moderate line, but commentators remarked that a feeling of achievement and "good will" seemed to emerge from the meeting.[81] Even *Bohemia* remarked that Prío appeared before the assembly as a "leader," not a *"caudillo."* The good feelings did not last more than a week.

On November 25, Policarpo Soler escaped from the Castillo del Principe prison. It was the most spectacular jailbreak in Cuban history, not only because it involved the so-called Public Enemy Number One but also because of allegations of official complicity in its successful execution. It reopened the *pistolero* issue in sensational fashion. A week earlier, Prío had asserted that the issue was in abeyance, but now it came roaring back with regime-threatening force. The newspapers gave dramatic accounts of the escape and provided detailed background information from the criminal records of Soler and the five convicts who fled with him. Three of the *pistoleros* (José Fayat Aguerres—*"El Turquito,"* Manuel Salgado

Rebollo—"*El Guajiro* Salgado," and Luis Matos Gilbes) were in prison for their role in the Orfila massacre, and another (Wilfredo Lara García) was serving time for the murders of "Wichy" Salazar and Justo Fuentes.[82] Contradicting the outcry about *pistolero* impunity, one may note that Mario Salabarría and the aforementioned participants in the Orfila affair been in prison for four years by that time.

UIR leaders were outraged that the assassins of their comrades were at large again. They suspected that it was another example of official collusion with Soler and León Lemus. How else might one explain the flight in broad daylight, one hundred feet down the side of the prison building, across a wide moat, and over the exterior wall that dropped another hundred feet to the street? How, indeed, was the obese Soler provided the time to descend rope ladders and reach the waiting auto of his partner in crime, "El Colorado"? Moreover, facilitating his escape, Soler had been admitted to the lightly guarded infirmary two days before for minor surgery. Segundo Curti, the minister of government, and Federico de Córdova, the prison warden, made the customary gesture of offering their resignations, which Prío, of course, did not accept. Soler, broadcasting from his hideout, explained that his escape was in response to his loyal supporters, who urged him to return to Matanzas and lead his campaign for Congress in person. "The entire matter has been a bold stroke by a group of my loyal friends of the province of Matanzas and nothing more."[83]

The opposition politicians saw it as a great deal more, and the claims of Curti that he would bring the fugitives to justice were met with scorn. Ramón Vasconcelos summed up opposition sentiment best, exclaiming, "Policarpo, and other *policarpos* more insincere and less daring will continue doing what they do. What we don't know now is if the meekness or the foolishness of our people will go so far as to contribute to the continuation of the Auténtico calamity in power! We trust in the contrary."[84] He predicted, in fact, that the opposition would win the 1952 elections "by ten in the morning." Barely recovered from the effects of Chibás's suicide and the September crisis, Prío and the Auténticos were set back again at the end of the year by the scandal of Soler's prison break.

Without the advantage of a crystal ball, *Bohemia* declared that 1951 was "one of the most critical years in the history of Cuba."[85] It was the beginning of what Luis Aguilar described as the "tragic decade," marked by the suicide of Eddy Chibás in August 1951, the coup by Fulgencio Batista in March 1952, and the seizure of power by Fidel Castro in January 1959.[86] Chibás's suicide set in motion a chain of events. Speaking as the outraged conscience of the nation, he overplayed his hand and killed himself, depriving Cuba of a people's champion to overcome the evils he had exposed and exaggerated. Only time would reveal the full impact of Eddy's persona and death on Cuban history, but *Bohemia* was correct to sense then that his passion marked a turning point in the history of the nation. What gave this fact particular weight was that he was not always honest in the charges he made. He had a "personal vendetta" against Prío, resenting the fact that Prío, not he, emerged to represent the Generation of '30 in the presidency, and he took old charges against Grau and heaped them on Prío.[87] Prío had enough sins of his own to warrant condemnation, but Eddy was irresponsible in his zeal, for example, jumping to a conclusion in the Manhattan skyscraper episode. At the same time, he left a great void the extent of which only the crisis of March 1952 would demonstrate.

There was a sense of loss but not immediately of hopelessness. Enrique de la Osa, editor of *Bohemia's* "en Cuba" section, testified grandly to Eddy's suicide as "an act of sacrifice that was an example of human selflessness and desire to open a new furrow of rich hope with blood sincerely shed."[88] There were, moreover, positive features of the year that provided a basis for hope. If the politicians were venal, the economic numbers were good. Felipe Pazos, the president of the National Bank, stated that in 1951 the country had achieved "the highest level of economic activity ever." He affirmed that the national income was 7.5 percent greater than the previous high of 1948. "In real terms," he continued, "the increase is even greater, because prices are still ten percent below the maximum level of that year."[89] And despite the strong-arm tactics of the Prío administration in September, Cubans continued to enjoy freedom of expression, as was manifest by radio, TV, and press commentary and by the creativity of Cuban artists. Virgilio Piñero might react to Cuban society with "absurdity," but the Auténticos never gave him cause to say, "I am afraid."[90] Prío complained that "the public liberties were abused by the radio and print media."[91] He went to excess in his red-baiting in September but quickly yielded to pressure both from within and outside his party, making the gesture of removing Minister Lomberto Díaz. Moreover, the controversial Decree 2273 (the "gag" decree) was scrapped after being used only once (against Chibás on "Bloody Sunday").

Finally, Soler was on the loose, but Cabrera Infante viewed Havana as "peaceable," and tourists were beginning to come. Ava Gardner and Frank Sinatra honeymooned there in November, and Gary Cooper and Ernest Hemingway celebrated New Year's Eve in La Floridita. *Bohemia* published Prío's "last" Christmas message to the people of Cuba in its December 16 issue, but it made no impression on the gunmen who seriously wounded the former army chief of staff General Genovevo Pérez Dámera in an assassination attempt on December 23. Contradictions abounded. Democracy was progressing and in peril. The year 1951 ended on notes of hope and disgust, but who foresaw impending disaster?

10

Conclusion: 1952

There was no strong indication at the beginning of 1952 that Cuba was on the brink of disaster. To be sure, there were rumors that discontented junior army officers were complaining about corruption and lawlessness in Cuban society and possibly planning a coup, but few appeared to be taking such talk seriously. Eufemio Fernández heard about "strange movements" at Fulgencio Batista's "medieval" estate, Kuquine, and suggested getting rid of the former dictator "once and for all," but Prío was "horrified" and would not hear of it.[1] According to Tony Varona, Prío was too "débil" (weak) to confront potential trouble, preferring to avoid unpleasantness.

Varona advised Prío to "decentralize" the armed forces as a means of making him less vulnerable to a military coup. He proposed eliminating the concentration of military forces in Havana by dispersing the various branches. He pointed out that the army ruled supreme, exercising control over the National Police and dominating the navy and air force. The latter two branches were small, he told the president, and were literally "under the guns" of the army. The main air base was next to Camp Columbia—all the army had to do was roll a few tanks onto the runway, and "there was no Air Force," he argued. Likewise, the navy was in Havana Harbor, but the army commanded the fortress La Cabaña and could effectively "blockade" any ship trying to reach the open sea. Varona suggested that Prío move air force headquarters to San Antonio, one of the air bases built by the United States during World War II, and that he increase the appropriations for the air force and navy and give them independent commands. Prío listened patiently but rejected the advice, saying that he did not want "to stir things up." He did not want to disturb the "tranquility."[2]

In the meantime, the political parties continued maneuvering in anticipation of the general elections in June 1952. The Auténtico Party held its national convention in November and drafted a substantial platform outlining its vision for Cuba's future. In peering into the future, it reprised the past as well. Tracing their roots back to the original Cuban Revolutionary Party (PRC) founded by José Martí in 1892, the Auténticos noted that the Spanish colonial masters kept Cubans divided through the system of slavery. Martí, in establishing the PRC, "took special care" to integrate whites and blacks in its composition, aware "that in their unity existed the very possibility of attaining national independence."[3] With the achievement of independence and the death of Martí, the PRC ceased to exist.

The PRC was born again in 1934, in the wake of the overthrow of Gerardo Machado and the one hundred days of Ramón Grau San Martín. During the interim, Cubans "discovered" that "foreign capitalists" had come not to "favor" them but in search of "raw materials and cheap labor." "The new character of imperialism, based on the economic exploitation of peoples, had its widest and most definitive expression in Cuba."[4] In initiating the "second stage" of its struggle, the PRC-Auténtico undertook to abolish the Platt Amendment and overcome economic imperialism. By 1951, the Auténticos boasted, they had enabled Cuba to gain control of its economy. They did so, in spite of their "decidedly and openly nationalistic policy," they insisted, without "unjust attacks" on foreign interests and without "frightening away" foreign finance capital. "We maintained free and faithful relations with our North American neighbor, without any surrender of our interests, or of our sovereignty, to its dictates."[5] The platform continued with the assertion that the PRC-A had secured the economic independence of Cuba with the creation of the National Bank and the Bank for Agricultural and Industrial Development, strengthened by the Tribunal of Accounts and the laws regulating state budgets and government accounting. Proud of these achievements, the Auténticos noted that when they began the second stage of their struggle, they had defined their doctrine as "nationalist, anti-imperialist, and socialist." They claimed that they had completed the first two, and now was the time for accomplishing the third.

The platform of the Auténtico Party for 1952 pledged to achieve "the socialization of the economy." To guarantee the Cuban people a decent standard of living and "indispensable well being," it would be necessary, the platform affirmed, "to empower the State, as the economic organ of the nation, to intervene directly in the production, distribution, and consumption of wealth." State intervention was necessary, it explained, because Cuba was a nation of "scarce capital resources." Because Cuban capitalists were technically disadvantaged and had limited resources, they were "at the mercy" of foreign capitalists and enterprises. Heavy industry was virtually out of the question because of the small scale of the national market and the lack of energy resources. Moreover, the problem of chronic and seasonal unemployment, owing to the organization of the sugar industry, required resolution through a more equitable distribution of wealth, an increase in per capita production, and the development of the Cuban economic order "within a sound economic plan." For this purpose, the platform declared, it was essential "to place the national savings in the hands of the State."[6]

Despite the Auténticos' claim that they had established the basis for a socialist economy, they pointed out the need to overcome certain "realities." "Cuba has more millionaires than England," the platform stated, "owing to the unjust distribution of the national income, while thousands of Cubans live in the grip of poverty, or are threatened by it."[7] Referring to the agrarian sector alone, the platform cited the agricultural census of 1946 to demonstrate the unjust distribution of income. Accordingly, 47 percent of the land was concentrated in 2,336 fincas, "probably owned by [an even] smaller number of persons or enterprises." In the sugar harvest of 1946, 50.2 percent of the cane was ground by 740 *colonos* and the existing mills (administration cane), whereas 32,769 *colonos* (97 percent of the total) ground the remainder, slightly less than half. "All this anti-democratic economic organization," the Auténticos proclaimed, "has caused unemployment and the stagnation of the development of our economy and forced the exile of more than 100,000 Cubans, who have had to emigrate in search of job opportunities in other countries."[8] In launching a "new stage" of its struggle, dedicated to the fulfillment of its "socialist doctrine," the PRC-A sought to provide certain reassurances.

The Auténtico Party reiterated its commitment to the free exercise of representative democracy and the absolute enjoyment of human rights. It condemned international communism and any other form of totalitarian government "as incompatible with the concept of American freedom." While it adhered to the principle of nonintervention as a unilateral action, the PRC-A endorsed the concept of collective intervention "in all cases of the violation of the basic principles affecting the rights of the individual within society." Finally, the party affirmed its respect for the principle of private property, but with the condition "that it serve the collective interests of the nation," applicable equally to domestic and foreign capital. Having pledged to maintain the democratic order and to respect the right of private property, the Auténticos presented their platform in detail, dividing it into seven principal planks.

Beginning with the "standards and guarantees of the State," the PRC-A reaffirmed its absolute determination to devote its full political activity to the fulfillment of the dignity of the individual and the broadening of possibilities for progress, from both a material and a moral standpoint. It pledged to continue fighting for democratic principles guaranteeing equal opportunity to all Cubans for the enjoyment of political freedom, social justice, individual and collective well-being, and human solidarity. The Auténticos vowed especially to expand the rights provided the citizen in Article 10 of the Constitution, particularly the right to enjoy economic security guaranteed by the state. Accordingly, the state would have the duty to provide all citizens with the minimum wealth necessary for the enjoyment of a standard of living contributing to the progress and refinement of the nation.[9]

The second plank, "economic policy," was divided into various subtopics, including economic development, finances, industries, tourism, public services, and commerce. Before dealing with these matters individually, the PRC-A covered them generally with overall guiding principles. It referred to private property in terms of individual well-being and social function. The exercise of private ownership was not unlimited, it avowed, being subject to regulation and "the needs of society," including nationalization, "when the public interest demands it."[10] The state, the Auténticos affirmed, had a duty to provide full employment. They pledged to increase the opportunities for employment through the creation of new industries, agricultural development, and the expansion of trade. The Auténticos maintained the payment of high salaries as a "fundamental policy," as a means of achieving the equitable distribution of income, but argued also for the need to increase productivity to keep prices down, resulting in the increase in real income and contributing to the nation's progress. Above all, the Auténticos proclaimed the principle of state intervention in the economy, proposing to use the national budget as a means of distributing wealth and allocating resources for agricultural and industrial development. "When the public interest demands it," the Auténticos emphasized, "the State may nationalize lands, industries, public services, and any other economic activity, managing them on the public's behalf."[11]

Turning to the "agrarian question" as its third major plank, the PRC-A reiterated its commitment to the agrarian reform program already in progress. The essential features included maximum efficiency in agricultural organization and productivity to fulfill the needs of the nation, while guaranteeing the farmer due compensation, specifically, "a decent standard of living and just participation in the fruits of the Cuban economy and the benefits of its culture."[12] While the program went into great detail describing aspects of the agrarian reform program, including land distribution, public credit, roads, health and sanitation, and marketing and storage facilities, it emphasized particularly the fight against latifundium (the corporately owned agroindustrial combine). Considering latifundium as "one of the fundamental ills" of the Cuban agrarian economy, the Auténticos pledged to eliminate it as a form of ownership, replacing it with "a system of small producers associated cooperatively for working the land."[13] The program set size limits for various types of landholdings (cattle ranches, sugar and rice farms, and so on), and the Auténticos declared their intention to expropriate properties in excess and distribute them at sale to farmers working the land, either individually or cooperatively. The Auténticos stated further their total opposition to the acquisition of agricultural lands by foreign corporations.

In the realm of "social policy," the fourth plank, the PRC-A reiterated its solid position in favor of employing Cubans "principally" in the workforce. It declared its intention to enact a labor code, incorporating "all the gains achieved by the national working class."[14] These included a six-hour day and thirty-six-hour workweek, the right to organize and bargain collectively, the right to strike, a minimum wage, and equal pay for equal work. The party pledged to establish a career civil service, recruited through competitive examination and promotion and salary increases based on merit. It proposed to create the Cuban Institute of Social Security, protecting citizens against the exigencies of life: accident, illness, disability, old age, and unemployment. One of the "principal efforts" of the Auténtico government, the platform declared, would be to provide inexpensive housing for employees and workers "by means of a broad plan of national character."[15] The Auténticos avowed finally that, in the event the national interest recommended the mechanization of an industry resulting in the displacement of workers, provisions would be made to provide opportunities for work to the dismissed workers, increases in salaries, and reduction of hours of work.[16]

In its fifth plank, defining "educational policy," the Auténticos fixed national education and instruction as "one of its essential concerns," relying on the quality of culture to solve the nation's political, social, and economic problems. The PRC-A believed that education was "the foundation of nationality and the most powerful instrument for shaping a people, nationally and internationally."[17] The party pledged to fight for the rights of children, meaning all measures that guaranteed the full development of their possibilities, personality, and culture. Specifically, it proposed to eliminate illiteracy, promote technical education, create the National Council of Education and Culture (to make the administration of education professional, not political), guarantee academic freedom at all levels, and create a career teachers system providing standards and certification and individual protections and benefits. Finally, the plank contained a lengthy list of construction projects designed to provide adequate school buildings in both rural and urban areas and to include new centers of specialized instruction in such fields as civil aviation, fisheries, and music.[18]

The sixth plank in the Auténtico platform addressed "health policy." The Auténticos did not offer a plan of socialized medicine but pledged to establish a firm economic base for providing hospital services to all social classes. They proposed to create "a social medical service to classify individuals requiring medical care and to secure payment in accordance with one's income, guaranteeing in this manner free care to the poor and extending it to the remainder of the social classes in accordance with one's ability to pay."[19] They determined to create a Career Health Service to protect the general health and public hygiene of the nation. As a public sector agency, the Career Health Service would be under the authority of the Superior Council of Health, responsible for administering a career system based on merit and providing employee benefits. The PRC-A expressed grave concern over the health infrastructure, promising to provide aqueducts and safe water systems to every Cuban city and town. It pledged to adopt the necessary measures to free the Cuban population of endemic illnesses through a program of preventive medicine, including vaccination, health education, and epidemiological studies. It intended especially to extend medical and dental services to rural areas, devising a plan for "the creation of a rural health school, the sanitation of the *bateyes,* and the improvement of farm housing."[20] Leaving no aspect of public health untouched, the party proposed finally to establish an Institute of Nutrition and to regulate all commerce in food, drugs, medicines, and cosmetics.

"International policy" was the final plank in the Auténtico platform. The party presented a list of thirteen points enumerating the "juridical and political principles" of its foreign policy and a twenty-point list of the "fundamentals and principles of international trade policy." The juridical and political principles of the Auténtico platform were essentially the response the Prío administration gave to the request by the Inter-American Peace Committee in August 1949 for information and suggestions concerning the situation prevailing in the Caribbean political areas. At that time, Cuba upheld the principle of collective intervention to liberate enslaved peoples from undemocratic regimes. Moreover, it stated the objective criteria for determining a functioning democracy, identifying at the same time the political standards the Auténticos had set for themselves. In that sense, the PRC-A reiterated its repudiation of international communism as "anti-democratic and interventionist."[21]

The Auténticos viewed international trade policy as an "extension" of their general economic policy. "Consequently," the platform stated, "international trade policy must take into account that the basic objective of domestic economic development is to maintain and expand employment and production to the maximum limits possible."[22] Placing foreign trade at the service of the planned economy, the Auténticos, in effect, were defending the economic nationalism and protectionism of previous Auténtico governments. They assumed an aggressive position for Cuban sugar in the United States market, demanding a guaranteed place, in recognition that "traditionally and historically" Cuba had supplied U.S. needs, "specifically in times of crisis." Similarly, the Auténticos argued that Cuba, "being a provider during world wars," deserved preferential treatment for its products on the part of recipient nations. The Auténticos spoke of diversification, while continuing to think of sugar exports as the engine of economic development and prosperity. The platform did not address the vexing problem of reciprocity that had been sacrificing the domestic market to King Sugar.

For all the talk of socialism, the Auténtico platform did not project a planned economy, but it was nonetheless a radical document by Cuban standards. It adhered to the admonitions of Ramiro Guerra y Sánchez for the preservation of Cuban culture in agricultural production and it buried deeper the aspiration of the U.S. State Department for a Treaty of Friendship, Commerce, and Navigation. The platform did not follow the moderate line that Prío advocated before the November convention, and it ignored both the warnings and recommendations of the Truslow mission of the World Bank. The Auténticos continued to abide by their social democratic philosophy, and if they failed it was because the concept was wrong, not because they did not make the effort. Eduardo Suárez Rivas described the program as a "New Social Contract." He claimed that the aim was not to abolish private property or free enterprise but to end class warfare through a more equitable distribution of wealth and a more humane form of capitalism.[23] Despite the powerful criticism of the Prío administration for corrupt practices and failure to overcome *pistolerismo*, the Auténticos showed maturity as a party and increasing political acumen. By the beginning of the year, they had assembled an electoral juggernaut, having negotiated pacts with the Liberal, Democrat, and Republican Parties. The struggle for the PRC-A nomination for president of the republic came down to two men: Carlos Hevia and Tony Varona. The others—Miguel Suárez Fernández, Félix Lancís, Oscar Gans, and Aureliano Sánchez Arango—never had a chance.

From all appearances, Varona won the battle for the platform, and Hevia got the nomination. Although Varona was deeply committed to the achievement of socialism, the third of the Auténticos' three watchwords, his zeal frightened Prío, who gave his support to Hevia. Varona gave in, principally because he placed party unity above personal ambition. He was a party man, and he extracted compensation from Hevia in the form of national and provincial candidacies for his friends and supporters, but he was unable to convert his party leadership into popular support. Varona's firm revolutionary credentials and reputation for honesty could not overcome a "brusque" personality that offended too many people. The "insurmountable barrier" to his presidential ambition, however, "was the fear that he would do to Prío, his associates and administration what Prío did to Grau San Martín, his associates and administration."[24] Prío regarded Hevia as a safer choice.

As president of the National Development Commission and minister without portfolio, Hevia also enjoyed a reputation for honesty, and he was more moderate politically. José Pardo Llada charged that he was "an accomplice" in the scandals of the Prío administration,[25] making a partisan attack that did not appear to stick. At the same time, even Grau praised him as "a revolutionary and good Auténtico."[26] A graduate of the United States Naval Academy, Hevia was more favorably disposed toward the United States than Varona. He endorsed the PRC-A platform without appearing extreme, promising, for example, "honesty in public administration, an agrarian reform program to help the farmer, an effective fight against racial discrimination, trade union democracy, protection of national industries, and a total war on gangsterism."[27] For Hevia's running mate, the Auténticos nominated Luis Casero, the upright minister of public works and former mayor of Santiago de Cuba, demonstrating that the PRC-A was aware of the necessity to propose honest men above all if it were to overcome the issue of corruption in government.

None of the other political parties presented a platform comparable to that of the Auténticos. Although embracing the aspirations of the Generation of '30, the Ortodoxos' message was essentially negative. Chibás, claiming to be more Auténtico than the Auténticos, had made corruption a central national issue, virtually a moral crusade, but provided no "serious analysis" of the causes of corruption in Cuba, engaging instead in "sloganeering" and bombast.[28] In addition, the Ortodoxos were divided within. Emilio "Millo" Ochoa challenged Roberto Agramonte for the nomination. Luis Aguilar maintained that the choice of Agramonte was "orchestrated" by the PPC's left wing (principally by Enrique de la Osa, the "destructive" editor of "en Cuba") and caused the Ortodoxos to lose "internal cohesion" and "external respect."[29] With the Ortodoxo nomination in hand, Agramonte led in the polls and might have won the election, but it would have been a personal victory for the "martyr" Chibás and a political victory for *autenticismo* and democracy.

The other political parties existed in name only, with scant grassroots organizations. The Unitary Action Party (PAU) was Fulgencio Batista's personal and electoral vehicle. Displaying posters bearing the slogan, "THIS IS THE MAN," Batista was running a distant third in the polls. According to the general consensus, he had little chance "of returning to power by the democratic route."[30] Protesting the "existing state of insecurity" in the country and wishing to appear as "the champion of order and peace," Batista could not erase the memory of him as the leader of a military dictatorship, "characterized by torture, murder, and fraud."[31] Like Batista, Grau San Martín was trying to draw on the "magic" of his name, but the magic was wearing thin, and his Cubanidad Party was an empty shell. The only one trying to preserve Grau's myth was Prío, and Grau did not have the sense to realize it.[32] Ineligible to run for the presidency in 1952, Grau gave the Cubanidad nomination to Miguel Suárez Fernández, another fickle-hearted Auténtico. Running farther behind and having even less substance was the Cuban National Party, with Havana mayor Nicolás Castellanos as presidential candidate, and Vice President Guillermo Alonso Pujol as éminence grise. Throughout January, this group of politicians considered uniting to form a "Third Front," only to have the talks break down over Batista's insistence that he should be the unity candidate.[33] As a result, Grau, Alonso Pujol, Castellanos, and even "Miguelito" returned to the Auténtico fold, endorsing Hevia. The Auténticos' chances of winning a third presidency looked good, if only they could overcome their corrupt image, which they could not.

The young Havana lawyer Fidel Castro was the person most responsible for keeping alive the allegations of venality on the part of Carlos Prío. Following the death of Chibás, Agramonte became the Ortodoxo presidential candidate, Pardo Llada took over Eddy's Sunday radio broadcast, and Fidel Castro assumed the role of chief accuser, becoming "one of the most fearless muckrakers in Cuba."[34] After earning his law degree, Castro started a practice, doing a great deal of pro bono work among the *solares* (slums) of Havana. Vowing not to repeat the error of Eddy Chibás, Castro was determined to have proof of any wrongdoing. On January 28, 1952, as a candidate for the Chamber, Castro delivered a speech, "I accuse" (also published in *Alerta*), in which he gave a detailed account of Prío's landholdings and how he had acquired them. He revealed that, in return for a presidential pardon for the crime of molesting a nine-year-old girl, Emilio Fernández Mendigutía, a *latifundista,* had "transferred" at least seven farms to Prío in three years (1946 to 1949).[35] Moreover, Fernández was serving as the civil secretary for the president. According to Castro, Prío had expanded his personal landholdings from 160 to 1,944 acres, consisting of "a chain of the best farms and most valuable lands in the vicinity of Havana."[36] Declaring that Prío had "prostituted the spirit of presidential pardoning" and was "promoting the system of latifundium," Castro further charged Prío with a variety of crimes in the way he managed his estates.[37]

Castro accused Prío of maintaining conditions of virtual slavery on his lands. He accused the president of using military personnel to work his farms, "turning soldiers into laborers and peons." By employing soldiers instead of civilians, declared Castro, Prío "contributed to unemployment." In addition, he worked his laborers (civilian and military) for stretches of twelve hours, violating all labor laws, subjecting them to the "most iniquitous exploitation."[38] For good measure, Castro added that Prío had "betrayed the national interest" by selling farm products below the market level (i.e., on the black market).[39] He concluded by characterizing Prío's administration as one of "corruption and moral decay." Hardly having delivered this bombshell, Castro produced another.

Through his collaboration with Ramón Vasconcelos, the editor of *Alerta*,

Castro published another exposé on February 20. Disguised as a gardener, Castro went onto the grounds of Prío's *finca*, La Chata, twenty kilometers from Havana, described as "a mini–Garden of Eden done with the understatement of a Busby Berkeley production."[40] He took photographs that showed "the fountains, the shooting range, the waterfall roaring into the huge swimming pool," and *Alerta* published them under the headline, "This is the way the President lives with the money he has robbed from the people."[41] Then, on March 4, *Alerta* published a devastating account by Castro that established the link between the Prío administration and the *pistolero* organizations by means of the "Pact of the Groups." Castro declared that presidential secretary Orlando Puente "actively" negotiated the pact in an effort to purchase peace "by means of the most ominous concessions."[42] He did so, Castro charged, by "distributing *botellas* in fabulous amounts" that escalated geometrically, as the groups "divided and subdivided," so that each petty chieftain got "his seat at the round table." The sinecures were parceled out, so that, for example, UIR received 120; ARG, 250; Colorado's group, 400; Masferrer's, 500; and Policarpo's, "the most dreaded," 600. In all, Castro counted, there were 2,120 positions "which received salaries without compensating services in the ministries of Health, Labor, Administration, and Public Works."[43] The ministry most put upon by this scheme was public works, with an envoy from each group coming around weekly to pick up the payoff. (Castro called upon his fellow *"oriental,"* Luis Casero, to resign his post in protest: "I know that the orders come from above."[44])

Even worse, Castro continued, additional payments were being made in cash directly by the Presidential Palace. Puente was distributing cash payments of $300 monthly to each of the sixty groups in the pact, for a total of $18,000 each month. The payments were enclosed in envelopes bearing the seal "President of the Republic" and marked "personal matter." Despite all this, Castro scoffed, Prío had been unable to impose order: "He bought peace, and they sold him crimes; he bought a truce, and they sold him gun battles and casualties." The groups, "dissatisfied with their share," rebelled against the agreement and renewed the warfare, Castro explained. The most recent example, he claimed, was the murder of Alejo Cossío del Pino. "Without money for the groups, there will be no more crimes," Castro concluded.[45] He added an unlikely pledge: "If everything that I have reported is not absolutely true, I shall keep silent for the rest of my life."[46]

Castro's findings may be interpreted in several ways. Either Prío was employing a private army of hoods and toughs to intimidate his political opposition and dominate the unions, or he was a victim of a vast protection racket—buy our insurance, or else. Is it reasonable to assume that the Presidential Palace could control sixty gangs? A third possibility was that Prío had a calculated plan to undermine the influence of renegades like Masferrer and Soler by providing their men with alternate means of employment and possible "rehabilitation" but got outsmarted in the process. In any case, the situation was damaging to the democratic order. And the murder of Cossío del Pino placed it in peril.

On February 12, Alejo Cossío del Pino, a former representative and minister of government and owner and director of Radio Cadena Habana, was assassinated. The murder was carried out in gangland style, as "several gunmen pumped twenty bullets into his body." The police suspected the UIR, which had sworn to get Cossío, as "responsible" for the death of Emilio Tró in the shoot-out at Orfila.[47] Nonetheless, there was a great deal of finger-pointing because of the prominence of the victim. Batista spoke out, "The Government says it knows who did it, but won't name names or make arrests."[48] His spokesman, Andrés Rivero Agüero, asked, "Gangsterism and *Autenticismo,* where does one end and the other begin?"[49] Ramón Vasconcelos and José Pardo Llada proclaimed, "The sickness is at the top."[50] ARG leader Eufemio Fernández, however, accused Rolando Masferrer directly of the crime. In an open letter to President Prío published on March 2, confirming Castro's suspicion of the motive for the murder, Fernández accused Masferrer of a "diabolical plan" to destroy the peace pact of the action groups and provoke gang warfare anew. "Masferrer lives to kill. And kills to live," affirmed Fernández, adding: "His secret plotting with Batista explains his conduct. That is why he provokes. That is why he wants a war of the groups. The elections are very near."[51] Here was a public warning that something more sinister was afoot. It was not the only one that Prío received.

According to Justo Carrillo, the murder of Cossío del Pino was intended as a cause célèbre.[52] In March 1951, Batista confided in Alonso Pujol about plans for a *golpe de estado* on the part of "young officers," to remove Prío from office and install the vice president (Alonso Pujol) in his place. Batista gave as reasons for the *golpe* a plot by Eufemio Fernández to assassinate him and the threat that gangsterism "was leading the nation to anarchy."[53] Alonso Pujol, no friend of Prío and at the time actively engaged in forming a political alliance with Batista, responded that Prío was "incapable" of sponsoring an assassination plot. "His record," Alonso Pujol stated, "whatever his political errors, will always be without the stain of bloodshed and will show him to be a jealous guardian of civil liberties."[54] Alonso Pujol conceded that gangsterism was a "national disgrace" but believed that its victims lacked distinction. He said that the victims were, "for the most part, members of the pseudo-revolutionary clans." The fighting was among themselves and had "not succeeded in affecting public sensibility deeply."[55] In a final effort to persuade Batista to abandon his plan, Alonso Pujol observed that "an event of sufficient magnitude has not yet taken place, such as that of the death of Calvo Sotelo in Spain that preceded the uprising of Generals [José] Sanjurjo, [Francisco] Franco, and [Emilio] Mola."[56] Batista did not go through with his planned coup in March 1951, but a year later, when Cossío del Pino was murdered, Alonso Pujol recalled his words and sensed "the imminence of a grave crisis."[57] Alonso Pujol went to Prío and, without telling him the details of the events of the year before, "begged him `to declare a state of emergency, surround Kuquine [Batista's *finca*], change the military commands!'"[58] In reaction, Prío convoked the cabinet in emergency session. Carrillo affirmed that Varona favored "drastic" action, such as arresting Batista and sending him into exile, but that Prime Minister Gans "advised him to do nothing."[59] Apparently, Prío took Gans's advice, following his pattern of not wanting to disturb the "tranquility." Varona tended to confirm this account.

Varona related to the author that he did not anticipate the coming coup, but he and Prío recognized the murder of Cossío del Pino as an "*acontecimiento*" (literally, "an event," in this case one of "sufficient magnitude").[60] When Prío asked him for his advice, Varona recommended that he suspend constitutional guarantees and expel Batista from the country, "as necessary precautionary measures." Prío shunned Varona's counsel, expressing concern about "public reaction and the stir it would create internationally."[61] As events proved, Prío's instincts betrayed him badly.

The standard accounts of Batista's March 10 coup relate that it took Prío by surprise and that it went like clockwork, being accomplished in less than an hour and a half. Actually, Prío had sufficient warning, if he had not avoided it, and once it started he had sufficient time to take countermeasures, if he had shown courage. Batista performed his part well. The plot was contained entirely within the army. A group of young officers thoroughly disgusted with the corruption and gangsterism of the Prío regime originated the plot and approached Batista to lead them, relying on his experience and influence to make the coup a success. They did not anticipate that his personal ambition would betray them and turn a movement "to save the republic" into a prolonged military dictatorship.[62] With the plan in readiness, Batista showed up at Camp Columbia a little before three A.M., Monday, March 10. The "lieutenants and captains" received him "enthusiastically" and notified him that "simultaneous" with his arrival their collaborators had seized La Cabaña fortress, taken over the air force and navy headquarters, and had "absolute control" of all police commands. Moreover, military personnel had occupied all radio and TV stations, keeping them off the air for the time being.[63] Everything went so smoothly that Afro-Cubans described it as "the coup of Sunsundamba ... Sunsundamba being in Congo myth a night bird possessed by a spirit which if properly petitioned will help human beings."[64] But there were some glitches.

Not all army commands joined the conspiracy. Unexpectedly, Colonels Eduardo Martín Elena and Manuel Alvarez Margolles, the military chiefs of Matanzas and Santiago de Cuba, respectively, maintained their loyalty to the constitutional president and "appeared ready to oppose the uprising."[65] Prío still had a chance when he arrived at the Presidential Palace at five in the morning, having been awakened at La Chata, where he had spent the weekend. He had been informed an hour earlier by the wife of Army Chief of Staff General Ruperto Cabrera that Batista had seized Camp Columbia and had arrested her husband. The scene at the Presidential Palace was one of bedlam, with ministers Lancís, Curti, Suárez Rivas, Megías, and Casero, among others, scurrying about and on the telephone, trying to find out what was happening and figure out what to do. According to eyewitnesses, Prío appeared "indecisive" and "disoriented."[66] Naval commander René Fiallo exhorted him, "What you ought to do, Carlos, is leave for one of the provinces loyal to the government, and resist until the end. The people will follow you in defense of the lawful order."[67] Prío should have left for Matanzas immediately. In delaying, he lost precious time.

Prío met with news reporters who had been converging on the Presidential Palace ever since his arrival. Although it seemed pointless to hold a press conference when all the news outlets were under Batista's control, he issued a release nonetheless. He reported that Batista had seized the army headquarters at Camp Columbia but affirmed that the commands of the distinct provinces remained loyal to the constitutional government. He condemned Batista's blind ambition and called on all Cubans—soldiers, workers, students, farmers, industrialists—to maintain their loyalty to the republic. "I have faith in the Cubans," he attested.[68] Certain Cubans fulfilled that faith.

At around 6:30 A.M., a delegation of students representing the FEU arrived to offer their support to the president. "Mr. President," declared Orestes Robledo, speaking for the group, "you know that on many occasions we have censured and criticized you publicly when we believed that your conduct deserved it, but on this occasion the FEU comes to offer you its assistance in defense of the Constitution of the Republic.... We are at your side, Mr. President, because we adhere to the Constitution and the law.... If you are prepared to resist, you can count on us."[69] Prío was deeply moved by the students' offer of support, but he had no clear idea of what he expected them to do. After additional dialogue, the students requested arms, "in order to defend the legal authority," and Prío instructed former minister of education and senator Diego Vicente Tejera to send a shipment of arms to the university. In the meantime, presidential secretary Orlando Puente arrived with word that tanks from Camp Columbia were approaching the palace.

At 8 A.M., Prío abandoned the Presidential Palace, traveling by automobile to Matanzas. Accompanied by Tejera, the Auténtico boss of Matanzas, and Minister of Commerce Sergio Megías, a Liberal Party leader, Prío arrived in Matanzas three hours later. He was too late. The garrison had fallen to the *golpistas,* and Colonel Martín Elena was under arrest, being held in the officers' club. Having established a temporary headquarters in a private residence in Matanzas, Prío received more bad news. "Tony" Varona, who had been sent to Las Villas to secure the loyalty of the military forces there, arrived with the report that the province had gone over to Batista. Camagüey and Oriente remained loyal, "with the popular masses in the streets and up in arms."[70] "Millo" Ochoa, the Ortodoxo leader, called Prío, offered to send a plane to fly the president to Santiago, and exhorted him to make a stand. But Prío was completely demoralized and decided to give up. He returned to Havana and took asylum in the Mexican embassy at 4 P.M., only twelve hours after he first received word of the *cuartelazo* (barracks revolt).

In the meantime, Batista solidified his control. The *golpistas* occupied the Presidential Palace at 8:30 A.M., and at 1 P.M. the Revolutionary Military Junta made its first radio broadcast to a largely passive, if confused, population. After being silent for several hours, the radio stations broadcast only music for most of the morning until the junta was ready to inform the public of the fait accompli. "We have acted," the members of the junta declared, "in order to rescue Cuba from a regime of bloodshed and corruption." These evils, they insisted, were compounded by the plans of President Prío and certain military chiefs to carry out a *golpe de estado* early next month, "reacting to evidence of having lost the elections."[71] In other words, they had carried out a preventive coup to head off a coup planned by Prío and the Auténticos. In setting the stage for this "infamy," continued the junta, Prío and his minions "were preparing personal assaults against the most notable figures of the opposition, with the intention of blaming them on the very gangsters that the government itself arms and protects." (The "Calvo Sotelo" gambit?) "Convinced of the preparation of these crimes," the junta declared, "we decided to confront the terrible situation in order to save the country from these tragedies, which were already inevitable."[72] Other broadcasts followed containing statements by Batista and laudatory descriptions of his career. Batista personally addressed the nation at 6 P.M.

He had released his address several hours earlier during a press conference at Camp Columbia, after which he permitted the afternoon newspapers to publish. Answering reporters' questions as to the motives for the *golpe*, Batista denounced again the venality and lawlessness of the Prío government and repeated the story that Prío was planning a coup on April 15, "if by that date there was no assurance that the people would elect Hevia." (He failed to mention that his chances of winning had faded long ago.) Batista declared a suspension of constitutional guarantees for forty-five days and announced the postponement of the June 1 elections, giving assurances that as soon as the country returned to normal, "elections would be held with full guarantees." In the interim, he proposed to govern Cuba under "Statutes of Government," outlining the political structure and powers of the de facto government. Batista assumed the position of prime minister and designated Miguel Angel Campa as president. To make sure of his base of support, he raised the monthly salaries of police officers to 150 pesos and of soldiers and sailors to 100 pesos, effective immediately.[73]

Aside from a brief skirmish outside the Presidential Palace at around 6 A.M. that left four dead, Batista's coup was bloodless. The only open sign of resistance to the *golpe* took place on the *Escalinata* of the university. There, students and professors displayed banners denouncing the coup and set up microphones and loudspeakers to appeal to those in listening range to resist. The FEU declared a strike, vowing to boycott classes until the Constitution was restored. Certain labor leaders representing the CTC arrived and confided preparations for "a general strike against the *cuartelazo*" but never followed through. Eusebio Mujal quickly made peace with Batista, choosing to switch rather than fight.[74] Among the *pistoleros*, only Masferrer rallied to the students' support, spending most of the morning at the University of Havana, although his subsequent service to Batista as security chief suggests that he may have been there to subvert the movement rather than to bolster it. The other "brave" gunsels went into hiding, never lifting a finger to rescue the fallen regime. Individuals such as Policarpo Soler and Jesús González Cartas ("El Extraño") fled Cuba and turned up in the Dominican Republic, hiring out their guns to Rafael Trujillo. Moreover, the guns that Prío had promised the students never arrived. The students continued to demonstrate, but their movement was contained and fizzled shortly. In the afternoon, soldiers and police, "armed with machine guns and rifles," surrounded the "hill."[75]

The rapid fall of the Prío government elicited general comment that the Auténticos deserved their fate. The Prío regime, affirmed Ramón Vasconcelos, "fell like a rotten fruit, almost by its own weight, victim of its political intrigues, of its intemperate ambition, and contempt for public opinion, the basis of democratic government."[76] *Bohemia* declared that the "entire government" of Carlos Prío Socarrás "fell without glory," condemning "the cowardice of the civilian officials that permitted the coup to succeed."[77] Luis Aguilar noted that the "loss of prestige of the Auténticos hit bottom with the quick stampede of its leaders toward Miami."[78] Rafael Estenger observed that the people reacted to the coup with contradictory emotions: sorrow and joy, satisfaction and displeasure. The *golpe*, he remarked, "has two faces, resembling the images of Janus. . . . On one side, there is the violation of legal principles, the breaking of the established constitutional rule; on the other, there is reality—the reality that indisputably represents the almost unanimous desire of the people, disgusted to the point of nausea with the corruption of the regime of Prío."[79]

The U.S. ambassador, Willard Beaulac, made the cruelest comment of all, proclaiming: "The Cubans get the kind of government they deserve. Until they learn discipline and sacrifice, the kind of thing that happened on March 10 will continue to happen."[80] For all his faults, Fidel Castro's reaction to Batista's coup was among the most noble at the time. He did not blame the victim. "The coup was not against Prío but against the people," he declared. "It was right to remove from office a government of murderers and thieves, and we were trying to do so peacefully with the support of public opinion and the aid of the people. But by what right do the military do so, they who have murdered and stolen without limit in the past?"[81]

There were those who believed that had Chibás been alive, he would have rallied the people against Batista. Sánchez Arango was brave but "without popularity," wrote Roberto Luque Escalona, adding that Pardo Llada was popular but "without daring."[82] Herminio Portell Vilá believed that the suicide of Chibás had affected Prío deeply and was critical in his failure to respond to Batista's challenge. "He was still feeling its effects when he needed most his characteristic fearlessness in the face of danger, which he had shown over the course of twenty-five years."[83] Perhaps this explained the contradiction between the image of Prío as one of the most intrepid fighters against Machado in 1933 and his failure of nerve in 1952. Maybe he had grown soft over the years, the accumulation of *fincas* undermining more than his courage. Some blamed Chibás more directly for the coup, suggesting that his attacks on the Auténticos weakened democracy as well.

Chibás's criticisms, according to Jaime Suchlicki, "helped to undermine not only the authority of the Auténticos, destroying what little prestige they still enjoyed, but the stability of Cuba's political institutions as well."[84] Suárez Rivas agreed, maintaining that Chibás's demagoguery and defection left the revolutionary power in a "vacuum." The military was just waiting for its opportunity. "Revolutionary unity was broken by the rupture of the Auténticos and Ortodoxos, and that was perhaps the principal reason why the power vacuum was filled again by Batista."[85] Luis Aguilar did not accept the thesis that in discrediting the Prío administration, Chibás went too far and undermined the democratic order at the same time. He contended, however, that his "vitriolic and excessive" attacks and suicide "poisoned the atmosphere" against the Auténticos and weakened the Ortodoxos, thereby encouraging the treachery of Batista.[86] Luis Ortega, the editor of *Prensa Libre*, stated categorically that the charges of corruption against the Auténticos were "exaggerated." His newspaper was as bad as the rest, even "inventing" stories. "We wanted to sell newspapers," he admitted.[87]

A great deal has been made of the assertions that the general public was apathetic toward the coup and made no effort to resist. According to Louis Pérez, "The toppled Auténtico government was not invested with the moral creditability to solicit national support. Its fall did not warrant public outrage."[88] This explained only partially the absence of public resistance. It was not true that all Auténticos fled the country. Tony Varona stayed behind and, as president of the Senate, tried to convoke the Congress to consider the "illegal situation" but was prevented by force from entering the Capitolio. Soldiers fired warning shots above the heads of the legislators. Civilians could not match the firepower of Batista.

Cuba was not the only Latin American country to succumb to military dictatorship in the late 1940s and early 1950s. The foibles of the Auténticos alone did not explain the trend. When the Auténticos fell, civilian government had been replaced by military rule in Argentina, Peru, and Venezuela, joining existing military dictatorships in Paraguay, El Salvador, Nicaragua, Haiti, and the Dominican Republic. And more military takeovers were imminent. The rise of the colonels and generals to power could not be blamed solely on public apathy or alleged corruption and inefficiency of civilian government; the Cold War and "softness" toward communism were additional excuses. The Auténticos and Ortodoxos of Vedado might wish to improve conditions for the poor of the *solares* and *bohios*, but the newly rich of Marianao and Miramar were scared to death of them. Democratic institutions in Latin America were fragile, particularly in the face of overwhelming economic and social problems. Underuse of human resources and poverty stalked the lands. The argument was made that a strong hand, not freedom of expression, was required to overcome poverty (unrest). Military "professionalism" and modern weapons reinforced *caudillismo*. As Rómulo Betancourt had said, "You can't go to the barricades in the era of tanks and bombing planes." If Prío had acted in a timely fashion, he might have had some of these weapons on his side and evened the odds. The students were ready to fight (give us arms, they had asked), and the people in Camagüey and Santiago were in the streets. Perhaps even the CTC might have shown some backbone. In a word, Prío failed to act as a president sworn to defend the Constitution. He ignored warnings of a pending threat and had no contingency plan to deal with a possible *cuartelazo*.

The fall of the Auténticos had unforeseen tragic consequences for Cuba. When Carlos Prío boarded a Mexicana Airways plane to go into exile, Cuban democracy departed with him, just as when Batista entered Camp Columbia on the morning of March 10, 1952, "there entered the camp as well the most sinister shadow of Fidel Castro."[89] The Auténticos failed the Cuban people miserably, but they gave Cuba a period of freedom it had not experienced before or, up to now, since.

The greatest gift was freedom of expression. Cuba had scores of newspapers, running the spectrum from the ultraconservative *Diario de la Marina* to the Communist *Hoy*. *Bohemia*, enjoying one of the largest circulations in Latin America, an unrelenting critic of the Auténtico governments, was published by the freewheeling Miguel Angel Quevedo, an unabashed admirer of Eddy Chibás. Enrique de la Osa, who allegedly had "a tragic ability to destroy personalities,"[90] edited the magazine's "en Cuba" section, containing astute insider political commentary, often with a satirical bite. *Bohemia*'s political cartoonists and caricaturists were equally good and irreverent. Juan Davíd was brilliant, and "Silvio," the creator of "El Reyecito Criollo," based on the U.S. comic strip "The Little King," expertly depicted the Auténtico presidents in royal robe and miniature crown, usually in contemporary dialogue with "Liborito," the everyman *guajiro*. *Bohemia* was one of the "five aces of Cuban democracy" that also included *El Mundo*, CMQ, *Diario de la Marina*, and *Alerta*. These media outlets combined their resources to interview political candidates, striving to be fair and stimulate voter interest. These eight years were a period of artistic flowering. Though the Auténticos placed no obstacles in the way of creativity, they were criticized for insufficient support of the arts. Contradictions abound. The Auténticos spent $335,828,146 on education from 1947 to 1952 (one-quarter of the national budget in each of those years), yet illiteracy stood at 23.6 percent in 1953.

Luis Aguilar wrote that the Auténticos "displayed an almost legendary capacity to steal public funds."[91] That may be so, but there was a difference between the Grau and Prío administrations, particularly after the departure of José Alemán. Although Carlos Prío and his brothers Antonio and Paco enriched themselves, there were more honest men than scoundrels in high office in the Prío administration. Tony Varona, Félix Lancís, Pepín Bosch, José Alvarez Díaz, Luis Casero, Aureliano Sánchez Arango, Carlos Hevia, Eduardo Suárez Rivas, Felipe Pazos, and Justo Carrillo performed their duties with distinction. Moreover, the Prío administration undertook to institutionalize honest government by making thievery more difficult through public budgets and standardized accounting procedures monitored by the Tribunal of Accounts (an independent office of the comptroller general), the National Bank, and the Agricultural and Industrial Development Bank. The charges of corruption in the Grau administration were well documented in "Case 82," whereas those against the Prío administration appeared to be warmed over and general in nature. Admittedly, both administrations failed to create a civil service system, leaving political patronage and *botellas* as prime sources of corruption. At the same time, Lowry Nelson wrote in *Rural Cuba* (1950) that he encountered "faithful, disinterested public servants who constitute one of the bright hopes for the future of the country."[92] The nominations of Hevia and Casero for president and vice president in 1952 demonstrated that the Auténticos recognized their problem and were determined to solve it. These were honest men, and civil service reform was a priority plank in the platform.

The Auténticos were blessed with good economic times that tended to mitigate or postpone the resolution of economic and social problems. They proclaimed a socialist philosophy, but the public sector was modest. If government was the second largest employer of the country, it was because of a patronage system that tolerated unproductive *botellas* (sinecures). The Auténticos did not nationalize public utilities or transportation or establish a national health system, as did their social democratic contemporary Costa Rica. Instead, the Auténticos maintained a highly regulated economy to achieve broadly nationalistic and anti-imperialist goals. Through a system of production quotas and guaranteed market share, the Auténticos sought to eliminate latifundium and check administration cane to promote Cuban ownership of land and industry. They chafed under the reality of having no control over the sugar quota set in Washington, D.C., but adopted measures to distribute the benefits to as many Cubans as possible, favoring small producers. Their policy was not limited to the sugar industry but extended to tobacco, cattle ranching, rice, and other agricultural products. It included highly nationalistic and protective labor policies as well. The Auténticos' relationship with the CTC was a classic example of politics dominating good sense. The PRC-A intended to liberate the Cuban economy and protect workers and small farmers, but, as many economists argued, its policies promoted inefficiency and stagnation.[93] Accordingly, the Cuban economy was in trouble not because the Auténticos failed to carry out their policy but because they put it into practice. The Auténticos were not disposed to follow the advice of the Truslow mission; the collapse of socialism, much less the mixed economy concept, was yet a long time in the future.

Swirling about all the woes of the Auténticos was the issue of *pistolerismo*. Grau had been indebted to "his boys," who stuck with him through the years of resistance, enduring the cruel reprisals of Batista. As president, Grau indulged them and found places for them in his government, mainly in the police and security forces. As the excuse for violence waned in the absence of repressive government, the role of the *pistoleros* as revolutionaries deteriorated into that of gangster and common criminal. Feuding among the "action groups" exacerbated this situation, particularly in the aftermath of the deadly Orfila affair. When in office, Prío tried to "take away their blue uniforms," ending police terror, but was inconsistent in his efforts to eradicate *pistolerismo*, and, like Grau, owing to his own thievery, lacked the "moral authority" to demand respect for the law.[94] He gave some of them a new reason for being by calling on Eufemio Fernández and the ARG to help in wresting control of the CTC from the Communists. Moreover, not all *pistoleros* were alike. They were a mixture of "romantics, revolutionaries,`gangsters' and terrorists."[95] Certain youths sought "glory and fortune," inspired by Hollywood gangster movies.[96] And others "believed sincerely that insurrection was necessary for installing a revolutionary government."[97] Eufemio Fernández (ARG) and

Rolando Masferrer (MSR), though both Spanish Civil War veterans, were contrasts in style and temperament. Both contested for influence and power in the labor movement, but Fernández was professional and ideologically motivated, whereas Masferrer was a brute and base opportunist. The post-coup activities of ARG's action chief Jesús González Cartas dictate a caveat. He hired out his gun to Rafael Trujillo and was arrested in Costa Rica in 1957 as a member of a three-man team sent to assassinate President José Figueres.

Although the public's outrage over *pistolero* violence was of long standing, there were not that many high profile gunmen left by 1952. The ARG appeared to have purpose and structure, but the MSR and UIR were fading and were essentially mercenary gangs. As Alonso Pujol implied, they were killing each other, and he told Batista that, although *pistolerismo* was a serious problem, it did not justify a *golpe de estado*. The Auténticos committed the gross error of failing to rein in their own leaders, namely, Miguel ("Miguelito") Suárez Fernández and Diego ("Dieguito") Vicente Tejera, who protected the desperados Policarpo Soler and Orlando León Lemus. *Pistolerismo* was a political issue, for which the Auténticos were primarily responsible. They could have removed it from the political realm at any time by cutting off its sources of public funding. After that, gangland killings would be criminal behavior exclusively and a law enforcement problem.

It is possible that a third free election and a decent presidency might have given democracy the final nudge it needed to survive in Cuba. Social injustice and economic disparity persisted, but the legal and political channels of redress would have stayed open under conditions of increasing confidence and opportunity. If Roberto Agramonte had been elected, he would have had a difficult time because the Ortodoxos would not have controlled Congress, but it is likely that he would have taken active measures against political corruption and *pistolerismo*. Hevia would probably have enjoyed a congressional majority and would have enacted important economic reforms, given his experience as president of the National Development Commission. He was also committed to civil service reform. But *pistolerismo* might have remained a problem because of Hevia's close ties to "Dieguito" Tejera, the Auténtico boss of Matanzas and protector of Policarpo Soler. It would have been interesting to see how Fidel Castro and Rolando Masferrer got along, both likely to win seats in the Chamber. Without Masferrer's threats, Castro's energies might have followed a less violent path. Tad Szulc believed that "even without" Batista's coup, Castro was "destined" to govern Cuba, possibly as an elected president.[98] Castro shaped his own destiny by contributing to the success of Batista's coup with his exposé of Prío in the first months of 1952.

Batista would have remained a threat regardless, meaning that either Agramonte or Hevia would have had to do what Grau and Prío failed to do: purge the army of Batista's influence and "restore" it to what it had been before Batista "politicized" it in 1933. The Liberation Army—the republic-in-arms—was not controlled by military men; "the military fought and the civilians directed the military movement."[99] Batista changed this circumstance with the "Sergeants Revolt" of 1933, creating a mercenary army dependent on his goodwill. By failing to bring in new officers who would stay out of politics, Prío was vulnerable to what happened to him on March 10. If that event had not occurred, and Agramonte or Hevia had been elected president, a major overhaul of the armed forces would have been essential. Unfortunately, Cuba did not get the opportunity to change these final paragraphs from the conditional to the past tense.

The eight years of Auténtico government were unique in Cuban history. They were a time of constitutional order and political freedom. They were not "golden years" by any means, but in two elections (1944 and 1948), Cubans had the opportunity to express their desire for a rule of civil liberties, primacy of Cuban culture, and achievement of economic independence. If there were sharp contradictions in Cuban society under the Auténticos, the circumstances differed only in degree from the complexities and dynamics encountered in free societies everywhere (how often did Cubans compare Havana with Chicago?). In Cuba before 1944, the experience had been little give and mostly take. José Alvarez Díaz stated that the governments of Grau and Prío were "characterized" by their respect for civil liberties, "even though [they] displayed an excessive tolerance that created a crisis of authority."[100]

In hindsight, Cubans would have fought like demons to resist Batista's *golpe* in 1952, but he was something of a known quantity at the time, leading most everyone to underestimate the consequences of his treachery. Few apparently regretted the departure of Prío, but few expected that democracy might be a permanent casualty as well. Even Fidel Castro's generation, the generation of "el cincuentenario" (the fiftieth year of the republic), reacted to Batista's coup with a declaration demanding "the restoration of the 1940 Constitution, the reestablishment of civil government, and the holding of free elections."[101] They wanted precisely what they had just lost, minus the corruption and violence. Castro himself attested to the evolving democracy of the Auténtico era, excoriating

Batista in 1952: "We have been accustomed to living within the Constitution, we have done so for 12 years without serious obstacles in spite of the errors and outrages. The superior state of civic peace is achieved only after long effort. You, Batista, have just cast to the ground in a few hours that noble dream of the Cuban people."[102] Emilio Roig de Leuchsenring affirmed that the "failure" of democracy in Cuba was not the fault of the people. "For all the political ills that we have suffered... the popular mass is innocent. The only guilty ones are the leaders and political bosses."[103] Cuban exiles sing the beautiful, haunting, "Cuando salí Cuba," expressing their nationality and yearning to return home and begin anew. Many of the Cubans who left their homeland after 1959 were either born or had their formative years in the Auténtico era. The Cuban democratic experience, 1944–52, is worth recalling for their children for its positive features as well as for its errors. It is a period worthy of the thoughtful consideration of all Cubans and students of Cuban history.

NOTES

Introduction. The Authentic Revolution

1. Louis A. Pérez, Jr., *Army Politics in Cuba, 1898–1958*, 5–6.
2. Justo Carrillo, *Cuba 1933*, 4.
3. Ibid., 110, n. 16.
4. Ibid., 6.
5. Ibid., 9.
6. Eduardo Suárez Rivas, *Los días iguales*, 46.
7. Carrillo, 15.
8. Marcela Mateo, "El ABC como opción reformista burguesa en la política neocolonial cubana," *La República Neocolonial*, 353.
9. Luis E. Aguilar, *Cuba 1933*, 125–26.
10. Suárez Rivas, 129. Jorge Ibarra, writing after 1959, asserted that the ABC followed Benito Mussolini's fascist line of "national renovation." ABC identified itself as "neither communist, nor fascist: Cuban." See Jorge Ibarra, *Historia de Cuba*, 59; also see Mateo, 372.
11. Carrillo, 17.
12. Ibid., 21.
13. Ibid., 22.
14. Ibid., 37.
15. Ibid., 44.
16. Pérez, *Cuba*, 262.
17. Ibid., 264.
18. Carrillo, 55.
19. Ibid., 85–86.
20. Ibid., 69.

21. Pérez, *Cuba*, 266.
22. Carrillo, 138.
23. Ibid., 139–40.
24. Ibid., 76.
25. Ibid., 148.
26. Ibid., 164.
27. Ibid., 162.
28. Aguilar, 200.
29. Carrillo, 182–83.
30. Aguilar, 184.
31. Carrillo, 232.
32. Ibid., 238.
33. Ibid.
34. Ibid.
35. Ibid., 253.
36. Ibid., 256.
37. Ibid., 258.
38. Ibid., 172.
39. Suárez Rivas, 139.
40. These decrees are highlighted in Eddy Chibás, "El Programa Auténtico: Las Leyes de Grau San Martín," *Bohemia,* April 16, 1944: 20–21.
41. Ibid., 20.
42. Quoted in Carrillo, 281.
43. Carrillo, 313.
44. Ibid., 315.
45. Suárez Rivas, 46.
46. Samuel Farber, *Revolution and Reaction in Cuba, 1933–1960,* 142.
47. Vicente Báez, ed., *Enciclopedia de Cuba,* 678.
48. Ramiro Guerra y Sánchez, *Sugar and Society in the Caribbean,* 74.
49. Suárez Rivas, 136.
50. Jaime Suchlicki, *University Students and Revolution in Cuba, 1920–1968,* 49.
51. *Bohemia,* November 26, 1944: 45.
52. Ibarra, 610.
53. Báez, 682.
54. Ibid., 679.
55. Ibid., 739.
56. Farber, 93.
57. Ibid., 94.
58. Báez, 593.
59. Suárez Rivas, 54.
60. U.S. Department of State, *Foreign Relations of the United States* (hereinafter cited as *FRUS*), 1942, 6: 299.
61. Ernest Hemingway, *Islands in the Stream,* 299. The novel is autobiographical in nature.

62. Chibás, "El Programa Auténtico," *Bohemia*, April 16, 1944: 20.
63. Ibid.

Chapter 1. "La Jornada Gloriosa"

1. en Cuba, "Balance," *Bohemia*, October 10, 1948: 107. "En Cuba," the political section of *Bohemia*, was divided into specific topics with titles such as "Balance." Note references to "en Cuba" hereinafter reflect the publication's format.
2. Irwin Gellman, *Roosevelt and Batista*, 228.
3. J. P. McEvoy, *The Saturday Evening Post*, quoted in Gellman, 212.
4. en Cuba, "Balance," *Bohemia*, October 10, 1948: 107.
5. Gellman, 212.
6. Hugh Thomas, *Cuba*, 735.
7. José López Vilaboy, *Motivos y culpables de la destrucción de Cuba*, 219.
8. Gellman, 206.
9. Ibid., 209–10.
10. Ibid., 210.
11. *Bohemia*, August 6, 1944: 28.
12. Steven J. Wright, *Cuba, Sugar, and the United States*, 46.
13. Gellman, 209.
14. Jorge I. Domínguez, *Cuba*, 103–4.
15. Wright, 46.
16. Domínguez, 102.
17. Ibid., 108.
18. Comments by Communist leader Blas Roca reported in *Bohemia*, November 28, 1943: 33.
19. Báez, 652.
20. Gellman, 83.
21. Eduardo R. Chibás, "El Autenticismo y las bases aéreas en Cuba," *Bohemia*, August 6, 1944: 31.
22. Spruille Braden, *Diplomats and Demagogues*, 290; Wright, 49–50.
23. en Cuba, "Balance," *Bohemia*, October 10, 1948: 108.
24. Ibid.
25. Guerra y Sánchez, 73–74.
26. Ibid., 167.
27. Oscar Zanetti Lecuona, *Los cautivos de la reciprodidad*, 120.
28. James O'Connor, *The Origins of Socialism in Cuba*, 18.
29. Zanetti Lecuona, 125.
30. Guerra y Sánchez, 177.
31. From 1939 to 1945, the number of Cuban-owned sugar mills increased from 56 to 83, the number of U.S.-owned mills declined from 66 to 59, and the total number of all mills remained steady at 174. See Wright, 249, table 10. Land distribution was still a concern in 1945, but there had been some success between 1931 and 1946, when the average *finca* declined in size from 188 acres to 140. The fact

that there were 28,000 *colonos* in 1936 and 40,000 by 1950 is further indication of the trend. See Thomas, 1145.

32. Juan Martínez Alier and Verena Martínez Alier, *Cuba*, 80.
33. Farber, 107.
34. Carlos M. Lechuga, "En 4 años el Congreso no trabajó más de 3 meses," *Bohemia*, October 10, 1948: 19.
35. Harold Dana Sims, "Cuba's Organized Labor from Depression to Cold War," 48.
36. en Cuba, "Balance," *Bohemia*, October 10, 1948: 108.
37. Ibarra, 598.
38. Farber, 22.
39. Robert Freeman Smith, *The United States and Cuba*, 170.
40. Wright, 54–55.
41. Suchlicki, *University Students*, 49.
42. Ibid.
43. Suárez Rivas, 160–61.
44. Ibid.
45. Ibid.
46. Báez, 731.
47. Farber, 109.
48. Gellman, 182.
49. Wright, 61.
50. Jacob Machover,ed., *La Habana, 1952–1961*, 145.
51. en Cuba, *Bohemia*, December 31, 1944: 24.
52. Lechuga, "En 4 años," 18.
53. Luis Conte Agüero, *Eduardo Chibás, el Adalid de Cuba*, 424.
54. en Cuba, *Bohemia*, November 26, 1944: 34.
55. en Cuba, "Ejército," *Bohemia*, January 7, 1945: 24.
56. en Cuba, "Balance," *Bohemia*, October 10, 1948: 129.
57. Ibid.
58. Vergara, "Picadillo a la criolla," *Bohemia*, July 8, 1945: 18.
59. *Bohemia*, June 4, 1950: 89.
60. Machover, 132–37.
61. Guillermo Cabrera Infante, *Mea Cuba*, 70.
62. Ibid., 337–38; see also Machover, 190–91, and *Bohemia*, February 27, 1949: 44.
63. en Cuba, "Política Americana. La reunión en México," *Bohemia*, February 11, 1945: 28–29.
64. Ibid.
65. Ibid.
66. See Wright, 91–100, for a full discussion of the 1945 sugar contract negotiations.
67. "Qué opina usted sobre Cuba en la postguerra?" *Bohemia*, September 2, 1945: 36–37.

68. Ibid., 36.
69. Ibid.
70. Ibid., 37.
71. "Señor Presidente de la República, nada tenemos que ofrecer a los turistas que nos visiten," *Bohemia*, September 16, 1945, supplement B, following p. 34.
72. Hemingway, 215.
73. "Señor Presidente," *Bohemia*, September 16, 1945, supplement B.
74. Conte Agüero, 391.
75. en Cuba, "Desconfianza," *Bohemia*, October 7, 1945: 28; en Cuba, "Balance," *Bohemia*, October 10, 1948: 114.
76. Ibid.
77. en Cuba, "Desconfianza," *Bohemia*, October 7, 1945: 28.
78. Rolando E. Bonachea and Nelson P. Valdés, eds., *Revolutionary Struggle, 1947–1958*, 16.
79. Suchlicki, *University Students*, 50.
80. Ibid., 51–52.
81. Suárez Rivas, 159.
82. Bonachea and Valdés, 18.
83. Nelson P. Valdés and Rolando E. Bonachea, "Fidel Castro y la política estudiantil de 1947 a 1952," 26–27.
84. Cabrera Infante, 366.
85. Bonachea and Valdés, 20.
86. Lionel Martin, *The Early Fidel*, 27.
87. Georgie Anne Geyer, *Guerrilla Prince*, 55.
88. Tad Szulc, *Fidel*, 143.
89. Martin, 28.
90. Valdés and Bonachea, "Fidel Castro," 28.
91. Conte Agüero, 400–1.
92. Ibid., 402.
93. Suchlicki, *University Students*, 54.

Chapter 2. The Ministry of Scandal

1. MacGaffey and Barnett, *Twentieth Century Cuba: The Background of the Castro Revolution*, 190–91.
2. en Cuba, "Balance," *Bohemia*, October 10, 1948: 123.
3. Ibid.
4. Ibid.
5. Ibid.
6. en Cuba, "Deceso. Un personaje de leyenda," *Bohemia*, April 2, 1950: 70.
7. Ibid.
8. Ibid.
9. en Cuba, "Balance," *Bohemia*, October 10, 1948: 124.

10. Ibid.
11. Ibid.
12. en Cuba, "Deceso," *Bohemia*, April 2, 1950: 70.
13. en Cuba, "Balance," *Bohemia*, October 10, 1948: 124–25.
14. Ibid., 124.
15. Carlos Del Toro, "Algunos aspectos económicos del movimiento obrero cubano," *La República Neocolonial*, 224–25.
16. Juan Pérez de la Riva, *El Barracón y otros ensayos*, 75–76.
17. en Cuba, "Deceso," *Bohemia*, April 2, 1950: 70.
18. en Cuba, "Balance," *Bohemia*, October 10, 1948: 125.
19. Inocente Alvarez, interview by author, February 27, 1980.
20. *Bohemia*, June 23, 1946: 44.
21. Conte Agüero, 466.
22. Suárez Rivas, 106; see also Wright, 111.
23. Suárez Rivas, 106.
24. Conte Agüero, 415.
25. Ibid., 422–23.
26. Ibid., 430.
27. Hemingway, 299.
28. Conte Agüero, 444–45.
29. Cabrera Infante, 141.
30. Conte Agüero, 455.
31. Ibid.
32. Ibid.
33. Ibid., 460–61.
34. Geoff Simons, *Cuba*, 259.
35. Ibid., 260.
36. Ibid., 261–62.
37. Martin A. Gosch and Richard Hammer, *The Last Testament of Lucky Luciano*, 311–12.
38. Ibid., 313.
39. Ibid., 284.
40. Simons, 261–62.
41. Gosch and Hammer, 324.
42. Conte Agüero, 491.
43. Ibid., 476–77.
44. Ibid., 486–87.
45. Ibid., 490.
46. Secret memo, October 9, 1946, R. Henry Norweb to Secretary of State, U.S. Department of State, *Confidential U.S. State Department Central Files: Cuba, 1945–1949*; hereinafter cited as *Cuba, 1945–1949*.
47. Conte Agüero, 483.

Chapter 3. The Torrid Season

1. Conte Agüero, 478.
2. W. Adolphe Roberts, *Havana*, 144.
3. Conte Agüero, 486.
4. en Cuba, "Balance," *Bohemia*, October 10, 1948: 114.
5. en Cuba, "Deceso," *Bohemia*, April 2, 1950: 70
6. José Duarte Oropesa, *Historiología Cubana*, 52.
7. Cabrera Infante, 148.
8. Ibid.
9. Conte Agüero, 502.
10. Farber, 124.
11. *FRUS*, 1947, 8: 621.
12. Conte Agüero, 506–7.
13. Ibid., 508.
14. Sebastian Balfour, *Castro*, 29.
15. Bonachea and Valdés, 29.
16. López Vilaboy, 234.
17. Bonachea and Valdés, 28.
18. Ibid.
19. Ibid., 132.
20. Szulc, 160–62.
21. Wright, 205.
22. *Bohemia*, October 10, 1948: 109.
23. Mario Lazo, *Dagger in the Heart*, 70.
24. *Bohemia*, October 10, 1948: 109; see also Serafino Romualdi, *Presidents and Peons: Recollections of a Labor Ambassador in Latin America*, 3–4, 108; and George Morris, *CIA and American Labor: The Subversion of the AFL-CIO's Foreign Policy*, 64–65, 157.
25. *Bohemia*, October 10, 1948: 109.
26. Ibid.
27. Enrique Vignier and Guillermo Alonso, *La corrupción política y administrativa en Cuba, 1944–1952*, 14.
28. Farber, 141–43.
29. Wright, 332; see also Sims, "Cuba's Organized Labor," 8–9.
30. Oscar Zanetti and Alejandro García, *Sugar and Railroads*, 367.
31. Quoted in Zanetti and García, 367.
32. Ibid.
33. Vignier and Alonso, 102–3. In 1959, with the triumph of Fidel Castro, Captain Castillas was arrested and executed for "this crime and others." Ibid., 17–18.
34. Farber, 139.
35. Wright, 334.

36. Ibid.
37. Angel Miolán, *El perredé desde mi ángulo*, 516–17, 98–99.
38. Ibid.
39. Charles D. Ameringer, *The Caribbean Legion*, 34.
40. Miolán, 120.
41. Szulc, 154–55; Martin, 32.
42. "Statement of Héctor Incháustagui Cabral." Dominican Republic. Documents furnished by the Organization of American States, Organ of Consultation, "Situation in the Caribbean, 1950," pertaining to Haiti, Cuba, Guatemala, and the Dominican Republic. Hereinafter referred to as OAS/OC.
43. Ameringer, *Caribbean Legion*, 43.
44. Ibid., 47.
45. OAS/OC (1950), Dominican Republic.
46. Ameringer, *Caribbean Legion*, 46.
47. Ibid.
48. Tulio H. Arvelo, *Cayo Confites y Luperón: Memorias de un expedicionario*, 65.
49. Ibid., 68.
50. Memorandum, W. W. Walker, September 12, 1947, *Cuba, 1945–1949*.
51. Dispatch 4382, U.S. Embassy to Secretary of State, September 30, 1947, *Cuba, 1945–1949*.
52. Norberto Fuentes, *Hemingway in Cuba*, 254.
53. Conte Agüero, 531.
54. Ameringer, *Caribbean Legion*, 55.
55. Ibid., 56.
56. Arvelo, 99.
57. Dispatch 4420, Norweb to Secretary of State, October 3, 1947, *Cuba, 1945–1949*.
58. Martin, 36–37.
59. Wright, 288.
60. Vignier and Alonso, 14.
61. Wright, 291.
62. Quoted in Wright, 294.
63. Wright, 269.
64. Ibid., 265.
65. Ibid., 264–65.
66. Ibid., 267.
67. Ibid., 268.
68. Ibid., 296.
69. Ibid., 286–87.
70. Ibid., 290.
71. Ibid., 292–93.
72. Ibid., 296.
73. Zanetti Lecuona, 143.

74. Ibid., 147.
75. Wright, 272.
76. Zanetti Lecuona, 123.
77. Cabrera Infante, 372.
78. Ibid., 488.
79. Ibid., 103.
80. Ibid., 56.
81. Machover, 207.
82. Ibid., 118.

Chapter 4. Passing the Torch

1. Duarte Oropesa, 92.
2. Francisco Ichaso, "El proceso Auténtico," *Bohemia*, June 26, 1949: 87.
3. Tony Delahoza, "Los cuatro años del regimén de Grau San Martín," *Bohemia*, October 10, 1948: 11.
4. Ibid.
5. en Cuba, "Balance," *Bohemia*, October 10, 1948: 127.
6. en Cuba, "Deceso," *Bohemia*, April 2, 1950: 70.
7. Dispatch 4421, October 9, 1947, *Cuba, 1945–1949*.
8. Juan González Martínez, "Porque hice Presidente a Carlos Prío," *Bohemia*, January 30, 1949: 58.
9. Báez, 734.
10. Raúl Lorenzo, "Promete Carlos Prío no continuar la obra del 'Viejo,'" *Bohemia*, September 12, 1948: 70.
11. Conte Agüero, 538–39.
12. Ibid., 541.
13. Ibid., 556.
14. en Cuba, *Bohemia*, May 30, 1948: 72.
15. Conte Agüero, 569.
16. Ichaso, "El proceso," *Bohemia*, June 26, 1949: 87.
17. José M. Illán, *Cuba*, 149.
18. *Bohemia*, May 30, 1948: 65.
19. en Cuba, "Balance," *Bohemia*, October 10, 1948: 125.
20. López Vilaboy, 242.
21. Conte Agüero, 571.
22. Ibid., 570.
23. Báez, 740.
24. Lorenzo, "Promete," *Bohemia*, September 12, 1948: 70.
25. Dispatch 447, September 2, 1948, *Cuba, 1945–1949*.
26. Ibid.
27. Dispatch 786, September 21, 1948, *Cuba, 1945–1949*.
28. Dispatch 447, September 2, 1948, *Cuba, 1945–1949*.

29. Telegram 364, August 25, 1948, *Cuba, 1945–1949*.
30. Lorenzo, "Promete," *Bohemia*, September 12, 1948: 70.
31. Office memo, September 9, 1948, *Cuba, 1945–1949*.
32. en Cuba, "Atentado. Una 'vendetta' más," *Bohemia*, August 29, 1948: 60.
33. Bonachea and Valdés, 133.
34. Szulc, 167–68.
35. Cabrera Infante, 312.
36. en Cuba, "Atentado," *Bohemia*, August 29, 1948: 60.
37. Delahoza, "Los cuatro años," *Bohemia*, October 10, 1948: 11.
38. Ibid., 206.
39. Ibid., 202.
40. Ibid., 12–13.
41. Ibid., 202.
42. Ibid., 201.
43. Ibid., 207.
44. Ibid.
45. Conte Agüero, 575–76.
46. Vignier and Alonso, 38.
47. Ibid., 44.
48. Ibid., 129.
49. Ibid., 136.
50. Guerra y Sánchez, xxxix.
51. International Bank for Reconstruction and Development (hereinafter cited as IBRD), *Report on Cuba*, 91.
52. Del Toro, 275.
53. Guerra y Sánchez, xliii.
54. Vignier and Alonso, 9.
55. Quoted in Thomas, 739.
56. Wright, 85, n. 57.
57. Ibid., 61.
58. Ibid., 281.
59. Zanetti Lecuona, 140–41.
60. Quoted in Vignier and Alonso, 34.

Chapter 5. The Cordial President

1. Báez, 746.
2. Herminio Portell Vilá, "Balance inicial en educación," *Bohemia*, November 20, 1949: 42.
3. *Bohemia*, October 9, 1949: 98–99.
4. en Cuba, "Balance. El primer año de la Cordialidad," *Bohemia*, October 9, 1949: 102.
5. *FRUS*, 1948, 9: 567.

6. Báez, 749.
7. *Bohemia*, March 20, 1949: 49.
8. Vignier and Alonso, 300–301.
9. Rafael García Bárcena, "El pistolerismo es un cáncer nacional," *Bohemia*, February 20, 1949: 69.
10. Francisco Ichaso, "La creación del Tribunal de Cuentas es un compromiso de honor del Congreso," *Bohemia*, June 19, 1949: 43.
11. Suárez Rivas, 115.
12. Zanetti and García, 371.
13. Suárez Rivas, 112.
14. en Cuba, "Balance," *Bohemia*, October 9, 1949: 102.
15. *Hispanic World Report* 2 (January 1949): 28.
16. *Cuba, 1945–1949*, September 9, 1948.
17. *FRUS*, 1948, 9: 576–77.
18. Ibid., 575.
19. Ibid.
20. González Martínez, "Porque," *Bohemia*, January 30, 1949: 58.
21. Ibid., 59.
22. *Bohemia*, February 13, 1949: 57.
23. en Cuba, "Controversia," *Bohemia*, February 6, 1949: 52.
24. Ibid.
25. Ibid.
26. Ibid.
27. Ibid.
28. Francisco Ichaso, "El proceso Auténtico," *Bohemia*, June 26, 1949: 87.
29. Conte Agüero, 604.
30. Ibid., 606.
31. Ibid., 619–20.
32. Ibid., 596–97.
33. Ibid., 621.
34. en Cuba, "Atentados. Apártese todo el mundo," *Bohemia*, January 23, 1949: 51–52.
35. Ibid., 52.
36. Ibid., 51.
37. en Cuba, "Atentado. El plomo habla de nuevo," *Bohemia*, April 10, 1949: 66.
38. Ibid., 65.
39. Martin, 67–68.
40. en Cuba, "Atentado," *Bohemia*, April 10, 1949: 66.
41. en Cuba, "Atentado. La policia protegó a los asesinos," *Bohemia*, April 24, 1949: 71.
42. Mario García del Cueto and Tony Delahoza, "Tres reportajes de gran actualidad," *Bohemia*, April 17, 1949: 62–63.
43. en Cuba, "Atentado," *Bohemia*, April 24, 1949: 72.

44. en Cuba, "La Capital. Marejada antidemocrática," *Bohemia*, May 15, 1949, supplement 1.
45. Ibid.
46. Ibid., supplement 2.
47. en Cuba, "Defensa. 'Ese código de agresión social,'" *Bohemia*, May 22, 1949: 60.
48. Ibid., 60–61.
49. Vergara, "Picadillo a la criolla," *Bohemia*, June 5, 1949: 47.
50. en Cuba, "Defensa," *Bohemia*, May 22, 1949: 61.
51. en Cuba, "La Capital. Vuelve la racha homicida," *Bohemia*, July 31, 1949: 67.
52. Fuentes, 254.
53. en Cuba, "Atentado. Por quinta vez," *Bohemia*, September 25, 1949: 71.
54. Ibid., 70.
55. Duarte Oropesa, 55.
56. Bonachea and Valdés, 27.
57. *Hispanic World Report* 2 (September 1949): 29.
58. Filiberto Rodríguez Angulo, "Actualidad universitaria," *Bohemia*, September 25, 1949: 11.
59. Tony Martín, "Así salió Caramés y entró Uría," *Bohemia*, October 2, 1949: 55.
60. Emeterio Santovenia and Raúl M. Shelton, *Cuba y su historia*, 3: 178.
61. Valdés and Bonachea, 38–39.
62. Ibid., 25.
63. *Bohemia*, October 9, 1949: 98–99.
64. *Bohemia*, "Balance," October 9, 1949: 101–2.

Chapter 6. The Democratic Bulwark

1. *Rómulo Betancourt: pensamiento y acción*, 284.
2. Ibid., 285.
3. Rómulo Betancourt, *Venezuela: política y petróleo*, 470.
4. Alberto Bayo, *Tempestad en el Caribe*, 123.
5. Charles D. Ameringer, "Leonardo Ruiz Pineda," 215.
6. Betancourt, 587.
7. For details of the Luperón affair, see Ameringer, *Caribbean Legion*, 95–116.
8. Enrique V. Corominas, *In the Caribbean Political Areas*, 53.
9. Ibid., 88.
10. Ibid., 89.
11. U.S. Department of State, *Peace in the Americas*, 5–6.
12. *Bohemia*, August 14, 1949: 68.
13. Corominas, *In the Caribbean Political Areas*, 70–71.
14. Organization of American States (OAS), *Aplicaciones del Tratado Interamericano de Asistencia Recíproca, 1948–1960*, 120.
15. "Selección de algunas transmisiones radiales. Transmisiones dirigidas a Cuba [Julio 29 de 1949]." Document furnished by Cuba, OAS/OC.

16. en Cuba, "Destitución. Aliado de sátrapa Trujillo," *Bohemia*, August 29, 1949, supplement 2.

17. "Este documento constituyó una de las causas de la caída de Genovevo Pérez," *Bohemia*, September 4, 1949: 79–81.

18. en Cuba, "Destitución," *Bohemia*, August 29, 1949, supplement 1–2.

19. OAS, *Aplicaciones*, 121–23.

20. Statement by Paul Giacometti, January 27, 1950. Documents furnished by the Dominican Republic, OAS/OC.

21. OAS, *Aplicaciones*, 81.

22. Petition to OAS Committee, February 7, 1950. Documents furnished by Cuba, OAS/OC.

23. OAS, *Aplicaciones*, 122.

24. Ibid., 115–24.

25. Ibid., 129.

26. Ibid., 128–30.

27. ORIT-CIOSL, *15 años de sindicalismo libre interamericano, enero 1948–enero 1963*, 123.

28. Betancourt, 531.

29. OAS, *Aplicaciones*, 139.

30. Letter from Luis Thomen, May 12, 1951. Documents furnished by the Dominican Republic, OAS/OC.

31. *FRUS*, 1950, 2:848.

32. Ibid.

Chapter 7. New Directions

1. Francisco Ichaso, "Persistencia del matonismo en nuestras contiendas electorales," *Bohemia*, May 14, 1950: 61.

2. Ibid.

3. Memo of conversation, May 16, 1949, *FRUS*, 1949, 631.

4. Assistant Secretary Paul H. Nitze to Ambassador Robert Butler (February 23, 1949), *FRUS*, 623–25.

5. Eduardo Chibás, "Carta abierta. De Eduardo Chibás a Carlos Prío," *Bohemia*, July 31, 1949: 55.

6. Editorial, *Bohemia*, August 28, 1949: 51.

7. Editorial, "Un paso decisivo hacia nuestra liberación económica," *Bohemia*, April 3, 1950: 51.

8. José R. Alvarez Díaz et al., *A Study on Cuba*, 463.

9. IBRD, 693.

10. Alvarez Díaz, 454.

11. Suárez Rivas, 116.

12. Guillermo Alonso Pujol, "Infundios y verdades," *Bohemia*, February 12, 1950: 69.

13. Francisco Ichaso, "Balance y replanteo," *Bohemia*, June 11, 1950: 85.
14. Ibid., 86.
15. Conte Agüero, 662–76.
16. en Cuba, "Deceso," *Bohemia*, April 2, 1950: 69.
17. Ibid., 71.
18. Conte Agüero, 682.
19. Editorial, "A la cárcel los pillos," *Bohemia*, July 2, 1950: 71.
20. en Cuba, "Asalto. En la madrugada del 4 de julio," *Bohemia*, July 9, 1950: 76.
21. Ibid., 78.
22. Ibid., 77.
23. *Bohemia*, July 30, 1950: 58.
24. en Cuba, "Asalto," *Bohemia*, July 9, 1950: 77.
25. Ichaso, "Balance," *Bohemia*, June 11, 1950: 98.
26. Raúl Lorenzo, "La batalla por la candidatura en el Autenticismo," *Bohemia*, July 16, 1950: 67.
27. Ibid., 96.
28. Báez, 774–76.
29. *Hispanic American Report* 3 (September 1950): 16–17. The *Hispanic American Report* is hereinafter referred to as *HAR*.
30. Ibid., 17.
31. en Cuba, "Clausura. El periódico 'Hoy' y el Artículo 35," *Bohemia*, September 3, 1950: 79.
32. Ibid.
33. Editorial, "Es que la Generación del 30 no ha aprendido las lecciones de la historia?" *Bohemia*, August 20, 1950: 71.
34. Ibid., 70.
35. "Texto integro del discurso del Dr. Miguel Suárez, ante el Senado," *Bohemia*, October 8, 1950: 83.
36. Ibid.
37. en Cuba, "Balance de los años de gobierno," *Bohemia*, October 15, 1950: 74.
38. Nestor Piñango, "Prío: La mascara y el rostro en el templo de los gatos," *Bohemia*, December 3, 1950: 89.
39. Kuchilan, "El Primier Lancís," *Bohemia*, January 7, 1951: 44.
40. en Cuba, "Balance," *Bohemia*, October 15, 1950: 73.
41. Roberts, 225.
42. en Cuba, "Esquina caliente," *Bohemia*, January 21, 1951: 57.
43. Cabrera Infante, 401.
44. Machover, 147.
45. Martínez Alier, 108.
46. Machover, 189–90.
47. Cabrera Infante, 393.
48. Machover, 189–90.
49. Cabrera Infante, 393.

50. Machover, 186.
51. *HAR* 3 (November 1950): 20–21.
52. Báez, 772–73.
53. Pamela S. Falk, *Cuban Foreign Policy*, 17.
54. Memo, January 11, 1951, *FRUS*, 1950, 2: 853.
55. Machover, 67–68.

Chapter 8. Sugar and Vinegar

1. IBRD, 1039.
2. Ibid., 194, 35.
3. Ibid., 51.
4. Ibid., 38, 51–52.
5. Ibid., 52.
6. Wright, 255.
7. IBRD, 795–98.
8. Guerra y Sánchez, 142.
9. Suárez Rivas, 103–4.
10. Thomas, 708.
11. IBRD, 806.
12. O'Connor, 18.
13. IBRD, 815.
14. See Wright, 90–107, for details of the negotiations of these sugar contracts.
15. IBRD, 819.
16. Suárez Rivas, 106.
17. Ibid., 107–8.
18. Ibid., 108.
19. IBRD, 7.
20. Ibid., 59.
21. O'Connor, 55.
22. IBRD, 195–96.
23. Ibid., 76.
24. Ramiro Guerra y Sánchez et al., eds., *Historia de la Nación Cubana*, 9: 387.
25. IBRD, 199.
26. Wright, 254.
27. IBRD, 357.
28. Ibid., 138, 372.
29. Ibid., 139–40.
30. Ibid., 144–45.
31. Ibid., 60.
32. Ibid., 148.
33. Ibid., 9.
34. Ibid., 365–66; O'Connor, 180.

35. O'Connor, 180.
36. IBRD, 388.
37. Ibid., 366.
38. Farber, 140.
39. Zanetti and García, 374.
40. Del Toro, 259.
41. Ibid.
42. Ibid., 236.
43. IBRD, 405.
44. Ibid., 425.
45. Emilio Roig de Leuchsenring, *Males y vicios de Cuba republicana*, 283, 285.
46. IBRD, 424.
47. Ibid., 425–26.
48. Ibid., 427.
49. Ibid., 431.
50. Ibid., 434–35.
51. Del Toro, 234–35.
52. IBRD, 455.
53. Ibid., 456.
54. Ibid., 723.
55. Lowry Nelson, *Rural Cuba*, 47.
56. IBRD, 202.
57. O'Connor, 6.
58. IBRD, 773.
59. Ibid., 771.
60. Ibid., 775.
61. Roberts, 3.
62. Ibid., 262–63.
63. IBRD, 766.
64. Ibid., 3.
65. Oscar Zanetti, "El comercio exterior de la república neocolonial," 104; Wright, 231.
66. Zanetti Lecuona, 151–52.
67. Martínez Alier, 95.
68. Ibid.
69. Zanetti Lecuona, 155.
70. Guerra y Sánchez et al., eds., *Historia*, 9: 386–87.
71. Zanetti Lecuona, 155–56.
72. IBRD, 9–10.
73. Ibid., 10–11.
74. Ibid., 11.
75. Ibid., 11–12.
76. Ibid., 13.

77. Ibid., 17.
78. Ibid., 400.
79. Ibid., 22.
80. Ibid., 262.
81. Ibid., 29–30.
82. Ibid., 441.
83. Ibid., 24.
84. Ibid., 678–79.
85. Ibid., 26–27.
86. Ibid., 28.
87. Ibid., 29.
88. Ibid., 29–31.
89. Ibid., 32.
90. Zanetti and García, 468, n. 13.
91. Ibid., 373.
92. Ibid., 402.
93. Ibid., 373.
94. Ibid., 375.
95. Ibid., 374, 370.
96. Ibid., 377.
97. O'Connor, 64.
98. Francisco Ichaso, "Panorama de los partidos ante las elecciones parciales," *Bohemia*, January 22, 1950: 49.

Chapter 9. "Crazy Eddy"

1. Cabrera Infante, 141.
2. Conte Agüero, 716.
3. en Cuba, "Política. Una gigantesca polémica," *Bohemia*, January 28, 1951: 61.
4. Ibid.
5. Ibid.
6. Ibid., 62.
7. Ibid., 61.
8. Ibid., 62.
9. Ibid., 64.
10. Ibid., 64–65.
11. en Cuba, "Atentado. Parece que fué ayer," *Bohemia*, January 21, 1951: 57–58.
12. Ibid., 58.
13. Conte Agüero, 735–37.
14. Duarte Oropesa, 158–59.
15. Conte Agüero, 742.
16. Roig de Leuchsenring, 355.
17. en Cuba, "La substitución del General Uría," *Bohemia*, April 15, 1951: 77.

18. Ibid.
19. en Cuba, "Atentados. Muerte en las calles," *Bohemia*, March 11, 1951: 57.
20. Rogelio Caparros, "Habrá terminado la guerra de los grupos," *Bohemia*, May 13, 1951: 72.
21. Ibid., 74.
22. Editorial, *Bohemia*, June 24, 1951: 61.
23. Vignier and Alonso, 248.
24. *HAR* 4 (May 1951): 16.
25. *Bohemia*, May 20, 1951: 53.
26. Conte Agüero, 751.
27. Ibid., 755.
28. Ibid., 680, 755–56.
29. *Bohemia*, May 27, 1951: 67–68.
30. Ibid., 68.
31. Mario Riera Hernández, *Un presidente cordial*, 4.
32. Conte Agüero, 761.
33. Ibid., 764–65.
34. Ibid., 770–71.
35. *HAR* 4 (August 1951): 24–25.
36. Conte Agüero, 772.
37. Duarte Oropesa, 170.
38. Conte Agüero, 779.
39. Geyer, 89.
40. Conte Agüero, 784.
41. Cabrera Infante, 143.
42. Aureliano Sánchez Arango, *Trincheras de ideas . . . y de piedras*, xi.
43. Geyer, 89.
44. Martin, 82–83.
45. Báez, 783.
46. *HAR* 4 (September 1951): 17.
47. Geyer, 90.
48. Cabrera Infante, 143.
49. Geyer, 91.
50. Conte Agüero, 773.
51. Rafael Estenger, "Sentido revolucionario de la muerte de Chibás," *Bohemia*, August 26, 1951: 55.
52. *HAR* 4 (October 1951): 16.
53. en Cuba, "Orden público. Viejos rumbos," *Bohemia*, September 30, 1951: 59.
54. Ibid.
55. Ibid., 60.
56. Ibid.
57. Ibid.
58. Ibid., 61.

59. Ibid.
60. Ibid., 62.
61. Ibid.
62. Ibid., 63.
63. Ibid.
64. Ibid.
65. *HAR* 4 (November 1951): 16.
66. en Cuba, "Orden público," *Bohemia*, September 30, 1951: 63.
67. Báez, 784–85.
68. *Bohemia*, October 7, 1951: 72.
69. *HAR* 4 (November 1951): 17.
70. en Cuba, "Gabinete," *Bohemia*, October 7, 1951: 72.
71. Ibid.
72. Francisco Ichaso, "La batalla de las afiliaciones," *Bohemia*, September 23, 1951: 44.
73. en Cuba, "Educación. Ambición frustrada," *Bohemia*, October 14, 1951: 71.
74. Zanetti and García, 378.
75. en Cuba, "Educación," *Bohemia*, October 14, 1951: 71.
76. *HAR* 4 (November 1951): 16.
77. Ichaso, "La batalla," *Bohemia*, September 23, 1951: 44.
78. *HAR* 4 (December 1951): 16.
79. "Gestos y tesis en la política cubana," *Bohemia*, November 25, 1951: 74.
80. en Cuba, "Orden público. Las raíces del gangsterismo," *Bohemia*, December 2, 1951: 67.
81. Báez, 787.
82. en Cuba, "Orden público," *Bohemia*, December 2, 1951: 67.
83. Ibid., 68.
84. Ibid., 71.
85. en Cuba, "Recuento y perspectiva, 1951–1952," *Bohemia*, January 6, 1952: 59.
86. Luis Aguilar, "La 'década trágica,'" in Machover, 67.
87. Cabrera Infante, 141.
88. en Cuba, "Recuento," *Bohemia*, January 6, 1952: 59.
89. Ibid.
90. For the relationship between Cuban artists and Fidel Castro in 1961, see Cabrera Infante, 69–70.
91. Santovenia and Shelton, 178.

Chapter 10. Conclusion: 1952

1. Duarte Oropesa, 198.
2. Manuel Antonio (Tony) Varona, interview by author, January 31, 1980.
3. *Partido Revolucionario Cubano (Auténtico)*, "Programa," part 1, 6.
4. Ibid., 9.

5. Ibid., 10.
6. Ibid., 18.
7. Ibid.
8. Ibid., 18–19.
9. Ibid., part 2, 1–2.
10. Ibid., 12.
11. Ibid., 13.
12. Ibid., 24.
13. Ibid., 30.
14. Ibid., 32.
15. Ibid., 38.
16. Ibid., 41.
17. Ibid., 42.
18. Ibid., 45–47.
19. Ibid., 52–53.
20. Ibid., 48–49.
21. Ibid., 54–56.
22. Ibid., 57.
23. Suárez Rivas, 63.
24. Duarte Oropesa, 184.
25. *Bohemia,* December 23, 1951: 76.
26. *HAR* 5 (March 1952): 16.
27. Ibid.
28. Farber, 124.
29. Aguilar, "La 'década trágica,'" in Machover, 72.
30. Francisco Marqués, "Crisis y brega del Autenticismo," *Bohemia,* December 23, 1951: 24.
31. Ibid., 25.
32. Ibid., 26.
33. *Bohemia,* February 3, 1952: 57–59.
34. Martin, 83.
35. Bonachea and Valdés, 143.
36. Szulc, 205.
37. Bonachea and Valdés, 143.
38. Ibid.
39. Szulc, 204.
40. Geyer, 96.
41. Ibid.
42. Vignier and Alonso, 246.
43. Ibid., 247.
44. Ibid., 250.
45. Ibid., 249.
46. Ibid., 242.

47. *HAR* 5 (March 1952): 17.
48. *Bohemia*, February 24, 1952: 68–69.
49. en Cuba, *Bohemia*, March 2, 1952: 78–79.
50. "Recopilación de criterios," *Bohemia*, February 24, 1952: 73.
51. Eufemio Fernández Ortega, "Carta abierta al Sr. Presidente de la República," *Bohemia*, March 2, 1952: 77.
52. Carrillo, 398–99.
53. Vignier and Alonso, 303.
54. Ibid., 300.
55. Ibid., 303.
56. Ibid., 306.
57. Ibid.
58. Carrillo, 399.
59. Ibid.
60. Tony Varona, interview by the author.
61. Ibid.
62. Pérez, *Army Politics*, 132.
63. *Bohemia*, March 16, 1952: 61.
64. Roberts, 144.
65. Báez, 9: 829.
66. en Cuba, "Golpe de estado," *Bohemia*, March 16, 1952: 62.
67. Ibid.
68. Ibid.
69. Ibid.
70. Ibid., 65.
71. Ibid., 64.
72. Ibid.
73. Ibid.
74. Duarte Oropesa, 201.
75. en Cuba, "Golpe," *Bohemia*, March 16, 1952: 64.
76. Ibid., 65.
77. Ibid., 61.
78. Machover, 73.
79. Rafael Estenger, "La doble cara del golpe de estado," *Bohemia*, March 16, 1952: 49.
80. Robert E. Quirk, *Fidel Castro*, 40.
81. Bonachea and Valdés, 147.
82. Roberto Luque Escalona, *The Tiger and the Children*, 81.
83. Báez, 815.
84. Suchlicki, *University Students*, 57.
85. Suárez Rivas, 166.
86. Machover, 72–73.
87. Luis Ortega, interview by the author, January 21, 1980.

88. Pérez, *Army Politics*, 131.
89. Carrillo, 401.
90. Santovenia and Shelton, 150.
91. Aguilar, *Cuba 1933*, 241.
92. Nelson, *Rural Cuba*, 20–21.
93. For example, see O'Connor.
94. Valdés and Bonachea, 25.
95. Ibid.
96. Ibid.
97. Ibid.
98. Szulc, 207.
99. Luque Escalona, 82.
100. Alvarez Díaz, 417.
101. Suchlicki, 60.
102. Vignier and Alonso, 320.
103. Roig de Leuchsenring, 266.

BIBLIOGRAPHY

Aguilar, Luis E. *Cuba 1933: Prologue to Revolution.* Ithaca, N.Y.: Cornell University Press, 1972.
Alienes y Urosa, Julián. *Características fundamentales de la economía cubana.* Havana: Banco Nacional de Cuba, 1950.
Alvarez, Alberto Inocente. Interview by author. Miami, Fla., February 27, 1980.
Alvarez Díaz, José R. Interview by author. Miami, Fla., February 5, 1980.
Alvarez Díaz, José R., et al. *A Study on Cuba.* Coral Gables: University of Miami Press, 1965.
Ameringer, Charles D. "Leonardo Ruiz Pineda: Leader of the Venezuelan Resistance, 1949–1952." *Journal of Interamerican Studies and World Affairs* 21 (May 1979): 209–31.
———. *The Caribbean Legion: Patriots, Politicians, Soldiers of Fortune, 1946–1950.* University Park: Penn State University Press, 1996.
Arvelo, Tulio H. *Cayo Confites y Luperón: Memorias de un expedicionario.* Santo Domingo: Universidad Autónoma de Santo Domingo, 1981.
Báez, Vicente, ed. *La Enciclopedia de Cuba.* Vol. 9. *Gobiernos Republicanos.* Madrid: Playor, S.A., 1975.
Balfour, Sebastian. *Castro.* 2d ed. London: Longman, 1995.
Bayo, Alberto. *Tempestad en el Caribe.* Mexico City: n.p., 1950.
Bengelsdorf, Carollee. *The Problem of Democracy in Cuba: Between Vision and Reality.* New York: Oxford University Press, 1994.
Betancourt, Rómulo. *Venezuela: política y petróleo.* Mexico City: Fondo de Cultura Económica, 1956.
Bohemia. Havana, Cuba.
Bonachea, Rolando E., and Nelson P. Valdés, eds. *Revolutionary Struggle, 1947–1958.* Vol. 1 of *Selected Works of Fidel Castro.* Cambridge: MIT Press, 1972.

Boorstein, Edward. *The Economic Transformation of Cuba.* New York: Monthly Review Press, 1968.
Braden, Spruille. *Diplomats and Demagogues: The Memoirs of Spruille Braden.* New Rochelle, N.Y.: Arlington House, 1971.
Cabrera Infante, Guillermo. *Mea Cuba.* Translated by Kenneth Hall with the author. New York: Farrar, Straus and Giroux, 1994.
Carrillo, Justo. *Cuba 1933: Students, Yankees, and Soldiers.* Coral Gables: University of Miami North-South Center, 1994.
Carrillo, Justo. Interview by author. Miami, Fla., January 28, 1980.
Casero, Luis. Interview by author. Miami, Fla., February 17, 1980.
Chester, Edmund A. *A Sergeant Named Batista.* New York: Henry Holt, 1954.
Conte Agüero, Luis. *Eduardo Chibás, el Adalid de Cuba.* Mexico City: Editorial Jus, 1955.
Corominas, Enrique V. *En las areas políticas del Caribe.* Buenos Aires: Editorial El Ateneo, 1952.
―――. *In the Caribbean Political Areas.* Translated by Charles Foresti. New York: Cambridge University Press, 1954.
Del Toro, Carlos. "Algunos aspectos económicos del movimiento obrero cubano." *La República Neocolonial. Anuario de Estudios Cubanos.* Vol. 1. Havana: Editorial de Ciencias Sociales, ca. 1973.
Diario de la Marina. Havana, Cuba.
Díaz, Lomberto. Interview by author. Miami, Fla., January 7, 1980.
Domínguez, Jorge I. *Cuba: Order and Revolution.* Cambridge: Harvard University Press, 1978.
Dozer, Donald Marquand. *Are We Good Neighbors? Three Decades of Inter-American Relations, 1930–1960.* Gainesville: University of Florida Press, 1959.
Duarte Oropesa, José. *Historiología Cubana. Desde 1944 hasta 1959.* Vol. 3. Miami: Ediciones Universal, 1974.
Falk, Pamela S. *Cuban Foreign Policy: Caribbean Tempest.* Lexington, Mass.: Lexington Books, 1986.
Farber, Samuel. *Revolution and Reaction in Cuba, 1933–1960: A Political Sociology from Machado to Castro.* Middletown, Conn.: Wesleyan University Press, 1976.
Fuentes, Norberto. *Hemingway in Cuba.* Translated by Consuelo E. Corwin. Secaucus, N.J.: Lyle Stuart, 1984.
Gellman, Irwin F. *Roosevelt and Batista: Good Neighbor Diplomacy in Cuba, 1933–1945.* Albuquerque: University of New Mexico Press, 1973.
Geyer, Georgie Anne. *Guerrilla Prince: The Untold Story of Fidel Castro.* Boston: Little, Brown, 1991.
Goldenberg, Boris. *The Cuban Revolution and Latin America.* New York: Frederick A. Praeger, 1965.
Gosch, Martin A., and Richard Hammer. *The Last Testament of Lucky Luciano.* Boston: Little, Brown, 1974.
Guerra y Sánchez, Ramiro. *Sugar and Society in the Caribbean: An Economic History*

of Cuban Agriculture. Translated by Marjory M. Urquidi. New Haven: Yale University Press, 1964.
Guerra y Sánchez, Ramiro, José M. Pérez Cabrera, Juan J. Remos, and Emeterio S. Santovenia, eds. *Historia de la Nación Cubana*. 10 vols. Havana: Editorial de la Nación Cubana, 1952.
HAR. See *Hispanic American Report*.
Hemingway, Ernest. *Islands in the Stream*. New York: Charles Scribner's Sons, 1970.
Hispanic American Report (formerly *Hispanic World Report*). Stanford University.
Ibarra, Jorge. *Historia de Cuba*. Havana: Dirección Política de las F.A.R., 1967.
IBRD. See International Bank for Reconstruction and Development.
Illán, José M. *Cuba: Facts and Figures of an Economy in Ruins*. Translated by George A. Wehby. Miami: n.p., 1964.
International Bank for Reconstruction and Development (IBRD). *Report on Cuba*. Baltimore: Johns Hopkins University Press, 1951.
Lancís, César. Interview by author. Miami, Fla., January 21, 1980.
Lazo, Mario. *Dagger in the Heart: American Policy Failures in Cuba*. New York: Funk and Wagnalls, 1968.
LeRiverend, Julio. *Breve Historia de Cuba*. Havana: Editorial de Ciencias Sociales, 1992.
Liss, Sheldon B. *Fidel! Castro's Political and Social Thought*. Boulder, Colo.: Westview Press, 1994.
Llarena, Mario. Interview by author. Miami, Fla., January 25, 1980.
Llovio-Menéndez, José Luis. *Insider: My Hidden Life as a Revolutionary in Cuba*. Translated by Edith Grossman. New York: Bantam, 1988.
López Vilaboy, José. *Motivos y culpables de la destrucción de Cuba*. San Juan, P.R.: ELPRIN, 1973.
Luque Escalona, Roberto. *The Tiger and the Children: Fidel Castro and the Judgment of History*. Translated by Manuel A. Tellechea. New Brunswick, N.J.: Transaction, 1992.
MacGaffey, Wyatt, and Clifford R. Barnett. *Twentieth Century Cuba: The Background of the Castro Revolution*. Garden City, N.Y.: Anchor Books, 1965.
Machover, Jacobo, ed. *La Habana 1952–1961: El final de un mundo, el principio de una ilusión*. Madrid: Alianza Editorial, 1995.
Martin, Lionel. *The Early Fidel: Roots of Castro's Communism*. Secaucus, N.J.: Lyle Stuart, 1978.
Martínez Alier, Juan, and Verena Martínez Alier. *Cuba: Economía y sociedad*. Paris: Ruedo Ibérico, 1972.
Masó, Calixto C. *Historia de Cuba*. Miami: Editoriales Universal, 1976.
Mateo, Maricela. "El ABC como opción reformista burguesa en la política neocolonial cubana." *La República Neocolonial. Anuario de Estudios Cubanos*. Vol. 2. Havana: Editorial de Ciencias Sociales, 1979.
Mecham, J. Lloyd. *A Survey of United States–Latin American Relations*. Boston: Houghton Mifflin, 1965.

Miolán, Angel. *El perredé desde mi ángulo.* 2d ed. Caracas: Avila Arte, S.A., 1985.
Morris, George. *CIA and American Labor: The Subversion of the AFL-CIO's Foreign Policy.* New York: International Publishers, 1967.
El Mundo. Havana, Cuba.
Nelson, Lowry. *Cuba: The Measure of a Revolution.* Minneapolis: University of Minnesota Press, 1972.
———. *Rural Cuba.* Minneapolis: University of Minnesota Press, 1950.
New York Times.
OAS. See Organization of American States.
O'Connor, James. *The Origins of Socialism in Cuba.* Ithaca, N.Y.: Cornell University Press, 1970.
Organization of American States. *Aplicaciones del Tratado Interamericano de Asistencia Recíproca, 1948–1960.* 3d ed. Washington, D.C.: Unión Panamericana, 1960.
———. Organ of Consultation. "Situation in the Caribbean, 1950." Documents pertaining to Haiti, Cuba, Guatemala, and the Dominican Republic. 4 boxes. Columbus Memorial Library, Washington, D.C.
ORIT-CIOSL (InterAmerican Regional Organization of Labor–International Confederation of Free Trade Unions). *15 años de sindicalismo libre interamericano, enero 1948–enero 1963.* 2d ed. Mexico City, 1963.
Ortega, Luis. Interview by author. Miami, Fla., January 21, 1980.
Partido Revolucionario Cubano (Auténtico). "Programa" (November 1951). Typescript. Pattee Library, Rare Books Room, Pennsylvania State University, University Park, Pa.
Pérez, Louis A., Jr. *Army Politics in Cuba, 1898–1958.* Pittsburgh: University of Pittsburgh Press, 1976.
———. *Cuba and the United States: Ties of Singular Intimacy.* Athens: University of Georgia Press, 1990.
———. *Cuba: Between Reform and Revolution.* New York: Oxford University Press, 1988.
———. *Essays on Cuban History: Historiography and Research.* Gainesville: University Press of Florida, 1995.
Pérez Dámera, Genovevo. Interview by author. Miami, Fla., August 9, 1967.
Pérez de la Riva, Juan. *El Barracón y otros ensayos.* Havana: Editorial de Ciencias Sociales, 1975.
Phillips, Ruby Hart. *Cuba: Island of Paradox.* New York: McDowell, Obolansky, 1959.
Quirk, Robert E. *Fidel Castro.* New York: Norton, 1993.
Riera Hernández, Mario. *Cuba Libre, 1895–1958: Resumen Histórico.* Miami: n.p., 1968.
———. *Un presidente cordial: Carlos Prío Socarrás, 1927–1964.* Miami: n.p., 1966.
Roberts, W. Adolphe. *Havana: The Portrait of a City.* New York: Coward-McCann, 1953.
Rodón, Lincoln. Interview by author. Miami, Fla., February 4, 1980.

Roig de Leuchsenring, Emilio. *Males y vicios de Cuba republicana: Sus causas y sus remedios*. Havana: n.p., 1959.
Romualdi, Serafino. *Presidents and Peons: Recollections of a Labor Ambassador in Latin America*. New York: Funk and Wagnalls, 1967.
Rómulo Betancourt: pensamiento y acción. Recopilado y editado por miembros de Acción Democrática en el exilio. Mexico City: n.p., 1951.
Ruiz, Ramón Eduardo. *Cuba: The Making of a Revolution*. Amherst: University of Massachusetts Press, 1968.
Sánchez Arango, Aureliano. *Trincheras de ideas . . . y de piedras*. San Juan, P.R.: Editorial San Juan, 1972.
Santovenia, Emeterio S., and Raúl M. Shelton. *Cuba y su historia*. Vol. 3. Miami: Rema Press, 1965.
Segre, Roberto, Mario Coyula, and Joseph L. Scarpaci. *Havana: Two Faces of the Antillean Metropolis*. New York: Wiley, 1997.
Simeon, Charles. Interview by author. Miami, Fla., February 4, 1980.
Simons, Geoff. *Cuba: From Conquistador to Castro*. New York: St. Martin's Press, 1996.
Sims, Harold Dana. "The Cuban Sugar Workers' Progress Under the Leadership of a Black Communist, Jesús Menéndez Larrondo, 1941–1948." In MACLAS (Middle Atlantic Council of Latin American Studies), *Latin American Essays*. Vol. 6. Bethlehem, Pa.: Lehigh University, 1993.
———. "Cuba's Organized Labor, from Depression to Cold War." In MACLAS. *Latin American Essays*. Vol. 11. Newark: University of Delaware, 1998.
Smith, Robert Freeman. *The United States and Cuba: Business and Diplomacy, 1917–1960*. New York: Bookman Associates, 1960.
———, ed. *Background to Revolution: The Development of Modern Cuba*. New York: Knopf, 1966.
Souza, Raymond D. *Major Cuban Novelists: Innovation and Tradition*. Columbia: University of Missouri Press, 1976.
Stokes, William S. "The 'Cuban Revolution' and the Presidential Elections of 1948." *Hispanic American Historical Review* 31 (February 1951): 37–79.
Suárez Rivas, Eduardo. *Los días iguales*. Miami: n.p., 1974.
Suchlicki, Jaime. *University Students and Revolution in Cuba, 1920–1968*. Coral Gables: University of Miami Press, 1969.
———, ed. *Cuba, Castro, and Revolution*. Coral Gables: University of Miami Press, 1972.
Szulc, Tad. *Fidel: A Critical Portrait*. New York: William Morrow, 1986.
Thomas, Hugh. *Cuba: The Pursuit of Freedom*. New York: Harper and Row, 1971.
U.S. Department of State. *Confidential U.S. State Department Central Files. Cuba: Internal Affairs and Foreign Affairs, 1945–1954*. Record Group 59, General Records of the Department of State: Decimal File 837 (Internal Affairs of Cuba) and Decimal Files 737 and 711.37 (Foreign Affairs of Cuba) for 1945–49; Decimal Files 737, 837, and 937 (Internal Affairs of Cuba) and Decimal Files 637 and

611.37 (Foreign Affairs of Cuba) for 1950–54. Microform, unedited. Frederick, Md.: University Publications of America.

———. *Foreign Relations of the United States: Diplomatic Papers*. Washington, D.C.: U.S. Government Printing Office. Selected volumes, 1940–52.

———. *Peace in the Americas*. Publication 3964. Washington, D.C., 1950.

Valdés, Nelson P., and Rolando E. Bonachea. "Fidel Castro y la política estudiantil de 1947 a 1952." *Aportes*, No. 22 (October 1971): 24–40.

Varona, Manuel Antonio. Interviews by author. Miami, Fla., January 31, 1980; February 5, 20, 1980.

Vega, Bernardo, ed. *Los Estados Unidos y Trujillo: Colección de documentos del Departamento de Estado y de las Fuerzas Armadas Norteamericanos. Año 1946*. 2 vols. Santo Domingo: Fundación Cultural Dominicana, 1982.

———. *Los Estados Unidos y Trujillo: Colección de documentos del Departamento de Estado y de las Fuerzas Armadas Norteamericanos. Año 1947*. 2 vols. Santo Domingo: Fundación Cultural Dominicana, 1984.

Vignier, Enrique, and Guillermo Alonso. *La corrupción política y administrativa en Cuba, 1944–1952*. Havana: Editorial de Ciencias Sociales, 1973.

Wright, Stephen J. *Cuba, Sugar and the United States: Diplomatic and Economic Relations During the Administration of Ramón Grau San Martín, 1944–1948*. Ann Arbor, Mich.: University Microfilms International, 1983.

Zanetti, Oscar. "El comercio exterior de la república neocolonial." *La República Neocolonial: Anuario de Estudios Cubanos*. Vol. 1. Havana: Editorial de Ciencias Sociales, ca. 1973.

Zanetti, Oscar, and Alejandro García. *Sugar and Railroads: A Cuban History, 1837–1959*. Translated by Franklin W. Knight and Mary Todd. Chapel Hill: University of North Carolina Press, 1998.

Zanetti Lecuona, Oscar. *Los cautivos de la reciprocidad: La burguesía cubana y la dependencia comercial*. Havana: Ediciones ENPRES, 1989.

Zayas, Jorge. Interview by author. Miami, Fla., February 28, 1980.

INDEX

ABC Revolutionary Society, 3, 4, 8, 191n.10
Acebal Betancourt, Sergio, 116
action groups, 22, 33, 34. *See also under specific groups* (e.g., ARG, MSR, UIR)
administration cane, 21, 123, 187
Agramonte, Roberto, 64, 69, 100, 146, 148; and 1952 election, 159, 175, 176, 188, 189
agrarian reform, 72–73, 171, 193n.31
Agricultural and Industrial Development Bank of Cuba (BANFAIC), 108, 133, 160, 161, 186
Aguado, Julio, 7
Aguerreberre, Alfredo, 37
Aguerreberre, Mario, 82, 86
Aguilar, Luis: commentary by, 3, 164, 175, 183, 184, 186
Aguirre, Francisco, 46, 47, 49, 102
Albizu Campos, Pedro, 119
Alemán, José Braulio, 33
Alemán, José Manuel: background of, 33, 34, 36, 46; corrupt practices of, 35, 41, 42–43, 72, 73, 77, 79, 130, 131; and Cayo Cofites affair, 50–51, 52, 53, 54, 55, 100; political machine of (BAGA), 60, 61, 62, 65, 79, 80, 109; death of, and legacy, 110–11
Alexander, Robert, 103
Alonso, Cruz, 91, 93, 94, 98
Alonso, Maritza, 100
Alonso Pujol, Guillermo: and Republican Party, 17, 34, 76, 80, 108, 109, 110; and 1948 election, 61, 62, 63; and 1952 election, 112, 162, 175, 176; and 1952 coup, 178–79, 188
Alvarez, Aurelio, 63
Alvarez, Danilo, 67
Alvarez, Inocente Alberto, 36, 38, 41; and *trueques* affair, 28, 29, 40, 43
Alvarez del Real, Evelio, 41
Alvarez Díaz, José, 160–61, 186, 189
Alvarez Margolles, Manuel, 180
American Chamber of Commerce of Cuba, 55, 57, 143
American Federation of Labor (AFL), 47
American Popular Revolutionary Alliance (APRA), 4, 12
Anslinger, Henry, 40

Arana, Francisco, 95–96
Ardévol, José, 118
Arévalo, Juan, 46, 47, 49
Arévalo, Juan José, 50; and Caribbean Legion, 66, 96, 101, 104; and Luperón affair, 92, 94, 100
ARG. *See* Guiteras Revolutionary Action
Auténtica Organization (OA), 12
autenticismo, 138, 149; as a concept, 12, 13, 41, 63, 69, 78, 79; wide appeal of, 142–43, 153, 162, 175
Auténtico Party, Auténeicos. *See* Cuban Revolutionary Party-Auténtico (PRC-A)
Auténtico Reaffirmation movement, 62–63
"Authentic Revolution," 5–6, 9–10, 15, 16, 60

BAGA. *See* Bloque Alemán–Grau Alsina
Baldwin, Roger, 103
BANFAIC. *See* Agricultural and Industrial Development Bank of Cuba
Baquero, Gastón, 25
bateyes, 123; reform of, 126, 161
Batista, Fulgencio: and 1933 Revolution, 6, 7, 8, 9, 11, 22; dictatorship of, 13–14, 39–40, 124, 129; presidency of, 14, 15, 17, 18; conduct of, as senator, 76, 78, 80, 107, 149; and 1952 election, 112, 113, 153, 175, 176, 182; and 1952 coup, 152, 167, 178, 179, 179–83, 184, 185, 188, 189
Bayer, Antonio, 147, 148
Bayo, Alberto, 91
Beaulac, Willard, 183
Beauvoir, Vilfort, 99
Becerra, Humberto, 111
Belt, Guillermo, 17, 55–57, 73, 75, 110
Benítez Valdés, Manuel, 18
Betancourt, Rómulo, 66, 185; exile of, in Cuba, 26, 50, 67, 90–92, 98, 102–4
Betancourt Doctrine, 90, 102
Bisbé, Manuel, 44, 100, 109

Bloque Alemán–Grau Alsina (BAGA): corrupt influence of, 35, 60, 62, 63, 64, 70, 72, 75, 79, 109, 160
"Bloody Sunday," 148, 165
Bohemia, 25, 28; and Eddy Chibás, 64, 147, 165; and Ramón Grau San Martín, 78, 110, 111; and presidency of Carlos Prío Socarrás, 86, 104, 115, 116–17, 149, 157, 160, 161, 163, 164; and *pistolerismo*, 150, 151; and 1952 coup, 183; and freedom of expression, 185, 186
bohios, 123
Bonachea, Rolando, 30, 87
bonches. See *bonchismo*
bonchismo, 22, 29, 82, 83
Bosch, Juan: exile of, in Cuba, 25, 26, 66, 103; and the Caribbean Legion, 50, 52, 66, 93, 98
Bosch, Pepin, 112, 160–61, 186
botellas, 23, 33, 35, 60, 69, 186; and Pact of the Groups, 177
Bowles, Chester, 103
Braden, Spruille, 14, 22; and election of 1944, 17, 18, 48; and Section 202e, 56–57
Briggs, Ellis, 56–57
Buck, Pearl, 103
Butler, Robert, 75, 117

Caamaño, Fausto E., 52
Cabrera, Ruperto, 88, 97, 180
Cabrera Flores, Tomás, 150
Cabrera Infante, Guillermo: commentary by, 23, 43, 68, 155, 165; and cultural scene, 58, 118
Caffery, Jefferson, 11
Campa, Miguel Angel, 182
Camp Columbia, 6, 7, 167, 179, 182
Capitol diamond, 45
Caramés, José Manuel, 76, 81, 83, 84, 88
Carbó, Sergio, 6–7, 85
Carías Andino, Tiburcio, 50

Caribbean Legion, 66, 67, 92, 95, 96, 101
Caribbean Pact, 66, 67
Carpentier, Alejo, 118
Carrillo, Justo: and 1933 Revolution, 3, 6–7, 8, 60; and BANFAIC, 108, 161, 186; and 1952 coup, 178, 179
Carrillo Lima, Mario, 150
Casanova, José Manuel, 28, 39, 73, 87, 135–36
Casas, César, 40, 42–43
Case, Clifford, 103
Case 82: and indictment of Ramón Grau San Martín, 111–12, 115, 152, 186
Casero Guillén, Luis, 117, 160, 177, 180; and 1952 election, 175, 186
Castellanos, Nicolás, 109, 162, 175, 176
Castillas, Joaquín, 49, 197n.33
Castillo, Mario, 41
Castillo del Príncipe (prison), 80–81, 161, 163
Castro, Fidel: and *bonchismo*, 29, 30–31; and Eddy Chibás, 44, 45, 64, 155, 164; and Cayo Confites affair, 51, 53, 54, 55; and *pistolerismo*, 68, 82, 83, 87, 88; muckraking activities of, 152, 176–77; and 1952 coup, 183, 185, 188, 189–90
Castro, Manolo, 29, 30, 34, 37; and Cayo Confites affair, 51, 100; murder of, 67–68, 81, 84
Cayo Confites (islet), 52
Cayo Confites affair: organization of, 50, 51, 52; failure of, 54–55, 97; aftermath of, 59, 66, 94, 97, 100
centrales (sugar mills), 20, 122–23, 124
Céspedes, Carlos Manuel de, 5, 6–7
Céspedes, Carlos Miguel, 38
"cetekarios." *See* CTK
Chapultepec Conference, 26
Chibás, Eduardo ("Eddy"), 4, 15, 16, 17, 26; relationship of, with Grau San Martín, 23, 24, 28, 31, 36, 37, 38, 40, 41, 54, 60, 69, 72, 111; personality of, 39, 40, 42, 87, 144; and Cuban People's Party (PPC), 44, 45, 59, 110, 112, 113, 149, 175; and election of 1948, 62, 63, 64, 65; and Prío presidency, 79–81, 107, 115, 152; popularity of, 112, 144, 153; suicide of, and its effect, 155, 156, 160, 164–65, 183, 184 ; —verbal attacks of: against President Prío, 144–45, 149, 152, 184; against Masferrer, 146, 147, 148; against Sánchez Arango, 153–155
civil service reform: as an issue, 131, 132–33, 139, 171
CMQ (radio station), 24, 25; and Chibás, 144, 147, 148; and freedom of expression, 186
COCO (radio station), 24, 84
Cofiño, Angel, 47, 48, 49, 70–71
Colón barrio, 117; cleanup of, 147, 149, 159
colonos (sugar farmers), 20, 123, 124, 136
Colonos Association, 10, 20, 124, 126, 136
Committee for University Supervision (CSU), 29–30
Commodity Credit Corporation (U.S.), 125
complementary laws. *See* Constitution of 1940
Congress (Cuba): and Grau San Martín, 21, 24, 43, 49; and Prío Socarrás, 74, 76, 89, 108
Consolidated Railways (Ferrocarriles Consolidados), 139, 141, 142
Constitution of 1940: drafting of, 14; and complementary laws, 18, 27, 88, 108; and Grau San Martín, 60, 72; provisions of, 24, 32, 36, 43, 128, 132
Conte Agüero, Luis, 44
Cooper, Gary, 165
Correa, Armando, 81
Cossío del Pino, Alejo, 177, 178, 179
Costa Rica: and Caribbean Pact, 66, 67
"Crazy Eddy." *See* Eduardo Chibás
Cruz, Agustín, 44

CTK (cetekarios), 48, 70
Cuba: and the Caribbean Legion, 94–95, 96, 99, 100, 101–2
Cuba Company, 55–56
Cuban Association of Theatrical, Cinematic, and Circus Artists, 71
Cuban Communist Party (PCC), 5, 8, 12, 14, 21. *See also* Popular Socialist Party (PSP)
Cuban Electric Company, 79–80
Cuban Farm Workers Confederation (CCC), 71
"Cubanidad," 16, 25, 117
Cubanidad Alliance, 109
Cubanidad Party, 159, 162, 175
Cuban National Party, 162, 175
Cuban Peoples Party (PPC) (Ortodoxo): founding of, 44; and 1948 election, 62, 63; and 1950 election, 109; and Chibás, 144–47, 149; and 1952 election, 162, 175, 176, 188; and 1952 coup, 184
Cuban Red Cross, 98
Cuban Revolutionary Association (ARC), 7
Cuban Revolutionary Party (PRC), 168
Cuban Revolutionary Party-Auténtico (PRC-A), 1; doctrine and policy of, 12–14, 27–28, 49, 143, 163, 174; and election of 1944, 15, 16, 21; activist foreign policy of, 25–26, 50, 65–66, 89, 90, 92, 102–5, 173; and *pistolerismo*, 30, 55, 59, 84, 87–88, 188; assessment of, 35, 110, 112, 118, 142, 160, 162, 164–65, 168, 183, 185–90; and defection of Chibás, 36, 41, 42, 43–44, 59; and election of 1948, 38, 62–64, 78; and CTC, 46, 48–49, 59, 128–30; and election of 1950, 106, 108–10; and 1952 election, 112–13, 149, 168–69, 170–74
Cuban Sugar Stabilization Institute (ICEA), 20, 123–24, 126
Cuban Tourist Commission, 134–35
Cuban Workers Conferation (CTC): founding of, 12; and Grau San Martín, 18, 21, 45; and struggle for control of, 46–49, 66, 70, 161; and IBRD mission, 129–30; and PRC-A, 143, 187; and 1952 coup, 182
Cuervo Navarro, Pelayo, 44, 152, 161; and Case 82, 77–78, 79, 111, 112
Cuervo Rubio, Gustavo, 17
cultural awakening, 25, 58, 117, 118, 186
Curti, Segundo, 36, 42, 180; as Minister of Defense, 88, 97, 159, 164

Democratic Action (AD) (Venezuela), 66–67, 90–92, 98, 104
Democratic Party, 62, 63, 162, 174
Democratic Socialist Coalition, 16, 21
Despradel, Arturo, 52
DEU. *See* University Student Directorate
Diario de la Marina, 185, 186
Díaz, Herminio, 82
Díaz, Lomberto, 117, 147–48, 152, 157–59, 165
Díaz Duque, Luis, 148
Diego, Eliseo, 25, 117
Diéguez, Jesús, 30, 34, 84
Domingo, Gloria Jaime de, 25, 100
Dominican Democratic Workers Committee in Exile (CODDE), 103
Dominican exiles, 50, 53, 104
Dominican Revolutionary Party (PRD), 50, 103
Duarte Oropesa, José, 87
Dupotey Nico, Hugo, 37
Duys, John, 55

economic diversification: as an issue, 133, 135, 140
election of 1952: in anticipation of, 153, 159, 162, 164, 168, 175–76; postponement of, 182
elections: of 1944, 15, 16–17, 71, 108; of 1946, 36, 37–38; of 1948, 60–65, 76, 108; of 1950, 79, 108, 109–110, 115, 119, 149
El Mundo, 186
"El Reyecito Criollo," 185–86
"en Cuba," 25, 64
Enríquez López, Roberto, 86
Escalante, Aníbal, 85, 109, 158

Escalinata, 29, 182
Espinosa Fernández, Leoncio, 86, 116
Estenger, Rafael, 155–56, 160, 183
Estévez, Antonio Jorge, 94, 95

Fernández, Frank, 27
Fernández Caral, Oscar, 67, 68
Fernández Mendigutía, Emilio, 176
Fernández Ortega, Eufemio: and ARG, 22, 46, 151, 188; and *pistolerismo,* 29, 37, 187; and Carlos Prío, 66, 76, 86, 97; and Caribbean Legion, 93, 94, 95, 96–97, 98; and 1952 coup, 167, 178
FEU. *See* University Students Federation
Fiallo, René, 87, 180
Figueres, José, 103, 188; and Caribbean Legion, 66–67, 94, 104
Flying Tigers, 51, 53
"Fourteen Conclusions," 95, 99, 101. *See also* Inter-American Peace Committee (IAPC)
Fuentes, Justo, 82, 83, 86

Gallegos, Rómulo, 26, 66–67, 90
gangsterism, 22. See also *bonchismo; pistolerismo*
Gans y Martínez, Oscar, 75, 112, 160, 174, 179
García, Alejandro, 48, 130, 142, 162
García Bárcena, Rafael, 6, 29, 44
García Marruz, Fina, 25
Gardner, Ava, 165
Garzón, Conchita, 25, 100
GATT. *See* General Agreements on Tariffs and Trade
General Accounting Law for the State, Provinces, Municipalities, and Autonomous Institutions, 108
General Agreements on Tariffs and Trade (GATT), 136
Generation of "el cincuentenario," 189
Generation of '30, 2–3, 9, 142; and Carlos Prío, 24, 60, 65, 74, 165
Geyer, Georgie Ann, 155
Giacometti, Paul, 98

Ginjaume, Jesús ("Pepe"), 151
Giraudy, Angel Alberto, 9, 10
golpe de estado. See March 10, 1952, coup
golpistas. See March 10, 1952, coup
Gómez, Miguel Mariano, 3
Gómez Wangüermert, Luis, 100
González, Rubén Darío, 81, 83
González Cartas, Jesús ("El Extraño"): and ARG, 83, 96–97, 147–48, 151, 183; and Rafael Trujillo, 188
González Chávez, Camilo, 96, 97
González Guerra, Alfonso, 71
González Tellechea, Ignacio, 70–71
"Government of 100 Days." *See* Grau San Martín, Ramón
Group for the Repression of Subversive Activities (GRAS), 85–86, 88, 148, 158
Gran Casino Nacional, 28, 39
Grant, Frances, 103
Grau, Paulina Alsina *viuda de,* 23, 34, 73
Grau Alsina, Francisco ("Pancho"), 35, 75, 79, 80
Grau Doctrine, 57, 70
Grau San Martín, Ramón: and 1933 Revolution, 4, 7, 9, 12–13; and "Government of 100 Days," 8–10, 11, 15, 20, 123–26, 168; and PRC-A, 12, 13, 14; and election of 1944, 15–17, 18; presidency of, 21, 24, 28, 31, 37, 40, 43, 57–59, 69–73, 135, 137, 139, 189; personality of, 23, 65; and *pistolerismo,* 30, 53, 187; and José Alemán, 32, 34–35, 40–41, 110; and election of 1948, 36, 38, 41, 60, 62, 64–65; and CTC, 45, 48, 49; and Cayo Confites affair, 51–52, 54, 100; and Carlos Prío, 66, 77, 78–79, 107, 112, 158–59; and Case 82, 111, 152, 186; and 1952 election, 162, 174–76
guajiros (Cuban farmers), 71, 72
Guerra, José Antonio, 20
Guerra y Sánchez, Ramiro, 19–20, 118, 123–24, 173
Guevara, Alfredo, 69
Guillén, Nicolás, 118
Guiteras, Antonio, 9, 12

Guiteras Revolutionary Action (ARG): founding of, 12, 22; program of, 47, 148; and Cuban labor, 49, 143, 161; and *pistolerismo*, 83, 147–48, 177, 187–88; and Caribbean Legion, 96–97

hacendados (sugar mill owners), 20, 123, 136
Hacendados Association, 10, 20, 126, 135
Haiti: and Rafael Trujillo, 99–101
Havana, University of, 2, 3, 29; and *bonchismo*, 87–88
"Havana Boys," 56
Haya de la Torre, Víctor Raúl, 4, 12, 103
Hemingway, Ernest, 28, 53, 86, 118, 165. *See also* Hudson, Thomas
Henríquez, Enrique Cotubanamá ("Cotú"), 12–13, 50, 52; and Carlos Prío, 66, 97–98; and Caribbean Legion, 93–94, 98, 100, 104
Henríquez, Federico ("Gugú"), 98
Henríquez, Rodolfo, 98
Hernández, Luis Miguel, 68
Hernández Garriga, Salvador, 148
Hernández Tellaheche, Arturo, 161
Hernández Vega, Rogelio ("Cucú"), 12, 67, 82
Herrera, Benito, 39
Hevia, Carlos, 9, 20; background of, 75, 77, 161, 174, 186; and 1952 presidential candidacy, 112, 147, 153, 162, 176, 182, 186, 188–89
Hotel Nacional, 8
Hotel San Luis, 91, 95, 96
Hoy, 48–49, 114, 116, 158, 185
Hudson, Thomas, 14–15, 38, 52. *See also* Ernest Hemingway
Huguet Domínguez, Humberto, 147–48
Hull, Cordell, 8, 11

IBRD mission. *See* International Bank for Reconstruction and Development mission
Ichaso, Francisco, 3; commentary by, 60, 64, 76, 79, 106, 109, 142–43, 160, 162; on *autenticismo*, 153
Incháustegui Cabral, Héctor, 51, 98
Inciso K (Paragraph K), 32; corrupt abuse of, 33, 36, 48, 60, 63, 69–70, 111
Independent National Workers Committee (CONI), 47, 48
Inter-American Association for Democracy and Freedom (IADF), 103
Inter-American Confederation of Labor (CIT), 47, 102
Inter-American Conference on the Maintenance of Peace and Security (Rio Conference, 1947), 51, 57
Inter-American Conference on Problems of War and Peace (1945). *See* Chapultepec Conference
Inter-American Peace Committee (IAPC), 94–95, 173; "Fourteen Conclusions" of, 95–97, 99, 101
Inter-American Regional Organization of Workers (ORIT), 47, 102–3
Inter-American Treaty of Reciprocal Assistance (Rio Treaty), 94, 99
International Bank for Reconstruction and Development (IBRD) mission: background of, 113, 120; report of, 121, 130, 132, 133–35, 143; and sugar industry, 126–27; and organized labor, 127–30, 133–34, 136–37, 140; recommendations of, 138–42; effect of, 162, 174, 187
International Confederation of Free Trade Unions (ICFTU), 102
International Monetary Fund, 76

Jáuregui, Arturo, 102
Jiménez Grullón, Juan Isidro, 26
Jones-Costigan Act (U.S.), 125
Justiniani y de los Santos, Federico, 111–12, 152

Kid Chocolate (Eligio Sardiñas), 38, 44
Kid Gavilán (Geraldo González), 153

Korean War, 104, 107, 113–14, 119
"Kuquine," 167, 179

labor: critique of, by IBRD mission, 127–28, 136–38, 140, 143; status of, under PRC-A, 128–30, 133–34, 171
La Cabaña, 167, 180
"La Chata," 177, 180
"la Coincidencia" ("the Concurrence"). *See* Cubanidad Alliance
La Floridita, 38, 51, 165
La Guardia, Miguel, 111
L'Amelie affair, 98, 100
Lancís, Félix, 23–24, 160, 180, 186; and 1952 election, 112, 116, 174
Lansky, Meyer, 39–40
Lara, Wilfredo, 86
latifundium, 12, 19, 123, 171, 187
Latin American Workers Confederation (CTAL), 47
Laura, Amado, 81
"La Voz Dominicana," 96
Law against Gangsterism, 74, 76, 78, 81–83
Leoni, Raúl, 103
León Lemus, Orlando ("El Colorado"), 12, 34; and *pistolerismo*, 82–83, 86, 150–51, 160, 164, 177, 188; and Carlos Prío, 84–85, 161
Leyva, Gilberto, 116, 151
Lezama Lima, José, 25, 58, 117
Liberal Party, 3, 5, 21, 62–63, 149, 162, 174
Liberation Army (Cuba), 1, 189
Liberation Army of America, 50
"Liborito," 186
Lombardo Toledano, Vicente, 47
López, Eddy, 71
López Fernández, José, 27
López Migoya, Manuel, 24
López Vilaboy, José, 64–65
Lovestone, Jay, 47
Luciano, Lucky, 39–40
Luperón, Bay of, 93
Luperón affair, 94–95, 98–100

Luque Escalona, Roberto, 183
Lyceum Lawn Tennis Club, 25, 99–100

Machado, Gerardo, 1–2, 5, 20, 168
Malavé Villalba, Augusto, 102
Mañach, Jorge, 3, 9, 26, 147
March 10, 1952, coup, 179–85, 188–89
Marianao, 53. *See also* Orfila shoot-out
Marinello, Juan, 14, 21, 63, 65
Maristany, Carlos, 84
Márquez, Juan Manuel, 49
Márquez Sterling, Carlos, 109–10, 112, 146
Marshall, George C., 51, 57
Martí, José, 168
Martin, Lionel, 30
Martín Elena, Eduardo, 180–81
Martínez, Florentino, 111, 160
Martínez, José Agustín, 85
Martínez Sáenz, Joaquín, 3
Masferrer, Rolando: and MSR, 22, 30, 34, 68, 147–48, 151, 177; and Caribbean Legion, 51–52, 54, 93; and *pistolerismo*, 81–84, 87, 116, 150, 158, 188; and 1952 coup, 178, 182
Massó, Gustavo, 81
McGovern, Maurice, 57
Megías, Sergio, 180
Mejías, Gustavo, 87
Menció Hernández, Carlos Rafael, 152
Mendieta, Carlos, 3, 9, 11
Menéndez, Jesús, 49
Menocal, Mario G., 3
Messersmith, George, 23
Military Intelligence Service (SIM), 85
Mills, R. G., 141
Miolán, Angel, 103
Miró Cardona, José, 152
Monroe, F. Adair, 55–56
Montes Armando, 6
Mora, José, 99
Morales, Angel, 50
Moré, Beny, 118
Moscoso, Alfonso, 100

MSR. *See* Revolutionary Socialist Movement
Mujal, Eusebio, 21, 46–49, 71, 112, 129, 143, 161–62, 182
Muñoz Marín, Luis, 119

National Association of Colonos. *See* Colonos Association
National Association of Journalists, 159
National Bank of Cuba, 74, 76, 107, 133, 139, 160–61, 186
National Congress, (CTC), 46–47
National Development Commission, 139–40, 161, 174
National Federation of Sugar Workers (FNTA), 49
Nationalist Union Association (AUN), 3
"nationalization of labor," 124
National Labor Confederation (CNOC), 2
National Workers Committee (CON), 46–47
Nelson, Lowry, 131, 133, 186
Norweb, R. Henry, 41, 43–44, 51, 54, 56
Novás Calvo, Lino, 58
novelas radiofónicas (soap operas), 58
Núñez Portuondo, Ricardo, 62–63, 65

OAS. *See* Organization of American States
Ochoa, Emilio ("Millo"), 41, 44, 175, 181
O'Connor, James, 142, 143
Olguín, Humberto, 98
Orfila shoot-out: description of, 53; consequences of, 55, 59, 67–68, 83, 87–88, 164, 178, 187
Organic Law of the Budget, 76–77
Organization of American States (OAS), 99–101, 104
Oriente, Province of, 35, 64
Orígenes, 25, 58
ORIT. *See* Inter-American Regional Organization of Workers
Ornes, Horacio, 93, 94
Orozco, Blas Andrés, 69–70
Ortega, Luis, 184

Ortiz, Fernando, 118
Ortodoxo group, 39, 41–42. *See also* Cuban Peoples Party (PPC) (Ortodoxo)
Ortodoxo Party. *See* Cuban Peoples Party (PPC) (Ortodoxo)
Ortodoxo Radical Action (ARO), 45, 88
Otero, Lisandro, 118
Otero y Ben, José, 148
Ovares, Enrique, 45, 51, 68

Pact of Florida, 62
Pact of the Groups, 151–52, 177
Palú, Félix, 47
Paniagua Recalt, Tulio, 115–16
Pardo Llada, José, 41, 183; commentary of, on behalf of PPC, 85, 115, 155, 159, 176, 178; and 1952 election, 153, 174
Patriotic League. *See* Porra
Pazos, Felipe, 9, 76, 107, 161, 165, 186
Peña, Lázaro, 12, 21, 46–48
Pentarchy, 7
Pequeño, Alfredo, 39
Pereda Pulgares, Ramón, 38
Pérez, Louis, 184
Pérez, Virgilio, 110
Pérez Dámera, Genovevo: rapid rise of, 24–25; conduct of, as army chief of staff, 52–53, 62, 65, 73, 75–76, 78–79, 85–86; removal of, 96–97; attempted assassination of, 166
Pérez Espinós, Luis, 32–33, 112
Pérez y González Muñoz, Rafael, 51, 56
Piñango, Nestor, 84
Piñera, Virgilio, 25, 117, 165
pistolerismo: character of, 22, 148; acts of, 37, 43–44, 47, 53, 65, 67–68, 150–51; and Grau San Martín, 60, 69, 187; and Carlos Prío, 88, 106, 115–16, 164, 174, 187–88; and Pact of the Groups, 151, 177
pistoleros. See pistolerismo
Planas, Angélica, 25
Platt Amendment, 1–2, 10, 11, 142, 168
Popular Socialist Party (PSP), 21, 44, 49, 88, 107; and elections, 17, 63, 109, 162;

and CTC, 46, 48, 66, 70, 129; crackdown of, by President Prío, 85, 114, 157
Porra (Patriotic League), 2
Portell Vilá, Herminio, 10, 26, 100, 146–47, 162, 183–84
PPC. *See* Cuban Peoples Party (Ortodoxo)
PRC-A. *See* Cuban Revolutionary Party-Auténtico (PRC-A)
Price, Waterhouse & Company, 108, 139
Prío Socarrás, Antonio, 75, 78, 84; and candidacy for mayor of Havana, 109, 112, 149; alleged corrupt practices of, 146, 160–61, 186
Prío Socarrás, Carlos: and Revolution of 1933, 2, 9, 10, 12, 23–24; and relationship with Grau San Martín, 36, 38, 78–79, 111–12, 175; and rivalry with Chibás, 38, 80–81, 115, 144–45, 147, 155–56, 165; and CTC, 46, 48–49; and election of 1948, 60, 61–63, 65, 73; and 1952 election, 113, 174; and 1952 coup, 167–68, 179–81, 183–85, 189; — presidency of: and relations with the United States, 57, 77, 104, 114, 136; and struggle for democracy in Latin America, 66–67, 89, 90, 92–98, 100, 102–4; and *pistolerismo*, 68, 84–88, 116, 150, 164, 187; and legislation, 74, 76–77, 106–7, 109; and anti-communism, 114, 119, 157; achievements of, 117–20, 153, 160, 163, 165; and IBRD mission, 120–21, 126, 130, 132–33, 137, 142, 161, 163; and charges of corruption, 139, 146, 149, 176–78, 186
Prío Socarrás, Francisco ("Paco"), 39, 78, 80, 83, 146, 186
PSP. *See* Popular Socialist Party
Puente, Orlando, 145–46, 151, 177, 181
Puerto Rican Nationalists, 119

Quevedo, Miguel Angel, 104, 185
Quillévéré, Marcel, 118
Quincosa Valdés, Segundo, 70

Radio Mil Diez (1010), 48–49, 70
Ramírez, Miguel Angel, 93, 95, 98
Ramírez Corría, Filiberto, 98
Reciprocal Trade Treaty (1934), 135
reciprocity (U.S.-Cuban trade relations), 57
Reciprocity Treaty of 1902, 125
Republican Party: and election of 1944, 16–17, 21; and PRC-A, 38, 106, 108–9; and election of 1948, 61–63; and 1952 election, 162, 174
Requeiro, Juan, 81
Revolutionary Insurrectional Union (UIR): general description of, 22, 29–30, 86, 188; and Fidel Castro, 44–45, 82–83, 87; and Orfila shoot-out, 53, 67; rivalry of, with MSR, 67–68, 81–83, 86–87, 115, 164, 178; and Pact of the Groups, 151, 177
Revolutionary Military Junta (1952), 181–82
Revolutionary Socialist Movement (MSR): description of, 22, 29–30, 86, 188; and José Alemán, 34, 62; and Orfila shoot-out, 53, 67; rivalry of, with UIR, 67–68, 81–83, 86, 115–16, 151
Revolution of 1933, 7. *See also* University Student Directorate (DEU) of 1930
Río Verde affair, 3
Rivero Agüero, Andrés, 153, 178
Roa, Raúl, 87, 100, 103
Roberts, Adolphe, 134
Robledo, Orestes, 180–81
Roca, Blas, 85
Rodón, Lincoln, 36
Rodríguez, Carlos Rafael, 14
Rodríguez, Conrado, 162
Rodríguez, Luis Orlando, 44, 146–47
Rodríguez Feo, José, 25, 58
Rodríguez García, Juan: and Cayo Confites affair, 50, 52, 54, 91; and Caribbean Legion, 65, 66, 92–93, 95, 98
Rodríguez Lora, Sebastián, 99
Roig de Leuchsenring, Emilio, 100, 131, 149, 190

228 / Index

Romualdi, Serafino, 47, 103
Roosevelt, Franklin D., 8, 11, 18
Rubio Padilla, Juan Antonio, 6, 10
Ruiz Pineda, Leonardo, 91–92
rural education: status of, 35, 71

Salabarría, Julio, 68
Salabarría, Mario, 29; and MSR, 30, 37, 44; and Orfila shoot-out, 53, 68, 82, 164
Saladrigas, Carlos, 3, 15, 16–17
Salazar Callicó, Luis Felipe ("Wichy"), 83, 86, 87
Sánchez Alonso, Eduardo, 111
Sánchez Arango, Aureliano: 74, 98, 103, 157–59, 161, 183, 186; work of, as minister of education, 75, 77–78, 88, 106, 130–31, 132; and 1952 election, 112, 153, 174; and Chibás, 146, 153–56
San Martín, José ("Pepe"), 60–61, 112, 153
Schlesinger, Arthur, Jr., 103
Seatrain Lines, Inc., 46, 156
Section 202e: of U.S. Sugar Act of 1948, 55, 56, 57
"Sergeants Revolt," 4, 6–7, 22, 189
Seventh International Conference of American States (Montevideo, 1933), 10–11
"Silvio," 185
Simeón, Charles, 44
Sinatra, Frank, 39, 165
Soler, Policarpo: and *pistolerismo*, 83, 86, 150, 160–61, 183, 188; and Pact of the Groups, 151–52, 177; prison break of, 163–64
Solís, José Ramón, 86
Somoza, Anastasio, 50, 90
Sotelo, Calvo, 179, 182
Soto, Lionel, 45
Soto Carmenatti, Eustaquio, 82, 86
Spalding, Hobart, 100
Spanish Civil War, 13
Student Left Wing, 4
Suárez, Pedro, 151

Suárez Aróstegui, Pablo, 37
Suárez Fernández, Miguel ("Miguelito"): and José Alemán, 34, 36; and election of 1948, 60–63; and Carlos Prío, 76, 78, 84; and 1952 election, 112–13, 152–53, 159, 162, 174–76; and *pistolerismo*, 115–16, 151, 188
Suárez Rivas, Eduardo, 9, 21, 29, 37, 126; and Liberal-Auténtico cooperation, 149, 152, 161, 174, 186; and 1952 coup, 180, 184
Suchlicki, Jaime, 31, 184
Sugar Act of 1948 (U.S.), 55–57, 59, 73. *See also* Section 202e
Sugar Coordination Law of 1937 (Cuba), 11, 20, 124
sugar differential, 37, 125–26
sugar industry: impact of, on Cuban economy, 19–20, 27, 57, 64, 73, 107, 113, 141; and PRC-A policy, 28, 169, 187; dominant position of, 121–22, 133, 135, 140, 143, 173; regulation of, 122–24, 126–27, 135, 138
sugar quota (U.S.), 14
Sunsundamba, 180
Supervielle, Manuel Fernández, 38, 43
Szulc, Tad, 188–89

Tabernilla y Dolz, Francisco, 24
Tabio, Evelio, 54
tanteo (preemptive bid): right of, 124
Tejera, Diego Vicente, 33–34, 181, 188
television: inauguration of, in Cuba, 118
"third floor": and corruption, 23, 33, 35, 43, 63
"Third Front," 62–63, 176
Thomas, Norman, 103
Thomen, Luis, 104
Toriello, Guillermo, 103
Torquay Conference, 136
tourism, 28, 133–35
Treaty of Friendship, Commerce, and Navigation (draft), 55, 57
Trejo, Rafael, 2
Triana, Jorge, 98

Tribunal of Accounts, 108, 160, 186
Tró, Emilio, 22, 30, 34, 53
trueques (barter deals), 28–29, 43, 126
Trujillo, Rafael, 183, 188; and Caribbean Legion, 50, 54, 93–94, 96, 98–100
Truman, Harry, 55, 57, 77, 107, 114, 119
Truslow, Francis Adams, 121, 141
Truslow mission. *See* International Bank for Reconstruction and Development mission

UIR. *See* Revolutionary Insurrectional Union
Ulloa, Juan, 27
Unione Siciliano, 39
Unitary Action Party (PAU), 162, 175
United Railways (Ferrocarriles Unidos), 139, 141–42
United States: and Cuban sugar production, 20, 27–28, 37, 55, 57, 64, 73, 77, 113, 119, 125, 127, 135–36, 173, 187; and conflict in the Caribbean, 52, 90–91, 94, 101, 104–5, 119; and Korean War, 104, 119; and Puerto Rican Nationalists, 104, 119
University Student Directorate (DEU): of 1927, 2, 4; of 1930, and the 1993 Revolution, 2–6, 9
University Students Federation (FEU), 29, 31, 83, 156; and 1952 coup, 180–81, 182, 183, 185
Uría, Quirino, 88, 147, 148, 149–50

Valdés, Isauro, 111
Valdés, Nelson, 30, 87
Valdés Daussá, Ramiro, 29–30
Varona Loredo, Manuel Antonio ("Tony"), 38–39, 46, 74, 109, 146; and 1933 Revolution, 2, 12; record of, as prime minister, 76, 83–85, 114, 116, 186; and 1952 election, 112, 153, 174; and 1952 coup, 167–68, 179, 181, 184
Varona Loredo, Roberto, 109
Vasconcelos, Ramón: commentary by, 24, 85, 114–15, 156–57, 159, 164, 178, 183; and Fidel Castro, 176–77
Vedado, 3, 23
Venezuelan military junta (1948), 90, 91, 92
"Vergara," 25, 85–86
Villa Yedra, Manuel, 86
Vitier, Cintio, 25

"Warm Springs Declaration," 11
Welles, Sumner, 4–5, 8–9, 11, 55
White, Walter, 103
Woll, Matthew, 47
Workers Palace, 45, 48
World Bank. *See* International Bank for Reconstruction and Development (IBRD) mission
World War II: effect of, on Cuba, 14

Young Cuba (Joven Cuba), 12

Zanetti, Oscar, 48, 130, 136, 142, 162

Charles D. Ameringer is professor emeritus of Latin American history at Penn State University. He is the author of five books, including *The Caribbean Legion: Patriots, Politicians, Soldiers of Fortune, 1946–1950* (1996) and *The Democratic Left in Exile: The Antidictatorial Struggle in the Caribbean, 1945–1959* (1974).

www.ingramcontent.com/pod-product-compliance
Lightning Source LLC
Chambersburg PA
CBHW032249150426
43195CB00008BA/378